PRIVATE OWNER WAGONS OF THE FOREST OF DEAN

IAN POPE

Copyright: Lightmoor Press and Ian Pope 2002
Reprinted 2004

British Library Cataloguing-in-Publication Data.
A catalogue record for this book is available from the British Library
ISBN 1 899889 09 4
All rights reserved. No part of this publication may be reproduced, stored in a retrieval system or transmitted in any form or by any means, electronic, mechanical, photocopying, recording or otherwise, without the written permission of the publisher.

Lightmoor Press
120 Farmers Close, Witney, Oxfordshire, OX28 1NR

Printed by Cromwell Press, Trowbridge

PRIVATE OWNER WAGONS OF THE FOREST OF DEAN

Lightmoor Press

A postcard view taken circa 1930 at Whitecroft on the Severn & Wye Joint Committee's line. Of interest here are the coal wagons with a rake of Parkend wagons closest to the camera – only one Phoenix Coal Co. wagon spoils the set! Behind is a second rake with some Norchard wagons discernible. The photographer was either lucky to catch a train heading south or, more likely at this time of depression in the coal trade with many collieries only working two or three days a week, the wagons are standing in the sidings with 'wait order' coal.
Neil Parkhouse collection

CONTENTS

INTRODUCTION	7
TRAMROAD DAYS	9
THE BROAD GAUGE	13
THE COLLIERIES: Part One: Housecoal	17
Parkend	18
New Fancy	23
Speech House Hill	25
Wimberry	27
Trafalgar	28
Crump Meadow	30
Foxes Bridge	32
Lightmoor	34
Pluds	39
Smaller Collieries	41
Nags Head	41
Dean Forest Navigation Coal & Fuel Co.	42
Forest Steam Coal Co.	43
Coleford Red Ash	43
Clement's Tump	44
Darkhill & Ellwood	44
Wallsend	44
Woorgreens	45
THE COLLIERIES: Part Two: The Deep Pits	47
Norchard	48
Princess Royal	52
Cannop	56
Arthur & Edward	60
Eastern United	65
Northern United	67
COAL FACTORS	69
Dean Forest Coal Co.	71
E. P. & R. L. Morgan	76
Edgar Jarrett & Co.	77
New Bowson Coal Co.	79
I. W. Baldwin & Co.	82
Phoenix Coal Co.	83
Sully & Co.	85
James Smith	88
Read & Son	92
Alfred J. Smith	94
Thomas Silvey	96
F. H. Silvey	98
Lowell Baldwin	99
Dunkerton Coal Factors	101
Clutton	101
Renwick, Wilton	102
Barker & Lovering	104
Baker & Kernick	105
Trevor Powell	105
COAL MERCHANTS: Forest of Dean	107
The Lydney Coal Co.	108
Mansfield Bros	109
Terrett Taylor	110
W. H. James	110
Non-Forest: Gloucestershire	
A. E. Moody	111
H. J. Mabbett	111
F. J. Holpin	111
R. E. Aldridge	111
H. Blandford	112
Dickinson, Prosser & Cox	113
Pates & Co.	113
W. Sawyer & Co.	114
Powell, Gwinnell & Co. Ltd	114
Alexander Crane	115
E. T. Ward	115
Non-Forest: Somerset	
G. Small & Son	116
William Thomas	117
Radstock Coal Co.	117
Somerset Trading Co.	117
Hartnell & Son	117
Non-Forest: Bristol	
Twining	118
Mark Whitwill & Son	118
S. Stone & Co.	119
H. Pepler & Son	119
Non-Forest: Wiltshire	
William Duck	119
G. Davis	119
Mortimore	120
Non-Forest: Others	
C & G. Ayres	121
Albert Usher	121
Ralls & Son	121
Spencer Abbott	121
Wye Valley	
Morgan Bros	122
John Yates	123
Samuel Llewellyn	123
Webb, Hall & Webb	123
John Hollins	123
Welsh Traders	
Wm Morris	124
Victor Grey & Co.	124
Leadbeter	124
James & Emanuel	125
Bedwas	125
Graham Roberts & Co.	125
Budd & Co.	125
INDUSTRIAL USERS	
Purified Flock & Bedding Co. Ltd	126
Wm Playne	126
Hillier's Bacon Curing Co. Ltd	127
E. A. Chamberlain	127
Stroud Gas Light	127
Samuel Jefferies	128
Stonehouse Brick & Tile Co. Ltd	128
S. J. Moreland & Sons	128
John Stephens, Son & Co. Ltd	129
Gloucester Gaslight Company	129
Gloucester Corporation	130
Borough of Cheltenham Electricity Dept	130
South Herefordshire Agricultural Co-op	130
Monmouth Steam Saw Mills Co. Ltd	131
Miscellaneous Wagons	132
COAL HANDLING	139
The Unknowns, Coal	144
STONE	149
E. R. Payne & Son	150
David & Sant	151
Forest of Dean Stone Firms	151
E. Turner & Sons	152
United Stone Firms	153
Clee Hill Granite Co.	154
Whitecliff Lime Co.	155
METALLIFEROUS	157
Easter Iron Mine	157
Richard Watkins	158
Forest of Dean Iron Co.	159
Parkend Tinplate Co.	159
Henry Crawshay & Co.	160
Great Western Iron Co.	161
Richard Thomas	162
The Unknowns, Metalliferous	163
TANK WAGONS	165
Berry Wiggins	165
Sharpness Chemical Co.	168
MISCELLANEOUS	169
Severn Ports Warehousing	169
Spillers	169
LOCAL WAGON BUILDERS	170
Cheltenham	170
Bullo Pill	170
Gloucester	171
APPENDIX ONE: Crawshay Orders	172
INDEX	182

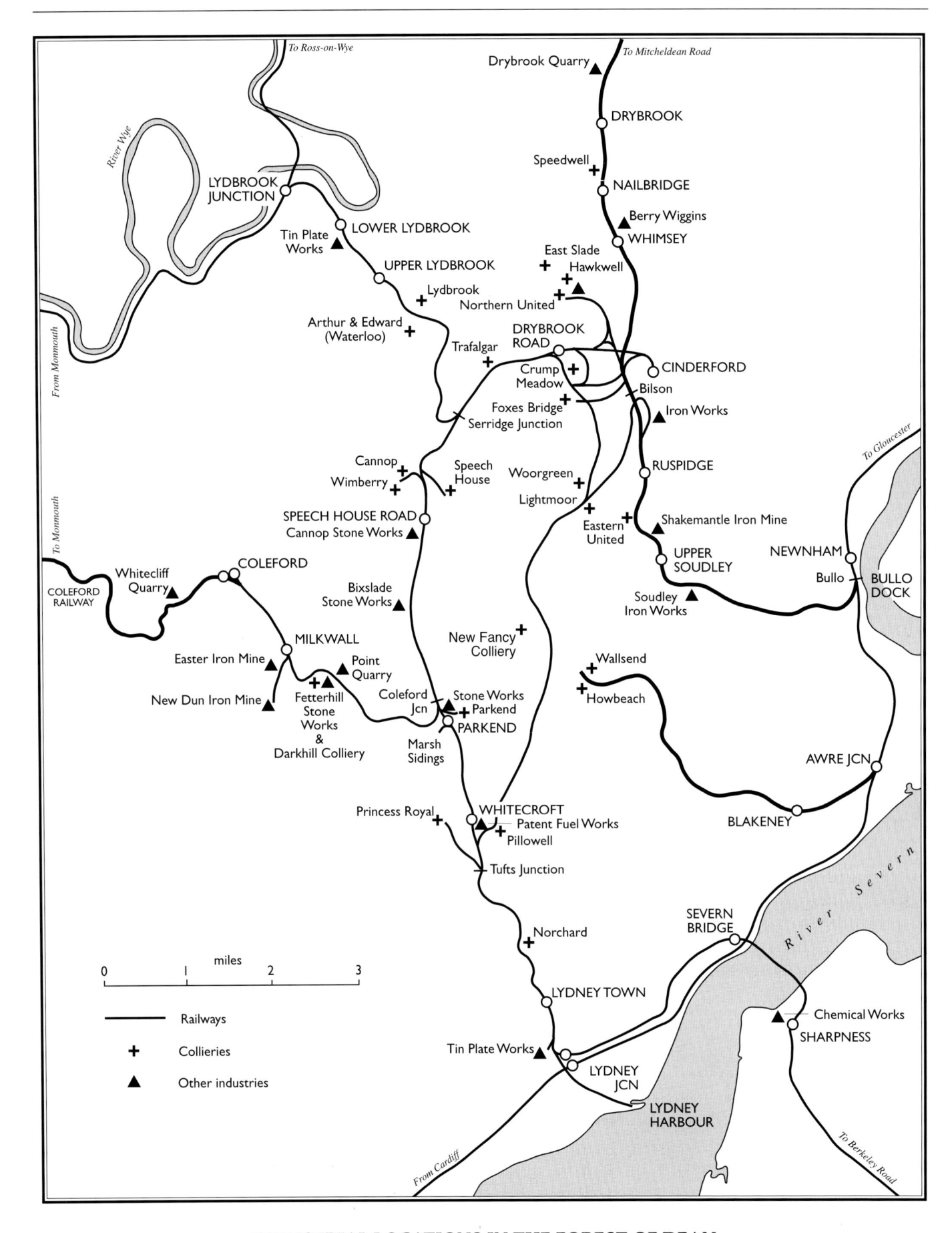

INDUSTRIAL LOCATIONS IN THE FOREST OF DEAN

INTRODUCTION

THE use of private owner wagons in the Forest of Dean goes back to the introduction of horse-drawn tramroads to the area. The first was laid in 1795 by James Teague but was really not much more than a colliery line. Following its success he built a second line to the River Wye at Lydbrook and thus it became more than just a colliery line but it was still owned and operated in connection with one colliery. It did, however, show the way forward for the transportation of minerals in the Forest. As a result, in the first decade of the 19th century three public tramroads were promoted and built in the Dean:

- The Severn & Wye Railway & Canal Co.;
- The Bullo Pill Railway; and
- The Monmouth Railway Company.

The Severn & Wye line served the western side of the Forest, from a harbour on the River Severn at Lydney to the River Wye at Lydbrook with several branches up side valleys. The Bullo Pill Railway served the eastern Forest from a small dock at Bullo Pill to north of the Cinderford area. The Monmouth Railway Co.'s line ran from around the Coleford area on the west of the Forest down to the town of Monmouth.

Other lines were built as private concerns linking into the main tramroad networks, a notable example of this is the Oakwood Tramroad, built by the ironmaster Robert Mushet, to take iron ore to the furnaces at Parkend but soon opened up for public use.

All of the tramroad companies operated their lines much as Railtrack do today. The tramroad companies provided the track and the various industrial concerns and traders along the route who wished to use it had to provide their own wagons. They were then charged a toll for the use of the line, the charge being dependent on the commodity carried and the weight. In order to keep a check on the traffic weighing machines were installed at various key points such as Lydney, Parkend and Bilson.

The types of traffic carried on the tramroads were wide and various but the staples of the Forest of Dean – coal, iron ore, stone and timber – were traffic types which were to remain, with the exception of iron ore, until the end of rail usage in the area.

The arrival of railways in the region, with the building of the South Wales Railway in 1851 along the banks of the River Severn from Gloucester down to Chepstow, began a period of change for the tramroads and the traders of the Forest. The first of the lines into the Forest to be converted was the tramroad between Bullo Pill and Cinderford. The operating company, the Forest of Dean Railway Co., was bought out by the South Wales Railway and conversion work soon began. Trade on the tramroad was not interfered with, even when the 1,064 yard long Haie Hill Tunnel was being opened out to broad gauge proportions. The conversion meant that the traders on the line had to go to considerable expense to provide new wagons for their trade. Unfortunately few records survive as to who was using the line.

As will be seen throughout this work the Gloucester Wagon Co's order books shed a great deal of light on the private owner wagons of the Forest of Dean, as do the minute books of Henry Crawshay & Co. Ltd which thankfully still survive. However, Crawshay's records do show that many wagons were acquired from other wagon companies, including some well away from the area such as the Lincoln Wagon Co., and here few records exist. Some which thankfully do survive are those for the Western Wagon Co. and these again have thrown fresh light on Forest wagons.

In the main, the traffic from Forest collieries was taken down to the River Severn for shipping to the West of England. The coal was shipped through the ports of Bullo and Lydney where mainly trows and ketches were used in the coastal trade to the West Country. Larger vessels used Sharpness, trains going via the Severn Bridge and some traffic also went to Newport. Other traffic to the West of England was rail borne over the Severn Bridge or via Gloucester.

Much of the traffic in stone would have gone the same way although finished dressed stone for architectural purposes would have gone by rail to its destination. Thus Forest of Dean based wagons could have been seen anywhere in the country where the architect of a building or a civil engineer working on a dock project required the use of the hard wearing Forest stone.

Details of tank wagon traffic is sparse to say the least until the arrival of Messrs Berry Wiggins in the Forest after the Second World War. This new traffic in bitumen was looked on by the train crews as 'the tank invasion'.

It is not the intention of this book to deal with design matters of private owner wagons as that has been amply covered elsewhere but to look at the liveries of the wagons which worked into the area and to give some idea of the dates at which the wagon owning concerns were operating.

I have tried to be as accurate as possible and to record as many known wagons which worked in and around the Forest of Dean as can be gained from photographic sources and the written record. That there will be others I am certain and if any reader can supply details I would be most grateful.

I would like to thank the staff at the Gloucestershire Records Office for their continuous production of the Gloucester Railway Carriage & Wagon records; Bristol Records Office; and Paul Karau, Bob Essery, Richard Kelham, Roderick Simm and Coombe Martin Museum, for information and photographs.

Ian Pope, Witney, August 2002

A wooden mineral type tram photographed on the Wimberry Tramroad in the 1930s. This line was built as a branch off the Severn & Wye Tramroad but was retained after the mainline was converted to a railway to serve several small collieries and some quarries at the head of the valley. It survived until the Second World War when military activity destroyed sections of the track.
Ian Pope collection

TRAMROAD DAYS

THE wagons used on the tramroads in the early 1800s were probably little different from those which remained in use on isolated sections of the system up until the 1940s and beyond. It was laid down in the various Acts of Parliament for the construction of the lines that every wagon used on the tramroads had to have the owners' name, his address and the wagon number painted on in white. On the Severn & Wye system their 1809 Act stated that the lettering had to be at least three inches high and of a proportional breadth. The provision of such information in a clear fashion was to enable the toll collectors to keep accurate records and also to ensure that the tramroad company's bylaws concerning the weight of wagons, width of wheels etc. were being adhered to. Here then were the origins of the private owner wagons with the name painted on the side.

In the early years of tramroad operation the wagons were supplied by the various mine and quarry owners and it can be assumed that the majority of colliery, quarry, iron mine and other industrial proprietors owned tramroad wagons to transport their produce. What is not known is whether there were any dedicated companies who may have hired wagons to those works, especially to the smaller operations. To help the traders the Severn & Wye purchased a stock of wagons in 1842 which were then leased out but the practice only lasted for two years, after which the wagons were sold. It was restarted in 1852 when the S&W again began to hire out wagons and by 1871 they had around 270 but with the demise of most of the tramroad after this date the number soon declined.

Those owners who can be traced can only be found by looking in the tramroad company's minute books where occasional transgressions against the bylaws are noted. For example, Messrs Trotter, Thomas & Co. and Edward Protheroe were recorded in 1840 as using wagons with too narrow a wheel rim which wore grooves in the tram plates.

The vast majority of the tramroad wagons were used for the coal and iron ore traffic. Each wagon carried between $1^1/_2$ and 2 tons and most were of timber construction. However, some do appear to have been built of iron as shown by the drawing below. The coal wagons also had an openable end to allow for tipping at Lydney and Bullo docks and also at tips alongside the South Wales Railway at Bullo and Lydney. A more specialist wagon was used by quarry owners for the transportation of large blocks of stone. These consisted of two four-wheel bogies connected by a flat platform as shown in the drawing and photograph on page 12. How numerous or widespread these wagons were is unknown. It is unlikely that there would have been many due to the cost of building such a vehicle which would have been high. It can only be said for certain that they were in use on the Bicslade Branch although they were undoubtedly used on all of the lines on which quarries were located.

Exactly how many wagons existed on the Forest's tramroads is unknown but given the Severn & Wye alone at one time had 270 there must have been several hundred more than this. If one takes a coal working, such as the Bixslade Colliery worked by David Mushet, which in 1841 had an output of 100 tons a day taken to Lydney, then at least 25 wagons would have been involved if one wagon made two round trips in a day. Multiply this across the whole of the Forest and a considerable number of wagons would have been involved. Sadly, how that amount of traffic was regulated is unknown.

The coming of the broad gauge railway to the Forest area spelt the beginning of the end for the tramroad systems. Between 1851 and 1854 the Bullo Pill line was converted to a broad gauge railway by the South Wales Railway Co. who had purchased the line from the Forest of Dean Railway Co., who had bought out the Bullo Pill Railway Co. in 1826. Those traders who had owned tramroad wagons now had to go out and purchase broad gauge wagons for the continuance of their traffic.

The Severn & Wye remained a tramroad until 1868 when its mainline was converted to a broad gauge railway which itself was soon to succumb when converted to standard gauge in 1872. Here some traders must have been worse off having provided broad gauge wagons at large expense and then within a couple of years having to convert them to standard gauge.

The use of privately owned tramroad wagons continued until the final demise of the tramroad in the Forest of Dean with the closure of the Bicslade Tramroad in 1947 – although a couple of the bogie stone wagons remained in use between the stone works at Bixslade and the wharf until the 1960s.

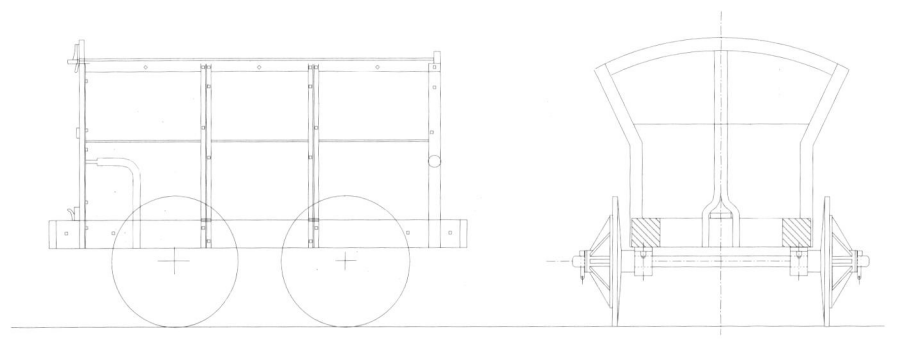

A drawing of what appears to be an iron-bodied tramroad wagon, probably for the carriage of coal. In shape it is very similar to some of the wooden-bodied vehicles.

A close-up of three mineral type wagons in use during the late 1920s on the privately-owned Crump Meadow Tramroad which joined the colliery of that name with the main Forest of Dean Tramroad on the edge of Cinderford. The wagons are typical of those used throughout the Forest, although all three here differ from one another! Notice also the variety of wheels with a couple of wagons having wheels of differing diameters. This is probably a case of make-do and mend as the tramroad was coming to the end of its working life. Unfortunately there is no trace of any lettering on the wagons recording owner and weight as was required by the mainline tramroad companies. By this date such refinements had been long forgotten.

A tramroad coal wagon photographed in 1947 standing on the siding for the Bixslade Deep Level. The siding was off another long-lived ex Severn & Wye tramroad, the Bicslade Branch (note, Bixslade was always spelt with a 'c' by the railway). The dimensions of the wagon were given as: wheels 23in. diameter, 31in. centres; body 36in. wide inside, 36in. height to hinge of end door, 81in. length. These wagons probably carried about 2 tons of coal.

An engraving of the upper basin of Lydney Docks showing a tramroad wagon standing on a tip awaiting discharge into the sailing vessel. The tip appears to be rather like a canal lift bridge but what cannot be ascertained is whether there was a lifting platform on which the wagon stood, or if a chain was simply attached to the rear of the wagon which was then lifted off the ground.

An accident on the broad gauge at Lydney reveals a glimpse of the tramroad coal tips on the right. These were provided to give an interchange facility with the South Wales Railway. Similar tips were built alongside the South Wales line at Bullo for interchange with the Forest of Dean Tramroad prior to its conversion to a broad gauge line.

To move large blocks of stone from the quarries to the various stoneworks, bogie flat wagons were employed. Two such vehicles are seen here posed on the Bicslade Tramroad with the three horse team taking a breather.

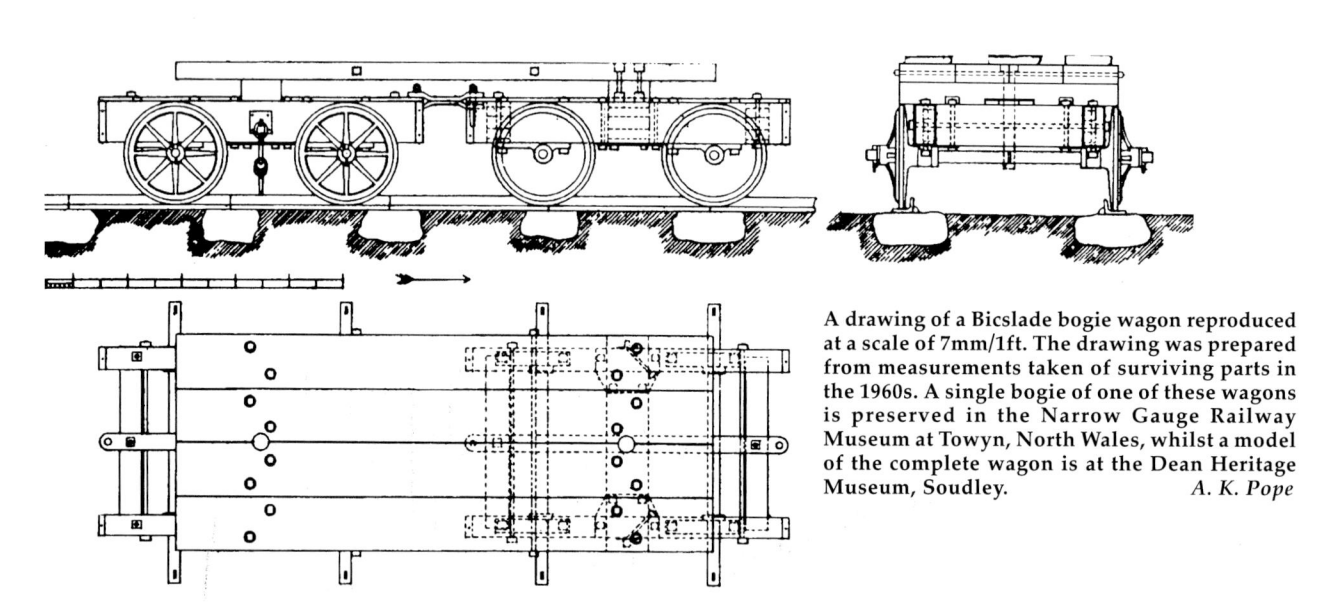

A drawing of a Bicslade bogie wagon reproduced at a scale of 7mm/1ft. The drawing was prepared from measurements taken of surviving parts in the 1960s. A single bogie of one of these wagons is preserved in the Narrow Gauge Railway Museum at Towyn, North Wales, whilst a model of the complete wagon is at the Dean Heritage Museum, Soudley. *A. K. Pope*

To move smaller rubble stone about, especially around the quarry areas, 'tipjack' wagons were employed. The upper frame seen here could be turned and fitted in various bearing mounts to enable a [missing] iron box to be tipped in whichever direction was necessary. The iron box itself was removable to allow it to be craned in and out of the quarries. A complete tipjack as seen here can be found in the Dean Heritage Museum.

THE BROAD GAUGE

LITTLE is known of the broad gauge private owner wagon situation. The surviving order books of the Gloucester Wagon Co.[1] reveal some orders placed for broad gauge wagons by Forest based traders. For example, on the 11th April 1865 an order was placed by Aaron Goold of Newnham for thirty secondhand broad gauge wagons, ex Hirwaun Aberdare Steam Coal Co., to be paid for over a period of seven years. Goold was a colliery proprietor, owning the Bilson and the Crump Meadow collieries on the Forest of Dean Branch. Another possible Forest order was placed on the 6th October 1866 by William Barrett for the hire of six 10-ton wagons for a three year period. Another was on the 4th June 1870 when Toomer Brothers, coal merchants from Reading, Berkshire, took out a contract with the wagon company for the repair of six broad gauge wagons for five years. Toomers also had connections with Speech House Hill Colliery.

Those dated prior to 1868 would only work to stations on the South Wales mainline – Newnham, Awre, Bullo and Lydney – or the Forest of Dean Branch. The Severn & Wye did not convert any of its tramroad to broad gauge until 1868, and even then it was only the line between Lydney and Wimberry and opening of that was delayed until April 1869.

The Severn & Wye however, had been beaten to it by a new broad gauge line completed in the Forest. The Forest of Dean Central Railway ran from a junction with the South Wales Railway at Awre, through Blakeney and up the Howbeach valley aiming for the Parkend Coal Co's New Fancy Colliery and other collieries around Howbeach. It opened in May 1868 but the traffic potential was not realised. It was not until early 1869 that the connection to New Fancy was completed. After this date Parkend Coal Co. wagons may have used the line for a while but soon the Severn & Wye completed their Mineral Loop on the standard gauge which gave a much better outlet through Lydney and traffic began using that route which left the Central with little business.

The Severn & Wye had, as already mentioned, converted the mainline of their tramroad between Lydney and Wimberry to a broad gauge line. They also laid in a branch to Pillowell on part of the Mineral Loop to serve the colliery of the Compressed Coal Co. who also had a works at Whitecroft and a line down to a tip in Lydney Docks. However, the Severn & Wye's broad gauge period was not to last long as it was converted to standard gauge in May 1872. The standard gauge had already existed between Whitecroft and Lydney in the form of mixed gauge following the opening of the standard gauge only Mineral Loop in April 1872.

The most detail on the broad gauge wagons can be found in The General Instructions for the conversion to standard gauge of the line between Swindon and New Milford in May 1872. The owners listed in this document are given in Table 1. There is much of interest in the list.

Gollop & Ridler were known in 1860 to have restarted work at the Staple Edge Brickworks on the Forest of Dean Branch but they were mainly known as colliery proprietors and they also had a coal merchants business in Lydney. They also had an interest in Wallsend Colliery which was in the Howbeach valley and connected to the Forest of Dean Central Railway. For conversion the wagons were to go to the wagon works at Bullo Pill which are dealt with on page 170.

Allaways of Lydney were the operators of the tinplate works at both Lydney and Lydbrook. They also held the Wigpool Iron Mine which was connected to the Forest of Dean Branch via a tramroad to Whimsey. The wagons would have been used in conjunction with the Lydney works as there was no broad gauge connection to

Table 1 Trader	Owned	Hired	Instructions for conversion
Gollop & Ridler	15		To be sent to Mr Joseph Boucher, Waggon Works, Bullo Pill
Allaway, Lydney	12	3	Please send our twelve private Waggons to Lydney, where they will be altered. The three Waggons, Nos. 22, 23, and 24, which we have on hire, and which we believe are marked Forester & Co., please send to the Cheltenham & Swansea Waggon Co., at Swansea.
Trotter, Thomas, and Co.	8	6	Trotter, Thomas & Co. say – 'Mr. Goold will take charge of the six Bristol Waggon Company's Trucks at Bullo, Nos. 56 to 65, and Mr Boucher will take 182 and 183, J. T. Thomas, owner;' and Sydney J. Thomas says, 'Please send my 6 trucks, Nos. 66 to 71, to Mr Boucher.'
Ridler & Weedon	20		No instructions
Parkend Coal Company	18		No instructions
Greenham & James (Forest of Dean Iron Co.)	6	23	All Waggons hired of the Western Waggon Company to go to Bridgwater, and those hired of the Bristol & South Wales Waggon Company to Bullo Pill.
H. Crawshay & Co.	3	13	To be sent to Cinderford Iron Works.
Goold Bros and A. Goold & Co.	250		A. Goold & Co. say, 'We would like all our trucks sent to Bilson Junction, subject to permission on their arriving at Bullo Pill, to be allowed to send some of them to the Docks at that place. This will apply to all the trucks bearing the name of 'Goold' in any shape.'
T. Brain, Trafalgar Colliery			No instructions
S. Holmes, Howbeach	5		To be sent to the Bristol Waggon Works, Lawrence Hill, Bristol.

Lydbrook. Some members of the Allaway family had had an interest in the Cinderford Ironworks but this was sold out to Henry Crawshay in 1862. The wagons would have been used to take iron ore from Whimsey to a furnace, possibly Cinderford, and the finished iron to the tinplate works at Lydney and then the finished product away from the works.

Trotter, Thomas & Co. worked quarries and collieries on the western side of the Forest in both the Bixslade and Wimberry valleys. It was this company, with their colliery at Wimberry, that campaigned hard for the Severn & Wye to convert their tramroad to a railway.

Ridler & Weedon had an interest, together with Messrs Lückes & Nash, in the Speech House Hill Colliery. A trade directory for 1876 lists Ridler & Weedon as 'coal merchants, Lydney Basin'. It is assumed that Weedon is connected to the family who had a coal business centred on Goring in Berkshire but this has not been confirmed.

The **Parkend Coal Company** was owned by the Sully family when the broad gauge Severn & Wye line arrived close to the colliery. The history of Sullys is dealt with on page 85. As 'no instructions' were given regarding the conversion of the wagons it is possible that they were added to the fleet of wagons operated by Sullys out of Bridgwater as it was to be another twenty years before the broad gauge was removed from the West of England.

Greenham & James (Forest of Dean Iron Co.) were also located at Parkend and were working the iron furnace there. They would have had direct access at Parkend to the broad gauge as the ironworks was alongside the Severn & Wye line. Around 1869 they built a broad gauge siding to the coke yard above the furnaces. Indeed coke was one of the first commodities carried on the Severn & Wye's broad gauge line coming up to Parkend from South Wales.

H. Crawshay & Co. are the biggest surprise here in the very low number of wagons owned and in the comparatively small number on hire. Considering that they had many interests in collieries, iron mines and blast furnaces in the Forest the number of wagons does not seem sufficient to operate their business. However, Crawshay had his own private tramroads between several of his iron mines and the blast furnace at Cinderford. He had also built their own broad gauge line between Lightmoor Colliery and Cinderford Ironworks in 1854 which was operated by their own locomotive. It is possible therefore that most of Crawshay's wagons were 'internal users' and that the finished iron from the ironworks was taken away in Great Western Railway Co's wagons. A photograph taken of the ironworks in the 1890s does show the sidings full of Great Western wagons only. Locally it is recalled that they also had some transporter wagons onto which tramroad wagons were loaded at Churchway at the northern end of the Forest of Dean Branch to bring iron ore from the western side of the Forest via the Severn & Wye Tramroad to Cinderford, these may have been broad gauge.

Goold Bros, by far the largest owners and operators had collieries in the Cinderford area and also Soudley Ironworks hence the request that all wagons be worked back to Bilson Junction from where they would be placed on the collieries own private sidings. Presumably most were to be converted here suggesting the presence of a wagon repair shed. It is also noted in the minutes of the Cheltenham & Swansea Wagon Co. Ltd[2] that Alfred Goold

The end of the broad gauge Severn & Wye line was at Wimberry. The colliery operated by Messrs Trotter, Thomas & Co. was on the hillside beyond the wagons. Immediately in front of the camera is the Wimberry Tramroad and on the interchange wharf stands the remains of a tip used to discharge the tramroad wagons into railway wagons below.

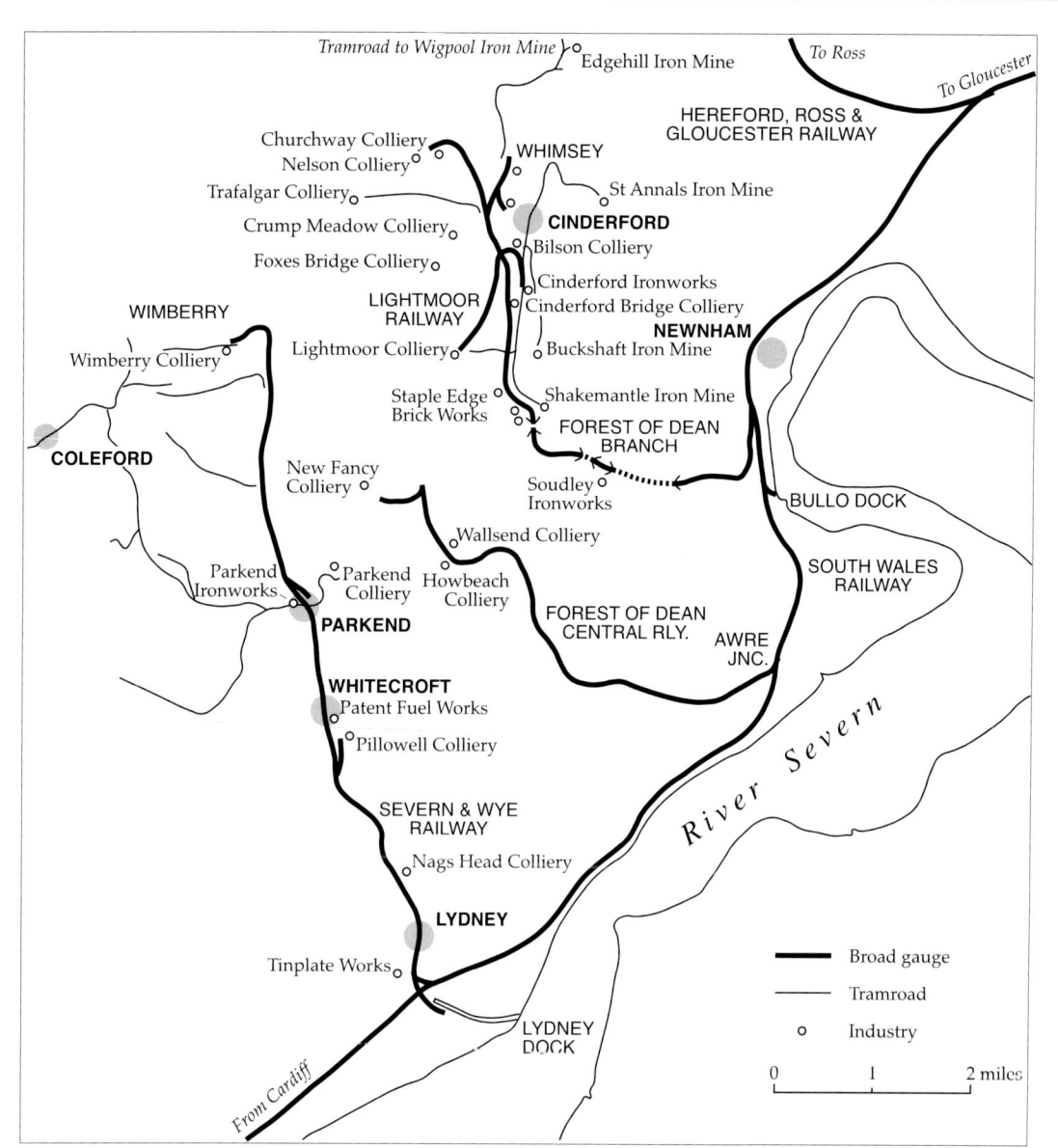

The extent of the broad gauge in the Forest of Dean. The Severn & Wye line from Lydney to Wimberry was to be fairly short lived. Note that not all of the industries were active at the same period.

was chairman of a meeting of owners of broad gauge wagons which was held at Gloucester in late 1871. With the impending conversion they were seeking compensation from the Great Western for the costs involved in rebuilding their wagons. The outcome of the meeting is unknown.

T. Brain & Co. were the owners of Trafalgar Colliery which was not connected directly to the broad gauge system. They did have sidings off Bilson Yard on the Forest of Dean Branch to which ran a tramway from the colliery.

S. Holmes was operating collieries in the Pillowell area and the Patent Fuel Works at Whitecroft. It was for his Pillowell Colliery that the Severn & Wye laid a broad gauge line on the route of the Mineral Loop.

There were possibly other traders on the Forest of Dean Branch as sidings were provided in several locations. One such was the **Cinderford Bridge Colliery**. The colliery was being worked by William Wagstaff when he applied for a broad gauge siding in 1854. In 1858 he was in difficulties and the concern was put up for sale which included '19 Adams & Co. Registered Railway Coal Trucks'. The sale did not proceed but another was arranged for August 1860 when Wagstaff was hoping to buy a colliery on Moseley Green which could have supplied business to the Forest of Dean Central Railway of which by this time he was Chairman. Wagstaff was, however, still in difficulties and his interests were sold off in late 1861. Cinderford Bridge appears to have been taken by a John Vincent who wished to give it up in 1876. At a sale of Cinderford Bridge plant in August there is no mention of any wagons but the siding was still laid to the broad gauge so obviously no traffic had passed for the last four years!

Another trader on the broad gauge working into the Forest may have been **James Smith** of Stroud, Glos. Certainly in May 1872 he had 42 wagons converted to standard gauge by the Gloucester Wagon Co. It is known that he later traded in the Forest so it is likely that he was doing so during this period as well.

[1] Gloucestershire Records Office ref D4791 6/1 to 6/16
[2] *Ibid.*, D2202

Lightmoor Colliery, Ruspidge, Near Cinderford. 1225.

One of the largest and most productive of the housecoal collieries was Lightmoor owned by Henry Crawshay & Co. Ltd. The colliery was started in 1836 and was producing coal by the early 1840s. By 1883 production stood at 104,811 tons, extensive screening plant had been erected and a large fleet of railway wagons had been acquired to enable the coal to be moved away.

In comparison, at Lydbrook Colliery a pair of sidings was provided and the coal was brought to them over the wooden bridge seen to the right of this view. The sidings were located where the small groundframe hut stands to the left of the bridge. Lydbrook Deep Level itself was off to the right towards the bottom of the valley. In 1883 production at the Lydbrook Deep Level Colliery stood at 15,234 tons.

THE COLLIERIES

Part One
Housecoal Pits

THE early coal workings in the Forest of Dean were in the Middle series of coals which were used in the main for housecoal purposes. With the construction of the tramroad system several larger collieries began to develop and the eventual conversion of the tramroads to railways in the 1850s and 60s, followed by the construction of new lines through the 1870s and 80s, led to them growing much larger. However, it could be said that it was the growth of the collieries which led to the construction of the tramroads and railways. What is certain is that the two were interlinked.

The largest of the housecoal collieries were situated just to the west of Cinderford on the ridge along which ran the Severn & Wye Railway's Mineral Loop. Here were to be found Trafalgar, Crump Meadow, Foxes Bridge, Lightmoor, New Fancy and several smaller collieries in the Yorkley/Pillowell area. Other housecoal collieries were in the southwest of the Forest between Lydney and Bream. Here lay the workings of Kidnalls, Princess Royal and Parkend and smaller concerns such as Venus & Jupiter, Park Hill and Wimberry. Note that not all of these collieries worked concurrently.

All of the collieries named above had direct rail connections but there were dozens of smaller pits, usually worked by the free miners and with fairly small workforces. These either sold their coal locally, known as 'land sales', or by moving it to a suitable rail transshipment point. Most of the Forest's railway stations had a loading wharf onto which horses and carts could be taken. There were also other points which were used such as the Marsh Sidings at Parkend, Bicknor Siding near Lydbrook and perhaps more unusually, one of the passenger platforms at Upper Lydbrook Station. Here the shelter on the down platform was temporarily removed in 1884 to allow wagons stood on the siding below to be loaded. Quite what intending passengers made of clouds of coal dust is unknown!

The larger housecoal collieries began to close down in the 1920s due to a combination of there being less workable coal and rising amounts of water to be pumped. One of the first to go was Speech House Hill which stopped production in 1906. Then Trafalgar closed down in 1925 after which the domino effect of the rising water soon impacted on Crump Meadow, closed 1929, Foxes Bridge 1930, Lightmoor 1940, and New Fancy in 1944. In part, their closures were compensated for by the development of the newer Deep collieries which are covered in the next section.

The smaller collieries which were not rail-connected moved their output using horse and cart to the nearest loading point. In this case coal is being loaded at Speech House Road Station on the Severn & Wye Joint line. The cart, carrying about 2 tons of coal, was owned by G. Davis of Broadwell Lane End near Coleford. The identity of the rail wagon being loaded cannot, unfortunately, be determined. The wagon standing on the siding behind the cart is interesting. Only a **B** is visible, possibly of **BRA** – British Red Ash Collieries?

Parkend Deep Navigation Collieries, Ltd.,

Telegrams: "NAVIGATION, LYDNEY."
Telephone: LYDNEY 4.

LYDNEY,
GLOUC.

The screens at Parkend were a rather rudimentary affair, it would appear that the colliery tubs were brought straight from the pit head at the Royal shaft, seen in the distance on the left, to the loading bank. Here they were tipped over the screens which would have consisted of just a set of perforated iron sheets through which the various sizes of coal fell. The coal could then be loaded into the waiting wagons. The photograph can be dated to pre-1892/5 as the wagons on the siding are lettered for the Parkend & New Fancy Collieries Co. This company was replaced by the Parkend Deep Navigation Collieries Co. Ltd in 1892 but the wagons would probably have remained in the original livery until the next repaint was due. Wagon numbers visible on the original print are 516, 573, and 521.

PARKEND

Parkend Colliery was originally owned by Edward Protheroe, one of the largest mining entrepreneurs in the Forest between the 1820s and the 1850s. His empire also included collieries in the Cinderford area and, for a while, the ownership of the Bullo Pill Tramroad and a share in the Severn & Wye system. By 1849 he had leased his Parkend interests to Messrs Trotter, Nicholson and Sully. In 1852 they formed the Parkend Coal Co. and following the death of Protheroe in 1857 they purchased the colliery from his executors. Thomas and James Wood Sully, who were partners in a Bridgwater, Somerset, firm of ship owners, colliery agents and coal factors (see page 85), soon bought out the other partners and traded as the Parkend Coal Co. In December 1878 the Parkend Coal Company Limited was formed but was not a great success and in 1881 Sully's sold out to a Mr Jackson.

In 1883 the collieries were bought by a syndicate including the manager, Thomas Deakin, who eventually came to control the entire concern. In 1885 a new company, the Parkend & New Fancy Collieries Co. was formed. In 1892 that company was wound up and replaced by the Parkend Deep Navigation Collieries Co. Ltd.

The company worked two main collieries, Parkend and New Fancy. Parkend consisted of the Royal Pit, which was the coal winning shaft, and Castlemain the pumping pit. The colliery closed for the production of coal in 1929 after which date all coal from the area was brought out through New Fancy Colliery.

THE WAGONS

The Parkend Coal Co. had a small fleet of broad gauge wagons as recorded on page 14. Some were supplied by the Cheltenham & Swansea Wagon Co. as in October 1868 two wagons were supplied on seven year redemption hire together with a repairing contract but at the same time a further repairing contract was signed for another eight wagons. It is possible that the previous wagons had been supplied by the Cheltenham Co's predecessors, Messrs Shakleford & Ford. In September 1871 the Parkend Co. wrote to the Cheltenham & Swansea Wagon Co. asking for revised terms for the future repair of their wagons. In May 1872 another twenty wagons were ordered on seven year redemption hire. October 1875 saw a repairing contract taken out for 22 wagons.

Photographed in November 1886, this wagon formed part of the batch of forty new wagons bought on seven years deferred purchase. The plate on the solebar is the GWR registration plate (D.3584) apart from which no other plate was carried. *GRC&WCo.*

Many of the standard gauge wagons for Parkend were provided by the Gloucester Railway Carriage & Wagon Co. The first record in the minutes is for November 1877 when six secondhand 10-ton wagons were let on hire for a period of three months to the Parkend Coal Co. Unfortunately there is no record of the livery carried.

The Great Western Railway registered some Parkend wagons in April 1879:
(Wagon No. followed by GWR Reg No.)

65	C.1998	66	C.1996	67	C.1989
68	C.1990	69	C.1992	70	C.1993
71	C.1994	72	C.1995	73	C.1997
74	C.1999	75	C.1962	76	C.1953
77	C.1966	78	C.1967	79	C.1979
80	C.1980	81	C.1981	82	C.1983
83	C.1985	84	C.1986.	all 10-tons.	

The Western Wagon Co. books show that in February 1883 Robert Jackson of London bought 42 10-ton wagons 'to be worked by the Parkend & New Fancy Colliery at Lydney'. These wagons had originally been sold to a George Holford but when he defaulted on payment they were seized by the wagon company and resold. However, in 1883 Jackson also defaulted and the wagons were again seized and in November 1883 were resold to R. Toomer & Co.

In January 1885 80 secondhand 10-ton wagons were let on hire for a year to the Parkend & New Fancy Collieries Co. The new company was obviously treading carefully, managing the capital and seeing how orders picked up before purchasing any new wagons. The following January saw them re-hiring 50 of the wagons. In March 1886 100 wagons were registered with the Great Western, running numbers 400-499. July 1886 saw the remaining 30 also re-hired, trade was obviously good. In September 1886 forty 10-ton wagons were bought new on deferred purchase over the usual period of seven years and with the Parkend Co. to keep the wagons in repair. These may have been the wagons registered by the Great Western in October 1866, running numbers 500-539:

500	D.3584	501	D.3585	502	D.3579
503	D.3583	504	D.3586	505	D.3588
506	D.3587	507	D.3590	508	D.3600
509	D.3589	510	D.3591	511	D.3592
512	D.3593	513	D.3594	514	D.3595
515	D.3596	516	D.3597	517	D.3598
518	D.3599	519	D.3601	520	D.3602
521	D.3603	522	D.3604	523	D.3605
524	D.3606	525	D.3607	526	D.3580
527	D.3608	528	D.3609	529	D.3611
530	D.3610	531	D.3612	532	D.3613
533	D.3614	534	D.3615	535	D.3616
536	D.3617	537	D.3618	538	D.3619
539	D.3620				

Wagon No. 111 photographed at Gloucester reveals that it was from a different builder. Of four planks and with rounded ends, the oval builder's plate on the left is annoyingly unreadable. *L. E. Copeland*

Wagon No. 249 photographed in January 1893 was part of the order placed in December 1892 for 50 new 10-ton wagons with payment over seven years. Internal dimensions were 14' 5" x 7' 0" x 3' 8". The wagon carries a Gloucester owner's plate as well as a GWR registration plate which shows that the wagon was also registered in 1893. *GRC&WCo.*

February 1888 saw a return to the Western Wagon & Property Co. when forty new 10-ton wagons were ordered on deferred purchase with the tenants agreeing to keep the wagons in repair. In January 1889 a total of fifteen 10-ton secondhand wagons were let on hire. The final order for the Parkend & New Fancy Collieries came in October 1890 when fifty secondhand 10-ton wagons were let on hire for three years.

In January 1892 the Parkend & New Fancy Collieries Co. Ltd offered to sell to the Gloucester Wagon Co. 200 10-ton wagons at £35 each which were then to be let back to the colliery company on an agreement for deferred purchase. The Gloucester Co. accepted this. In March the Parkend Co. cancelled agreements for eighty wagons held by them and for three held by Hockaday & Co., both being on deferred purchase, and to sell them to the Gloucester Co. and also to sell to Gloucester 125 other wagons for the sum of £7,505 13s. 4d. and then to take the whole number on an agreement for deferred purchase. From these two agreements it would appear that the Parkend Co. had a fleet of over 400 wagons. Quite what the purpose behind the financial manoeuvring was is unclear but as the Parkend Co. was about to go into voluntary liquidation it may have been a way of protecting its assets ready for the takeover by the Parkend Deep Navigation Collieries Co. Ltd in 1892.

April 1892 saw the letting on deferred purchase of two 8-ton and 206 10-ton wagons to the new company and in December fifty new 10-ton wagons were let on deferred purchase over seven years.

In October 1893 a further 30 10-ton wagons were bought new on deferred purchase and the same number of secondhand wagons were also hired for three weeks. It may be that the purpose of short term hirings were to tide the company over whilst business was brisk. In this case it might have been a stop-gap measure until the new wagons were delivered. Two months later, in December, seventy-five secondhand 10-ton wagons were hired 'temporarily'.

What is uncertain is just how long a period of hire had to be to see the wagons painted with the hirer's livery. Some may have remained in the hiring company's lettering whilst others may have received a very simple form of lettering which was easy and quick to apply. An example of a wagon painted in this fashion appears on page 90.

The next batch of new wagons were ordered in July 1896 with thirty new 10-ton wagons being let on deferred purchase. In December 1898 thirty new 10-ton wagons were let on deferred purchase and with the tenants agreeing to keep them in repair.

After this there were no more orders placed with Gloucester apart from some sundry ironwork and wheel retyring. What is unknown is whether any more wagons were ordered from any other builder.

Other details of Parkend wagons appear in a set of Severn & Wye Joint Committee letter books which mainly deal with wagons off the road or damaged. On the 17th March 1898 wagon No. 12 was damaged. On the 11th June 1902 wagons No's 73 & 118 were off the road at the turntable for tip No. 6 in Lydney Docks. On the 31st March 1904 wagon No. 399 was off the road at Speech House Road. In December 1907 wagon No. 70 suffered a broken drawbar on the 27th. On the 30th April 1908 wagon No. 104 was damaged as was wagon No. 199 on the 3rd October.

The next details of the wagon fleet appear in 1942 when a mortgage was raised on railway wagons owned by the Parkend Co. and details of the wagons involved were given:

No's: 209-252 inc.; 255-258 inc.; 319; 370-399 inc.; 259-287 inc.; 289-303 inc.; 305-315 inc.; 317-318 inc.; 320-323 inc.; 325-363 inc.; 365-369 inc.; 400-402 inc.; 1; 15; 19; 33; 86; 112; 113; 115; 124; 128; 151; 156; 174; 184; 189; 206; 207; and 885.

This gives a total of 178 which would have been involved in traffic from New Fancy Colliery which itself was in decline by this time and was to close two years later.

Photographed in October 1896, this wagon was part of the lot ordered in the previous July. It has a steel underframe and a seven-plank body with internal dimensions of 14' 5" x 6' 11" x 4' 0". Note the new style of axlebox. *GRC&WCo.*

One of the final batch of wagons built by Gloucester for Parkend, photographed in March 1899. Note the subtle changes in lettering and styles between the wagons, especially the 'Forest of Dean' and the '*Empty to*' branding. *GRC&WCo.*

Wagon No. 383, photographed in the sidings at Lydney Dock in 1909. It is not a Gloucester-built wagon and whilst similar in lettering style to No. 380 on the opposite page it differs in having the prefix 'Nº.' in front of the 383. Annoyingly its earlier running mate alongside with dumb buffers does not reveal its running number.

Enlarged from the same original image are the two illustrations below which again reveal subtle differences in the lettering style. Notice also that wagon No. 357 on the left has outside strapping, whilst wagon No. 203 below appears to be of 4-plank construction.

Two views of Parkend wagons included to show that it can be worthwhile studying views of goods yards and of locations far removed from the wagons home. On the left is a commercial postcard of Milford Haven Docks in Pembrokeshire. Sat on the quayside is a rake of private owners, from the left a North's Navigation, Cardiff; a Rock Collieries, Swansea; two more North's wagons and then a Parkend wagon No. 101 (enlarged in the inset). The two detached wagons are both Fernhill Merthyr Collieries, Cardiff. Quite what a Parkend wagon was doing at Milford is uncertain. Possibly it was supplying steam coal to a part of the large fishing fleet which used this port, possibly it had brought housecoal for a merchant in the town or it may have been delivering coal to one of the local businesses such as the South Western Ice Co. Ltd immediately behind the wagon. We shall probably never know unless in Milford Haven are receipts surviving. The right-hand view shows a Parkend in the yard at Monmouth Troy station. The wagon is full so is probably delivering for a local business. Alternately, it may have arrived at Monmouth on a Ross-Pontypool Road goods, having been picked up at Lydbrook Junction, and be awaiting forwarding on a Monmouth-Chepstow freight down the Wye Valley to a destination such as the Wire Works siding at Tintern. A commercial postcard does exist which shows a Parkend wagon on this siding, albeit very much 'in the distance'.

NEW FANCY

In 1855 it was reported that New Fancy was being 'opened with all vigour' and by 1860 it was producing about 250 tons a day which went to Lydney over the tramroad. From about 1888 onwards some coal from the Parkend gale was being brought to the surface at New Fancy, this increased over the years as the workings got further away from the Parkend Royal shafts until in the 1920s all output came out through New Fancy. The colliery was connected in 1868 to the ill-fated Forest of Dean Central Railway but with the opening of the Severn & Wye's Mineral Loop in 1872 a new connection was made which really sealed the fate of the FoDCR as it lost the majority of its traffic.

Between 1940 and 1944 the colliery was producing virtually all the tonnage for the Mineral Loop apart from ammunition traffic. Some 350 wagons per week were sent out until final closure of the colliery came in August 1944. It is likely that the wagons to be seen at this period were from a real mixture of owners as this was the period of wartime wagon pooling. Thus the last time that Parkend wagons would have been seen exclusively at their home colliery was pre-war.

Above: The pit head at New Fancy showing a fine selection of buildings. On the right are two Cornish engine houses, both with rotative beam engines, and between them a pair of egg-ended boilers. The main winding engine house is on the extreme left.

Wagon No. 331 in the yard at New Fancy shows an alternative livery and appears to be lettered in white on a black body, it is not possible to define whether the lettering is shaded. 'PARKEND' occupies the top four planks, '*FOREST OF DEAN*' is in italic capitals on the right. It appears that the wagon may recently have had a replacement wheel set as the left hand wheel rims seem to be painted white. The photograph dates from *c.*1935.

The loaded wagon sidings at New Fancy Colliery with a rake of wagons lettered in the same style as No. 331 on the opposite page. Note the lettering 'NEW FANCY COLLIERY' on two planks of the side door which is also probably on 331. On the nearest wagon, a six-planker No. 360, there does appear to be an oval builder's plate on the solebars between the two arms of the brakegear V hanger, it also has steel solebars. Close inspection of the original print also reveals shading to the lettering, probably red. Wagon 374 is of 7-planks, No. 185 appears to be of 4-planks. The sidings curve round to join the Severn & Wye Mineral Loop. The photo dates from around 1935.

A view taken at the Parkend Co's wagon repair shop at New Fancy showing a freshly repainted wagon No. 350. The wagon has a steel underframe but sadly the proud workmen obscure any builder's plates upon it and the axleboxes which might also give the builder away. The wagon has outside strapping on the bodywork which would be unusual for a Gloucester-built wagon and so we are left again to speculate whether Parkend sourced its wagon fleet from several builders.

The Speech House Hill Colliery locomotive stands with two wagons in front of the pit head. Both of the wagons, No's 234 and 232 are built by the Gloucester Carriage & Wagon Co. Both have steel underframes and are 6-plank with end doors. They are probably in black livery, lettered white but they also show traces of shading.
collection Alan Corlett

SPEECH HOUSE HILL

The Speech House Hill Colliery had a very chequered history. Work was started on the site at some point between 1832 and 1841 by a Richard James. Ownership then passed to a William Jordan who set up the Royal Forester Colliery Co. Ltd in October 1861. In September 1869 a new company, the Speech House Hill Colliery Co. Ltd, was set up to purchase the colliery. Behind this company were Messrs Lückes and Nash, Ridler, a coal merchant from Lydney and Weedon a coal merchant of Stroud and Lydney. In 1873 control passed to the Great Western (Forest of Dean) Coal Consumers Co. Ltd and at this point Edwin Crawshay, the son of Henry, became involved with the concern. It was this company which laid in a siding to connect with the Severn & Wye in 1875. The company was wound up in 1883 but not before the Great Western (Forest of Dean) Collieries Co. Ltd had been set up. Connected with this company was Toomer, a coal merchant of Reading, who came to have a controlling interest. The company was wound up following the bankruptcy and death of Toomer to be replaced by the Speech House Collieries Co. Ltd in December 1892. In the prospectus for the new company it was said that for the sum of £207 10s. forty wagons worth £1,200 could be acquired. These still had a portion of the deferred payment, amounting to £578 5s. 0d., to be paid. In 1896 a new owner for the colliery was found when Whittaker of Keighley, Yorkshire, bought the concern and set up the Speech House Main Collieries Co. Ltd. The use of the word 'Main' in the colliery title shows the Yorkshire influence, many collieries in that coalfield being given this name. However, like so many companies before it was soon in difficulties and closure threatened. The colliery was then bought by Henry Crawshay & Co., mainly to protect their adjacent Lightmoor Colliery. Coal winning ceased in 1906 and the siding was soon removed.

THE WAGONS

It is possible that some of the orders in the Gloucester Wagon Co's books for Messrs. Lückes & Nash were actually for Speech House Hill although it must be said that they had many other colliery interests in the Forest. Sadly, no photographs have been found which show a Lückes & Nash wagon so no idea of the livery carried can be given. Again, Messrs Ridler & Weedon may have used their own wagons bearing in mind that they had some on the broad gauge (see page 14). Between 1868 and 1872 traffic from Speech House Hill would have been able to take advantage of the Severn & Wye's broad gauge line to Wimberry.

R. Toomer may also have used his own wagons whilst the Great Western (Forest of Dean) Collieries Co. Ltd was in

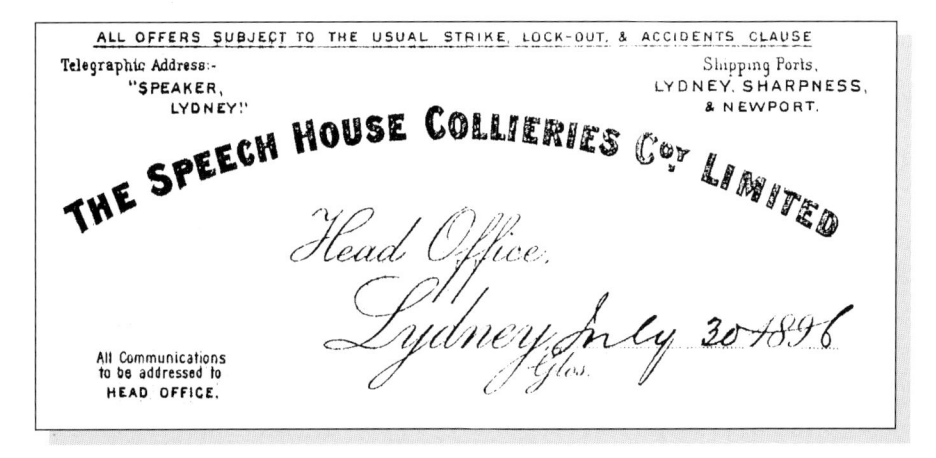

A Gloucester official photograph of wagon No. 101 taken in March 1893. The description boards give the livery as a black body, lettered white but there does appear to be a trace of shading around the lettering and it is possible that this wagon is a repaint. The company changed hands the previous year and maybe the new owners were cutting back on the painting costs. *GRC&WCo.*

existence as at his bankruptcy in 1892 the Gloucester Wagon Co. held 142 of his wagons. Toomer certainly had 42 wagons from the Western Wagon Co. which were acquired at the end of 1883 from R. Jackson and which had previously been worked by the Parkend & New Fancy Colliery (see page 19). No trace has so far been found of a wagon lettered up for the Great Western Collieries Ltd.

The Speech House Collieries Co. Ltd ordered 150 new 10-ton wagons in February 1893 which suggests that they acquired no wagons from the previous owners – especially as they took 25 10-ton wagons at the same time on temporary hire. The photograph above is of a wagon from this batch but as discussed in the caption, there are traces of shading around the lettering which may indicate a repaint of an existing wagon.

With another change of owner in 1896 the livery may have changed again as seen below. However, it is unknown whether any wagons were actually provided by Charles Roberts directly for Speech House or if the wagon was merely a repaint of an existing wagon belonging to Whittaker.

A wagon built by Charles Roberts of Wakefield for the Speech House Main Collieries Co. Ltd shows Whittakers northern interests. The livery, apparently grey with black lettering shaded red, may only have been applied as a 'sales pitch'. Many companies did this and the wagons may not have run in service in these colours. The size of the order is also unknown. *HMRS*

26

A 7-plank 10-ton wagon photographed in December 1896. It was part of an order for six new wagons placed in August. The livery is black with white lettering, the door was probably natural wood or grey with either a black or red 'W', although one source states that the door was 'chromium yellow'. Steel underframe with Gloucester builders, owners and repairer's plates. Registered with the GWR. *GRC&WCo.*

WIMBERRY

Wimberry Colliery was situated on the Old Furnace Level gale which was first granted to Aaron Hale and Edward Baldwin who in turn leased it to David Mushet in October 1821. Following his death in 1847 it passed to his sons William and Robert. In 1864 the lease passed to Messrs Trotter, Thomas & Co. who began work around 1867. In 1868 the colliery was important enough to be the terminus of the Severn & Wye's broad gauge line. In 1872 Mr Thomas was pressing for narrow gauge accommodation and in 1874 was requiring to extend the siding. However, by 1885 the concern was in difficulties, probably with water, and by 1890 the colliery was said to be disused. The gale was surrendered back to the Crown and was regranted to a committee of Free Miners in 1891 and they formed the Wimberry Colliery Co. Ltd. By April 1900 the workings had reached the barriers leaving little coal to be worked. From July 1901 the colliery was leased to Amos Brown but he gave up three years later. No more work was done and eventually the colliery became part of Cannop Colliery (see page 56).

THE WAGONS

As already mentioned in the broad gauge section Messrs Trotter, Thomas & Co. were operating wagons into Wimberry. In 1872 they owned eight and hired six wagons but unfortunately no further details have come to light apart from the fact that they had some wagons from the Cheltenham & Swansea Wagon Co. These however, cannot be ascribed directly to Wimberry Colliery and so have been included in the 'Unknowns' section (see page 145). Previous to the conversion of gauge the company also operated standard gauge wagons, again some were supplied by the Cheltenham & Swansea Wagon Co. but again they cannot be put down to Wimberry Colliery.

The first reference to wagons for the Wimberry Colliery Co. comes in August 1894 when six 10-ton secondhand wagons were let on hire for 14 months by the Gloucester Railway Carriage & Wagon Co. In August 1896 six new 10-ton wagons were let on deferred purchase over seven years with the wagon company to keep them in repair. The following month saw twelve secondhand 10-ton wagons let on hire for 2 months.

In June 1897 a further twelve 10-ton secondhand wagons were let on deferred purchase over seven years. These were previously let to the Speedwell Colliery (presumably that at Nailbridge and covered in the 'unknowns' section on page 144). The GRC&WCo. bought them back for £480 and resold them for £619 9s. 9d. In October 1897 a further eighteen 10-ton secondhand wagons were let on seven years deferred purchase followed in November by a further six wagons over five years and in December the same contract was taken out for yet another six wagons, these being said to be 'of the old type'. Work was obviously going well at the colliery at this period to warrant such an increase in the wagon fleet.

It was not to last and with the decline of the colliery from c.1900, with work ceasing in 1904, a lot of the wagons were still within the deferred purchase period so they presumably returned to the ownership of the Gloucester Wagon Co.

One mention of a Wimberry Coal Co. wagon can be found in the Severn & Wye letter books where it is recorded that on the 22nd November 1901 No. 100 was off the road at Lydney Docks. This suggests that the company numbering policy was not consecutive as they certainly never owned 100 wagons.

The sidings at Trafalgar Colliery with the pit head and the screens in the background. A rake of empty wagons stands on the left which includes several non-Trafalgar but unidentifiable wagons. In the centre is the loaded wagon weighbridge with a rake of wagons about to pass over it. On the right stands a Trafalgar wagon which appears to be of 5-plank construction and has obviously just been moved by means of the shunting horse.

TRAFALGAR

The Trafalgar gale was granted in 1842 and remained in the hands of the Brain family until 1919. Until the colliery was connected to the Severn & Wye in 1873, when the Mineral Loop was opened, the only rail outlet for Trafalgar was via a privately owned steam-worked tramway to transshipment sidings off the Great Western yard at Bilson. In 1890 new sidings were laid in from Drybrook Road Station. The Trafalgar Colliery Co. Ltd was formed by the Brains in 1881 and continued to run the colliery until in 1919 ownership of Trafalgar passed to the New Trafalgar Colliery Co. Ltd, which had been set up by the owners of Foxes Bridge Colliery and Lightmoor Colliery in an attempt to keep Trafalgar working and to protect the other two collieries from the threat of water from Trafalgar itself. However, the colliery proved to be a major drain on finances and was finally closed in 1925.

Right. **A rake of Trafalgar wagons standing on Speedwell Siding at Nailbridge near Drybrook. This siding was used as a land sales wharf by Trafalgar. The wagons are of a slightly different livery pattern to that seen above. In this case they have their running numbers centrally above the side door.**

THE WAGONS

No record has yet been found as to where Trafalgar obtained its wagon stock. All wagons appear to be either 4 or 5-plank and to be in black livery, lettered in white. A repair agreement was taken out with the Gloucester Wagon Co. in February 1895 for eight 6-ton, one 7-ton, seven 8-ton, and two 10-ton wagons for the sum of £3 15s. 0d. per annum for a period of seven years. In February 1896 twenty-two 10-ton wagons were added for seven years at £2 0s. 0d. Both of these agreements were renewed at the expiration of seven years although the prices had increased to £4 0s. 0d. and £2 12s. 6d. In July 1908 a repair agreement for 61 10-ton wagons was signed at £3 0s. 0d. with a 5s. advance. This contract was renewed in July 1915 although at that date it was only for 51

A fine study of wagon No. 330 at Lydney Junction in 1908. A five-plank 10-ton capacity wagon with end door, the builder is unknown although the builder's plate is obvious in the centre of the solebar. It does have a Gloucester Wagon Co. repairer's plate affixed, a contract first taken out in 1895. Interestingly, the wagon has both the *Tare* and *Load* details painted on the left-hand side. Livery is black with white lettering.

courtesy Bob Essery

wagons. In May 1909 ten wagons were 'converted' at a cost of £125. 'Conversions' were the alteration of elderly dumb-buffered wagons to sprung buffers. This work was necessary under the regulations of the Railway Clearing House which laid down that no dumb-buffered wagons were to remain in traffic after 1913. Also in May 1909 a repair contract was signed for seven 6-ton and four 7-ton wagons for 4 years 11 months, for 51 10-ton wagons over 6 years and 5 months, 11 10-tonners and 5 8-tonners for 10 years and one 10-ton wagon for repair and 'conversion'. In April 1910 a contract for repairing 22 10-ton wagons for seven years was signed, again probably a renewal of the earlier contracts and it was again renewed in May 1917. This was the last mention of Trafalgar in the Gloucester minutes as it was not to be long before the company ceased to exist.

The Severn & Wye letter books reveal that on the 6th April 1901 wagons 79 & 99 were off the road at Lydney Docks. Also off in the same place on the 5th January 1903 was wagon No. 110. Finally, on the 8th January 1911 wagon No. 1 was reported off at Sharpness.

Other known wagon numbers for the period 1891-1904 are: 76, 115, 118, 119, 120, 122, 128, 129, 130, 131, 138, 139, 140, 142, 145, 146, 147, 148, and 150.

All remittances and Inland Orders must be sent direct to Cinderford

TELEGRAPHIC ADDRESS;- "CRUMP, CINDERFORD."

Collieries.
FOREST OF DEAN.

Shipping Ports.
LYDNEY, SHARPNESS,
& BULLO.

LYDNEY & CRUMP MEADOW COLLIERIES Co. Ld.

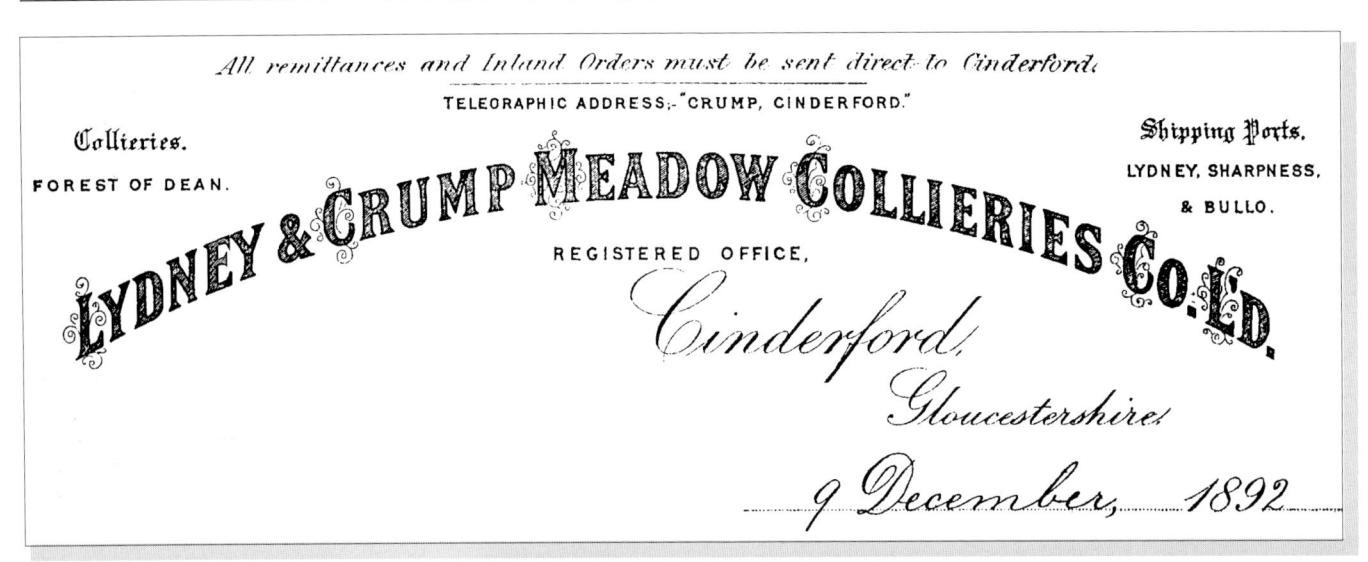

REGISTERED OFFICE,

Cinderford,
Gloucestershire,
9 December, 1892

CRUMP MEADOW

The colliery was started circa 1829 by Edward Protheroe with coal first being produced in 1839. By 1847 Aaron Goold & Co. were the owners of the colliery, Goold had been Protheroe's agent at the Bilson Colliery which was worked in conjunction with Crump Meadow. In 1866 output was given as 12,000 tons per month, all of which would have gone out over the Great Western's Forest of Dean Branch. Obviously this output shows why Goolds had 250 broad gauge wagons by 1872. In 1874, following the death of Aaron Goold, the Bilson & Crump Meadow Collieries Co. Ltd was formed. The largest shareholder was a John Richardson of Swansea. In 1884 a new company, the Lydney & Crump Meadow Collieries Co. Ltd was formed to take over the concern. In 1907 the company bought an area of the newly formed 'deep' gales and began developing the Arthur & Edward (Waterloo) Colliery (see page 60). Work stopped at Crump Meadow in July 1929 due to a combination of thin coal reserves and increasing water from other closed collieries.

The earliest known view of a Crump Meadow wagon, lettered for the Lydney & Crump Meadow Collieries Co. Ltd. Probably a five or six-plank wagon with an end door and a raised plank on the fixed end. The bodywork appears quite light and thus the livery may have been grey with white lettering. *Neil Parkhouse collection*

A general view of the Crump Meadow pit head. In the distance can be seen the chimneys of the adjacent Foxes Bridge Colliery.

An enlargement of a postcard dated 1914 which shows a rake of Crump wagons standing on the siding down into Bilson Yard on the GWR's Forest of Dean Branch. This shows all the wagons to be of 5-plank construction with a raised rounded end. The livery is black with plain white lettering. The two grey wagons are interesting and frustrating as it is just not possible to determine their ownership.

THE WAGONS

The earliest wagons known in connection with Crump Meadow Colliery would have been those belonging to Aaron Goold. On the 11th April 1865 an order was placed with the Gloucester Wagon Company by Aaron Goold of Newnham for thirty secondhand broad gauge wagons, ex Hirwaun Aberdare Steam Coal Co., to be paid for over a period of seven years. By the end of the broad gauge in the Forest in 1872 Goold Bros and A. Goold & Co. had 250 wagons. These were to be worked to Bilson Yard and then presumably onto the Crump Meadow sidings for either conversion to standard gauge or scrapping. Care has to be taken though with references to Goolds as they were also involved in working Soudley Ironworks, trading as Goold Bros., between 1863 and 1873 (see page 161).

The first reference to standard gauge wagons in the Gloucester books comes in May 1876 when Tom Goold purchased ten 10-ton wagons for cash secondhand.

On the 13th November 1878 the Bilson & Crump Meadow Colls. Co. Ltd hired ten 10-ton secondhand wagons. This order appears to have been renewed every three months up until January 1879 and then in July comes the note: 'Bad debts written off:- C. A. Goold'.

The next reference in Gloucester minutes comes well after the formation of the Lydney & Crump Meadow Collieries Co. Ltd which suggests that they may have acquired wagons from elsewhere. On the 12th December 1893 fifty 10-ton secondhand wagons were let to the company for 3 months at £13 0s. 0d. That wagons were sourced from other companies is shown by 40 wagons on simple hire from the Western Wagon Co. in June 1898.

The Company appears again in Gloucester minutes in August 1905 when ten secondhand 10-ton wagons were taken on deferred payment over 4³/₄ years with the tenants keeping the wagons in repair. A further secondhand 10-ton wagon was taken in October 1910 and another in November. After that date there are no further references to Lydney & Crump Meadow in Gloucester's minutes. The last couple of entries are interesting in that they were for single wagons showing piece-meal additions to the wagon fleet. They were also noted as being ex coal merchants. Were these cases of wagons being taken by the colliery in payment for debts? The deferred payment being transferred to the colliery co. thus giving them cheaper wagons. Of note is that whilst some wagons were supplied by the Gloucester Wagon Co. no official photographs appear to have been taken.

Wagons on hire from the Western Wagon & Property Company are again noted in December 1910 (50 wagons), December 1911 (50 wagons), December 1912 (100 wagons), December 1913 (50 wagons), December 1914 (150 wagons) and December 1920 (100 wagons). There was also an order for 10 new 12-ton wagons in August 1916 which were built in the WW&PCo's works at Cardiff and paid for over 7 years on deferred payments of £16 13s. 0d. per wagon per annum.

The wagons seem to have carried various liveries over the years. The earliest Lydney & Crump Meadow lettered wagons, of which only the example seen on the previous page has been found, appear to have a grey body with plain white lettering. Then came a change to the single word 'CRUMP' in white on a black body.

On the 29th July 1899 wagons No's 254, 428, 594 were off at Lydney Docks and on the 28th December wagon's 148 and 262 were noted as off at Lydney. On the 2nd February 1904 wagon No. 630 was off road at Lydney Docks and wagon No. 600 was damaged there on the 13th October. The 17th January 1906 saw wagon No. 633 off road Lydney Jct. Yard. A number of wagons were involved in an incident at Tufts Jct. on the 11th November 1907 with wagons No's 622, 541, 505, 288, 222 off road. The 4th July 1908 saw wagon No. 235 off at Cinderford Old Station and on the 20th January 1911 wagon No. 716 was off at Lydney Jct. Crump Meadow Colliery Co's hired wagon No. 563 was derailed Sharpness on the 10th April 1919.

After the closure of Crump Meadow in 1929 the wagon fleet would have been transferred to Arthur & Edward Colliery bearing in mind that the wagons between 1908 and 1929 would have served both collieries.

See also page 60.

From the opposite end of the same original postcard as at the top of the page comes this enlargement showing what is probably wagon No. 290. It can be seen that it has dumb buffers and a rounded top to the non-opening end.

A view over the screens at Foxes Bridge with loaded wagons emerging. Furthest right are a couple of Foxes Bridge wagons, then one belonging to Small's of Taunton, and a Leadbeter of Newport. The rest appear to be colliery wagons.

FOXES BRIDGE

A start was made on this site following an abortive beginning further south in 1855. The men behind the colliery were William Montague of Gloucester and Moses Teague, a free miner. Edward Protheroe was also claiming an interest, probably through a mortgage. By 1868 Protheroe's interest had passed to Osman Barrett and Teague's to William Crawshay. In that year Barrett and Henry Crawshay, William's son, were granted a license to build a connection to the Great Western's Forest of Dean Branch at Bilson Yard. In 1870 the output of the colliery was some 50,000 tons. In 1872 a connection was also made to the Severn & Wye's Mineral Loop line after which most traffic went that way. In December 1881 Barrett and others conveyed their interest in the colliery to Charles A. Goold, brother of Aaron Goold who operated the adjoining Crump Meadow Colliery. In 1889 the Foxes Bridge Colliery Co. Ltd was formed with Goold, Henry Crawshay and John Richardson of Swansea as the biggest shareholders. In 1904 the concern was transferred to the ownership of Henry Crawshay & Co., although remaining an independent company until the colliery closed in late 1930.

THE WAGONS

No details are known of builders but photos tend to indicate that most wagons were of 4 or 5-plank, painted black with white lettering. Wagon No's 6-8 were registered by the GWR in 1877 and they are also known to have registered No's 60, 61, 63, 66, 336-8, 342. In February 1888 there was a report of a Court case between one Mountjoy, a Newnham wagon builder with works at Bullo Pill, and Goold. The claim, of £59 4s., was for repairs to wagons under a contract entered into in 1879 with the Foxes Bridge Co. The defence was that the work was either not done or was done badly. The only real detail of the wagons was that some were of 8-ton capacity. The case went to arbitration and sadly no further details are known.

On the 28th December 1904 wagon No. 340 was reported off at Tufts Jct. and on the 21st July 1905 wagon No. 101 was mentioned in the S&W letter books.

Another enlargement from the series of postcards showing the lines down into Bilson Yard, this time giving details of a Foxes Bridge wagon. Apparently of 6-plank construction and very simply lettered.

Livery appears to have been black with white lettering and with a triangle and white dot on the side doors. The triangle probably being grey.

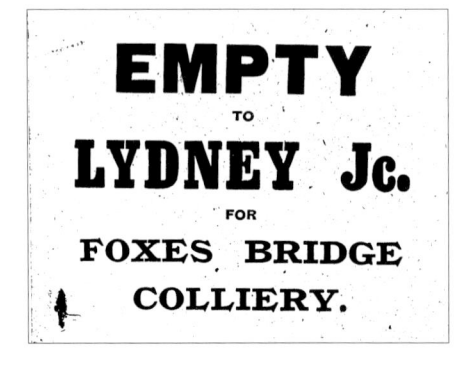

EMPTY
TO
LYDNEY Jc.
FOR
FOXES BRIDGE
COLLIERY.

A view over the sidings and pit head at Foxes Bridge. The screens are on the right, just to the left of the headframe. Several Foxes Bridge wagons can be made out on the left, together with a couple of Midland Railway wagons. The only other wagon which can be clearly defined on the original print belongs to Messrs Weedon Bros of Goring, Berkshire, it is not known if there was a connection with the Weedon of Stroud previously mentioned at Speech House Hill.

A closer view of the sidings, again with a good assortment of wagons visible. Several Forest coal factors' wagons are collecting orders including Sully & Co. of Lydney (see page 85) and Edgar Jarrett of Bream (page 77). From outside the Forest are wagons of William Thomas of Wellington, Somerset (page 117). The strangers are the Parkend wagons. The question might be asked as to why another Forest colliery company's wagons could be found collecting coal from a rival concern? The answer is found in the minutes of Henry Crawshay & Co. and also in the recollections of some of the Lightmoor Colliery office staff. Apparently if one colliery was suffering a shortage of wagons to complete an order then fellow members of the local Coal Owners Association would hire out wagons to assist.

Lightmoor Colliery, nr. Cinderford

A fine view of the pit head at Lightmoor with the main pumping engine on the left and the headframes of the North and South shafts in the background. In front of the headframes a rake of Sully & Co. wagons stand on the screens sidings. Sullys were a major coal factor and are dealt with later. On the left of the rake is one for – Williams & Co.

LIGHTMOOR

Work at Lightmoor commenced circa 1836 with coal being won from 1841. The Crawshay family was involved, firstly through William Crawshay, an ironmaster from Merthyr Tydfil, and then his son Henry. In 1879 Henry died but it took ten years and an Act of Parliament to sort out the family affairs, after which the works were continued on under the title of Henry Crawshay & Co. Ltd.

On the opening of the Great Western's Forest of Dean Branch in 1854 a broad gauge line was made between the colliery and Cinderford Ironworks, also owned by Crawshays, with a connection to the FoD Branch at Bilson. The building of the Severn & Wye Mineral Loop in 1872 gave Lightmoor a new outlet, especially to Lydney Docks, and most traffic then went this way.

Lightmoor was one of the most important housecoal collieries in the Forest. Thankfully, the minute books of H. Crawshay & Co. Ltd have survived which give a good impression of the trade to and from their various collieries. This information is reproduced in Appendix One. The minute books also reveal some of the orders for wagons.

The colliery did not quite reach its centenary of coal production as it closed early in 1940.

THE WAGONS

The earliest reference found to Crawshay's wagons is in July 1867 when a repairing contract for one wagon was taken out with Shackleford & Co. Ltd of Cheltenham. It is likely that this would have been broad gauge.

The first mention in Gloucester records of an order connected with Henry Crawshay comes in April 1875 when four mineral wagons were bought for cash.

In 1879 it is known that the Great Western Railway attached registration plates to wagon numbers 12, 17, 19, 20, 23 and 24.

The Western Wagon Co. supplied ten 10-ton wagons on 7 years deferred purchase in January 1880. In September 1881 a further twenty 8-ton wagons were ordered from the same source. In March 1894 Crawshay's minutes record

A Lightmoor wagon built by Gloucester in 1899. It is unusual in that the livery is grey with white lettering shaded black. At some point after this date the company standardised on a black body with white lettering, shaded red (see next page) and ex-Crawshay staff interviewed could not recall ever seeing any grey wagons. *GRC&WCo.*

Wagon No. 283 was part of the lot ordered in November 1907 which consisted of ten 10-ton wagons. The oval solebar plate, to the right of the 'V' hanger, is a Henry Crawshay & Co. owner's plate. This suggests that the wagons were paid for in cash by the trustees of Henry Crawshay as with an order in 1899. *GRC&WCo.*

a payment to the British Wagon Co. for wagon hire. In April 1894 the same source records an offer from the Standard Wagon Co. (of Bullo, see page 172) to purchase 30 old coke wagons (probably no longer needed due to the closure of Cinderford Ironworks) at £18 each or £540, or to convert them into coal wagons at £6 each, £180, or to exchange them for twenty secondhand 8-ton coal wagons at £25 each, £500, or 11 new wagons valued at £54 each, £594. Crawshays noted that if the wagons were sold then £20 each could be obtained. The outcome is unknown.

In March 1895 payment was made to the British Wagon Co., whether for wagons or for hire or for repairs is unknown. In November 1898 payment was made to the Bute Supply Co. for wagon hire. In May 1899 it was noted that additional wagons were needed and quotes were sought for the supply of thirty 10-ton wagons 'of new specification', probably to the 1897 Railway Clearing House specifications. The wagons were to be paid for by 'the trustees'. The quote from the Gloucester Wagon Co. was for £63 per wagon to be delivered in October and the Gloucester Records record that this was to be paid in cash, the sum being £1,890.

In July 1902 an arrangement was entered into with Messrs Edwards & Brown for the purchase of six new 10-ton wagons at £52 10s. each. An attempt was made by Mr Edwards to get the company to take a further four steel framed 10-ton wagons at £62 10s. each but this was considered too dear.

Crawshays returned to the Western Wagon Co. again in April 1904 with an order for thirty 10-ton secondhand wagons on 7 years redemption purchase and again in June with another order for 30 10-ton wagons on 7 years deferred purchase with a repairing agreement, a total contract price of £2,205.

November 1907 saw ten new 10-ton wagons supplied for £665 cash by the Gloucester Wagon Co. This is the last order which can be attributed to Lightmoor as after this date Crawshays other colliery, Eastern United, began to be developed and wagons were supplied lettered for that colliery also.

In the Crawshay minutes there then

A view of a Lightmoor wagon in the sidings at Eastern United. Builder unknown. Above the running number is a letter C on a square background and to its right is a ★. These symbols relate to Railway Clearing House commuted charge schemes and show that Crawshays had signed up to these. *L. E. Copeland*

35

A portion of a Lightmoor wagon in Bilson Yard showing a different lettering layout. From the running number of 1789 it would appear that it was one of the batch supplied in September 1915 by the Western Wagon & Property Co. The wagon displays a slight variation in the lettering style with the H. Crawshay and Cinderford not being aligned to the left but following the diagonal strapping. *L. E. Copeland*

Wagon No. 46 seen on the same occasion in 1933 as 1789 above displays the more normal arrangement of lettering. *L. E. Copeland*

appear several monthly listings of wagon hire: The Western Wagon & Property Co. in December 1907, Geo. Bryant & Co. in September 1908, New Bowson Coal Co. and Western Wagon Co. in March 1909 and New Bowson again in April 1909. Certainly Bryant and New Bowson were also customers at Lightmoor and it is possible that these are listings for Lightmoor wagons hired by those customers; income rather than payments.

In February 1910 it was stated that it had been decided to purchase Parry's wagons No's 7 & 8 from Mr J. W. Kilmister at the best price 'not to exceed £35'.

In December 1912 it is recorded by the Western Wagon & Property Co. that Henry Crawshay & Co. had had 66 wagons on simple hire.

At a Board Meeting in October 1913 it was further decided to get 20 new railway wagons on redemption hire as soon as possible. In November it was decided to purchase those 20 new twelve-ton wagons from the Gloucester Wagon Co. on seven years redemption hire at £14 13s. per wagon per year and £1 12s. 6d. per wagon per year for keeping same in repair. The draught agreement for the purchase of the wagons was approved in December and the order finally placed in January 1914. Apart from a later order for some wagon ironwork this is the last reference in the Gloucester books.

In December 1914 one secondhand coal truck was purchased from Mr J. W. Kilmister for the sum of £41 5s. January 1915 saw a decision to purchase seventeen 12-ton wagons from the British Wagon Co. on seven years redemption lease at £13 7s. 5d. per wagon per annum including repairs, the agreement being signed in February. In October it was reported that a further thirteen 12-ton wagons had been bought from Messrs Edmunds & Radley, Cardiff and that they were 'now being built by Messrs Harrison & Camm, Rotherham' at the rate of £87 15s. each net cash on delivery.

In September 1915 a further 76 10-ton wagons were ordered from the Western Wagon Co. on 7 years deferred purchase together with a repairing contract as from the 1st October. The cost per wagon was £9 7s. 6d. – a total cost of £4,987 10s. The wagons were taken from the stock of the WWCo. at £34 each. According to the order they were painted with the running numbers 1720 to 1825 but this totals to 105 wagons. Owner's plates with WWCo. numbers on were attached for the period of hire purchase. These plates were removed from the wagons in October 1922.

A letter was received from the Gloucester Wagon Co. in December 1916 asking Crawshays to consider the payment of an additional amount for the repairs of the 20 wagons leased on redemption hire. Crawshay's decided to purchase the wagons outright and do the repairs themselves. These would be undertaken at their wagon repair shed at Lightmoor.

Some idea of the size of the wagon fleet is given in March 1917 in a report:
'As to the 282 trucks owned by us it was considered that £80 per truck was a fair value and that they should be entered on the stock sheets at this price which amounted to £22,560.
As to wagons on redemption hire, the time they still had to run to complete purchase was fully considered. What was thought fair value proportioned as follows:
50 ten tonners on redemption hire from the Lincoln Wagon Co. at £80 each; £4,000
20 twelve tonners on redemption hire from the Gloucester Wagon Co. at £50 each; £1,000
17 twelve tonners on redemption hire from the British Wagon Co. at £30 each; £510
76 ten tonners on redemption hire from the Western Wagon Co. at £20 each; £1,520'

An unidentified wagon at Lightmoor showing a slightly different lettering style and presenting a rather scruffy appearance. Possibly it is in use as an 'internal user' and could well be loaded with small coal for use in the collieries own boilers.

In February 1818 it was reported that the redemption hire due on 30 wagons hired from the Lincoln Wagon Co., numbers 295 - 324, had now been paid off and that their owner plates on the wagons could be removed.

With the strain of the First World War beginning to tell on the infrastructure of the country it was reported in April 1918 that the Government intended appealing to all owners of private coal wagons to let the railway companies have 5% of their wagons for the duration of the war until otherwise arranged. Crawshays were going to be paid 6/6 per wagon per week for an 8-ton, 7/3 per wagon per week for a 10-ton, and 8/3 per week for a 12-ton. These rates included maintenance by owners of the wagons in all cases. Objections were raised as to Crawshays letting the railway company having any of their wagons but finally in June it was decided to let the railway company have 8 or 9 wagons when they wished them which was the amount due from Crawshays.

There was also a lot of correspondence relative to the painting of 76 wagons which were kept in repair by the Western Wagon & Property Co. Ltd. It was explained that they were trying to get out of painting the same, although according to their agreement it was plainly stated that the wagons should be painted once every three years, and that therefore they were due to be painted that summer [1918]. The matter was only shortly discussed, then it was arranged that the Secretary would write to them upon the matter and that they must carry out the terms of their agreement.

With new regulations being brought in by the Railway Clearing House regarding wagons it was reported that the cost of altering the brakework on the wagon fleet to suit would be about £10 per wagon which would involve a total outlay of about £4,000. There was no way out of it and it would have to be complied with.

In April 1922 another seventeen wagons become the property of Crawshays on the expiration of a seven year lease from the British Wagon Co. Ltd.

In September 1922 it was mentioned at a Board Meeting that Crawshays had been offered fifty-four railway wagons by Mr James Smith of Stroud (page 88) at £20 each and that arrangements were being made to have them inspected by the wagon foreman. It was thought that at this figure they ought to be a bargain worth considering but it is unknown if in fact they were purchased. They were certainly not on offer because Smith was ceasing trading so one can only suppose that he either had surplus wagons for his trade or was trying to get rid of wagons which needed work doing to them.

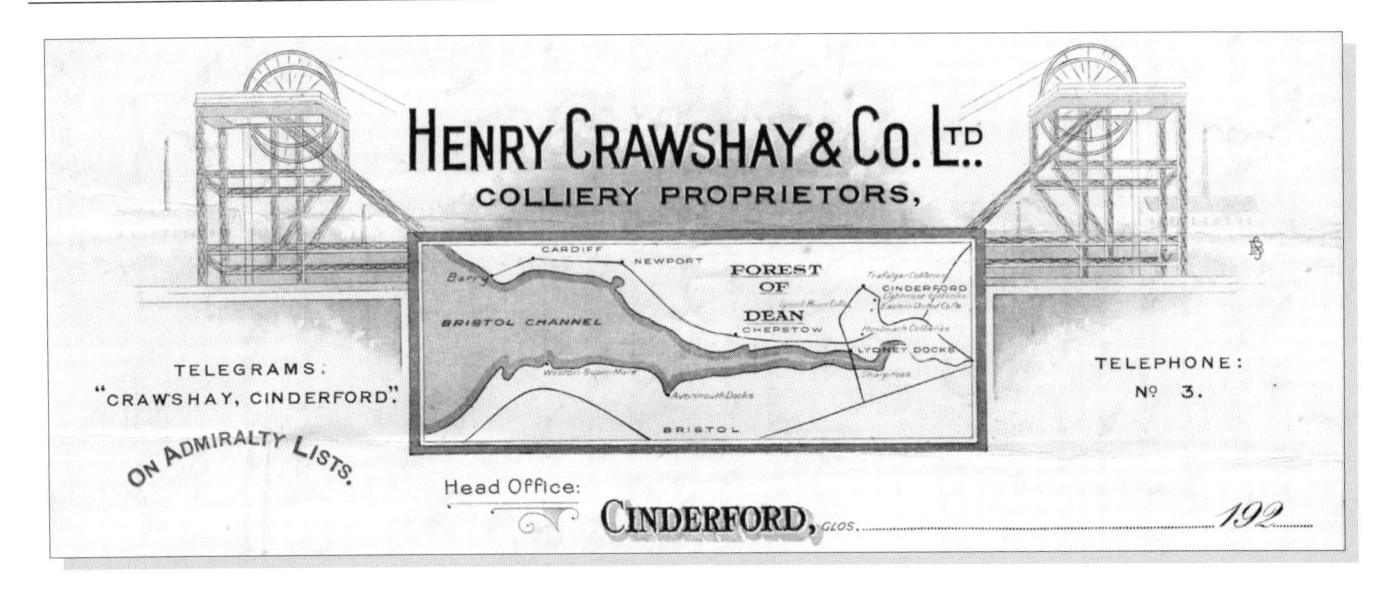

Crawshays could certainly have used the wagons as in February 1923 they were experiencing great difficulty in working their collieries in consequence of a scarcity of wagons. They had somewhat relieved the situation by insisting that as far as possible customers should send their own empties in but the question of hiring or purchasing additional wagons was bound to arise in the near future. Strangely, there are no further mentions of wagon shortages, possibly because trade was on a downturn.

The next mention of wagon matters in the minutes comes in June 1937 when a proposal was received from Messrs Wagon Repairs Ltd to acquire all of the wagons belonging to Forest of Dean collieries. They offered to buy from Crawshays a total of 310 mainline trucks and 70-80 'converted' trucks. The idea was that the wagons would then be re-hired back to the collieries on simple hire. Crawshays felt that it would be unwise to do this.

Another report in September 1938 reveals that when the Central Selling Scheme commenced in 1936 Crawshays had 406 wagons but that the fleet was down to 349 by that date. This included forty 'converted' type of which twenty-five would be taken out of traffic at the end of the year. The company would have liked 100 new wagons but they seem to have settled for 50 new wagons which were provided for their recently developed Northern United Colliery (see page 67).

With the international situation deteriorating plans had obviously been laid by the Government for the use of the railways in case of war, possibly learning from the conflict 20 years earlier. In October 1939 it was reported that the Government was requisitioning all coal wagons and would be paying for repairs to them during the time that they were under Government control. The rental charges for the wagons had not yet been agreed. Thus it was not long before the Crawshay wagons were spread around the country. None were destined to return to Lightmoor for long as the colliery closed in 1940.

Crawshays had their own wagon repair depot at Lightmoor Colliery. Here major repair work could be done, including the construction and fitting of new solebars and headstocks. Wagons were also painted here, on average once every three years.

Apart from the one batch of grey wagons it is believed that all Crawshay wagons were painted black, lettered white and shaded red. Certainly the men who worked in the wagon repair shed latterly can only recall black wagons.

Two partial Lightmoor wagons under the screens at Eastern United Colliery. The nearest wagon is one built by Gloucester Carriage & Wagon Co., the other is unknown. They display variations in lettering with the left-hand wagon being similar to that on page 37 whilst the other has a completely different lettering layout to any other seen. Its three-figure running number appears to end in 76.

The pit head at the Pluds Colliery. Situated at the top of a hill, it was connected to the screens at Waterloo sidings in the valley below by means of an incline.

courtesy Ron Scrivens

PLUDS

Although not destined to become a major colliery high hopes were entertained of the Pluds Pit (Lydbrook Colliery) by Richard Thomas & Co. when they began work there in 1891. New sidings were laid in off the Severn & Wye's Lydbrook Branch at Waterloo and screens erected. Thomas sold his interest in a failing colliery in 1912 to the British Red Ash Collieries Ltd. The sidings were removed by 1917.

THE WAGONS

Unfortunately nothing is known of where Richard Thomas sourced his wagons. He also had wagons in connection with his tinplate works in Lydney (see page 162). It is presumed that once Thomas's interest in Lydbrook Colliery ceased the wagons so lettered were absorbed back into his general fleet.

Wagons mentioned in the S&W letter books which can with certainty be ascribed to the colliery are No's 51 & 82 off road at Waterloo Sidings 13.10.1902.

A partial view of a Richard Thomas wagon lettered for the Lydbrook Collieries seen at Lydney in 1908. The only clue as to the wagon builder is the rounded end. The wagon number, ending in a 2, appears to be on a diamond-shaped background. The livery is probably black with white lettering and a red diamond behind the number. Frustratingly, the small lettering on the door cannot be read but it could well be a 'For Repairs Advise' plate.

courtesy Bob Essery

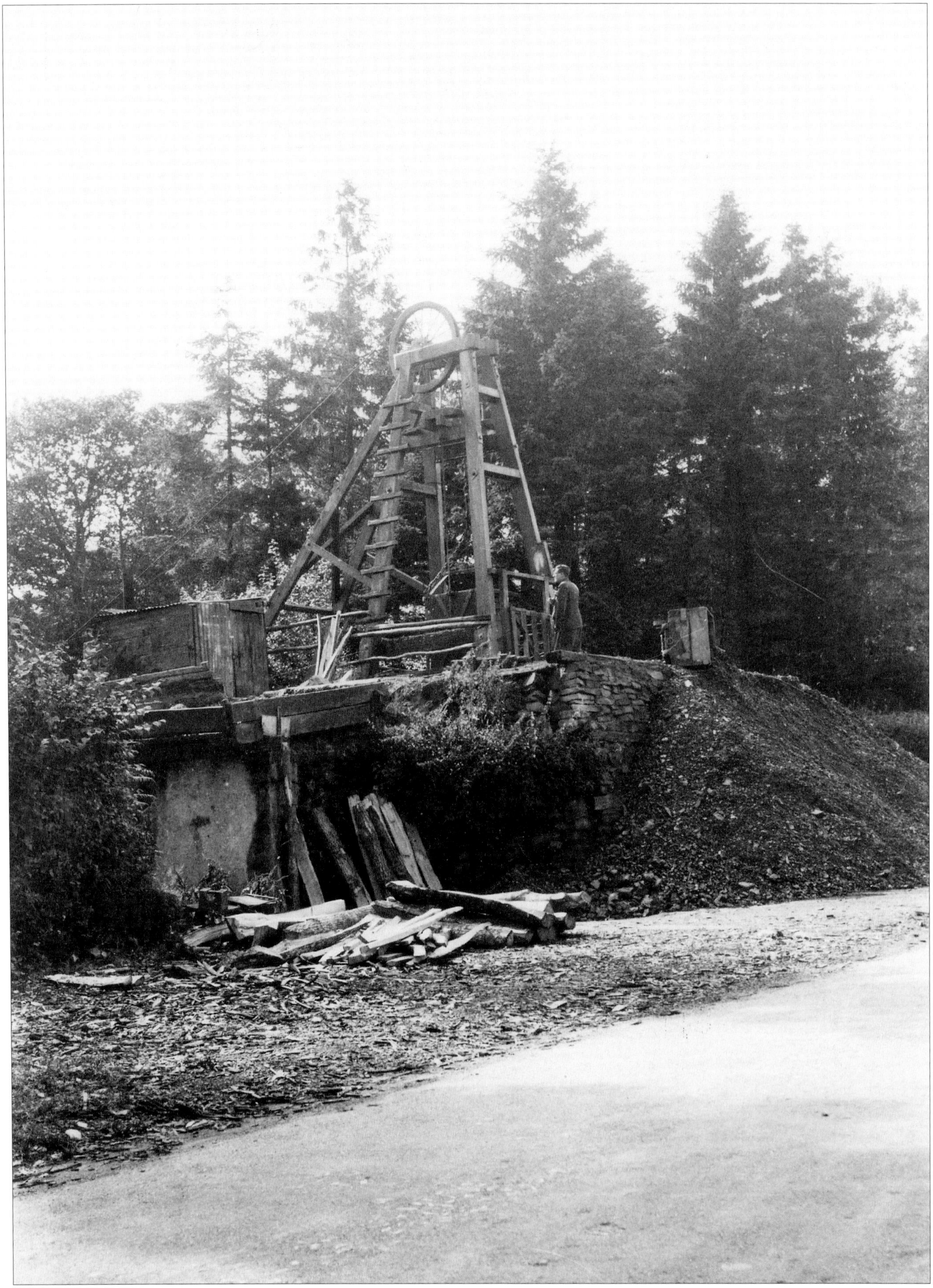

Smaller Collieries

UNLIKE the larger housecoal collieries, which could weather periods of depression in the coal trade or the temporary 'loss' of a seam of coal due to a geological fault or a washout, the smaller collieries were much more at the mercy of the vagaries of trade or nature. Many were small concerns employing a couple of dozen men, they were worked far more on a cash basis and when times were hard they often went to the wall.

Few of the smaller concerns could afford their own wagons, those that did had risen for a period to what in Forest terms might be called a 'middle-sized' colliery but often the end was bankruptcy for the owners and a loss of money for any investors. Many, many, small Forest businesses went this way. Records for them are few, one minute book that does survive is for the Coleford Red Ash Colliery Company Ltd but it gives only scanty information. Otherwise the business records held in the Public Record Office have to be relied upon for the dates of the start and end of a limited company (Board of Trade records, class BT31).

It is these smaller collieries which have, in the main, gone unrecorded photographically and thus any wagons they may have had escaped the lens. Wagons would probably have been bought secondhand, possibly from a smaller wagon company which did not record its products as did the larger wagon producers such as the Gloucester Wagon Co. One such small wagon company existed at Bullo Pill where Joseph Boucher built wagons but how many and for whom are unknown.

The 'unknown' owners of coal wagons are recorded on page 144.

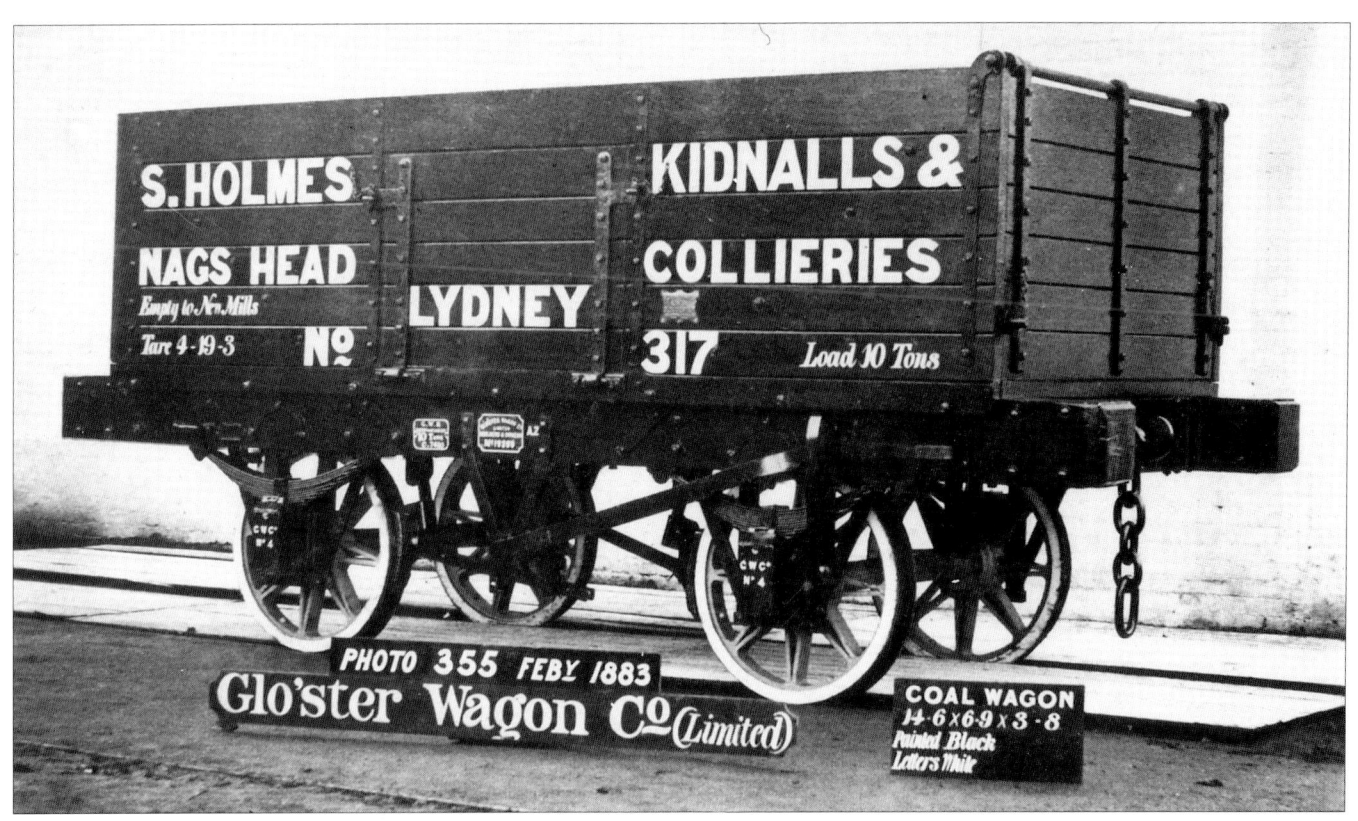

One of the eight wagons ordered in February 1883 and displaying a fleet number designed to impress customers! The fleet probably started with wagon number 310. Wagons built with dumb-buffers were due to be outlawed in 1887 when new Railway Clearing House specifications were introduced. Companies who had such wagons already in service were given until 1913 to get them converted to sprung buffers. Painted black with white lettering and branded *'Empty to New Mills'*. This was a siding on the site of the present day steam centre of the Dean Forest Railway. *GRC&WCo.*

NAGS HEAD COLLIERY

Simeon Holmes worked the Nags Head gale and started development work on it in 1877 in partnership with a Mr Smith, a coal factor. The Smith was probably James Smith of Stroud (see page 88). The colliery had a siding at New Mills which was later to be used in conjunction with Norchard Colliery (page 48). Holmes died in 1884 after which his grandsons continued the business, trading as Holmes Bros. The colliery was eventually taken over by the Dean Forest Navigation Coal & Fuel Co. The gale was surrendered in 1903.

THE WAGONS
As seen in the broad gauge section S. Holmes had five wagons which were to be sent to the Bristol Waggon Works suggesting that they had been obtained from that company.

There is one order in the Gloucester Wagon Co's minutes and that is dated the 13th February 1883 and is for eight new 10-ton wagons let on deferred purchase to Simeon Holmes over 7 years at £13 per year each. The Wagon Company were to keep them in repair.

The builder's portrait of Dean Forest Navigation's wagon number 150. The wagon carries a Gloucester builder's plate but no company registration plate. Registration presumably took place after the photo was taken and would undoubtedly have been with the GWR. Livery black with white lettering.
GRC&WCo.

DEAN FOREST NAVIGATION COAL & FUEL CO.

The Dean Forest Navigation Coal & Fuel Co. worked several small collieries in the Whitecroft/Yorkley area, together with a Patent Fuel works at Whitecroft which was connected via a long siding to the Severn & Wye. Managing Director was Simeon Oaks Holmes, a grandson of Simeon Holmes (see previous page). The company was in difficulties by 1893, although described as one of the most prosperous in the coalfield, and was mortgaged to the bank. Attempts were made to sell the concern in 1897 and 1898 but both were unsuccessful. When work ended at Whitecroft is unknown although the DFNC&FCo. was said to have closed its Pillowell Colliery in 1901 and removed its siding.

THE WAGONS

In February 1891 an order was placed with the Gloucester Wagon Co. for fifty new 10-ton wagons over 7 years deferred purchase at £11 19s. 6d. per wagon per year. The tenants were to keep them in repair. This is the only order which appears and the fact that the DFNC&FCo. were in difficulties in 1893 is recorded on the 11th July 1893: Bad debts written off - Dean Forest Navigation Coal & Fuel Co. £2 13s. 0d.

At a proposed sale of the works and collieries in 1898 it was stated that there were 113 6, 8 and 10-ton wagons and on the 8th November 1900 the S&W letter books mention wagon No. 104.

A view of the Patent Fuel Works at Whitecroft, owned by the Dean Forest Navigation Coal & Fuel Co. The photograph was taken for inclusion in an auction catalogue and shows the end of the siding into the works and Whitecroft Station off to the left beyond the buildings.
courtesy Gloucestershire Records Office D2299/584

Wagon No. 25 was photographed in September 1891 at Gloucester. It was probably part of the order for ten wagons placed in August. Of interest is the 'Empty to Bilson' which suggests that the company was also getting coal from the Cinderford area. *GRC&WCo.*

when in July 1892 the following appeared in the Gloucester Wagon Co's minutes: *'Forest Steam Coal Co. A cheque for £80 12s. 9d. given by Mr W. L. Hockaday in payment of a dishonoured bill having been returned unpaid. 15 wagons held by him on deferred payment.'* By July 1893 the Gloucester Co. gave up and records: *'Bad debts written off. Forest Steam Coal Co. £20 10s. 0d.'*

FOREST STEAM COAL CO.

It would appear that the company was working the Birchen Grove Colliery in Lydbrook on a lease for a period around 1890. Sidings for the colliery were located close to Lydbrook Church and can be seen in the lower view on page 16. In November 1890 one of the wagons ran away from the siding south of Upper Lydbrook Station and travelled two miles to Lydbrook Junction where it damaged a stop block and another wagon. The company was not a success and appears to have stopped trading by the end of 1892. Difficulties had surfaced earlier

THE WAGONS

In August 1890 twenty secondhand 10-ton wagons were let on hire by the Gloucester Wagon Co. to the Forest Steam Coal Co. for $1^1/_{16}$ years. A year later, August 1891, saw the company purchase ten new 10-ton wagons over 7 years on deferred purchase and a further five 10-ton wagons over 7 years were ordered in October.

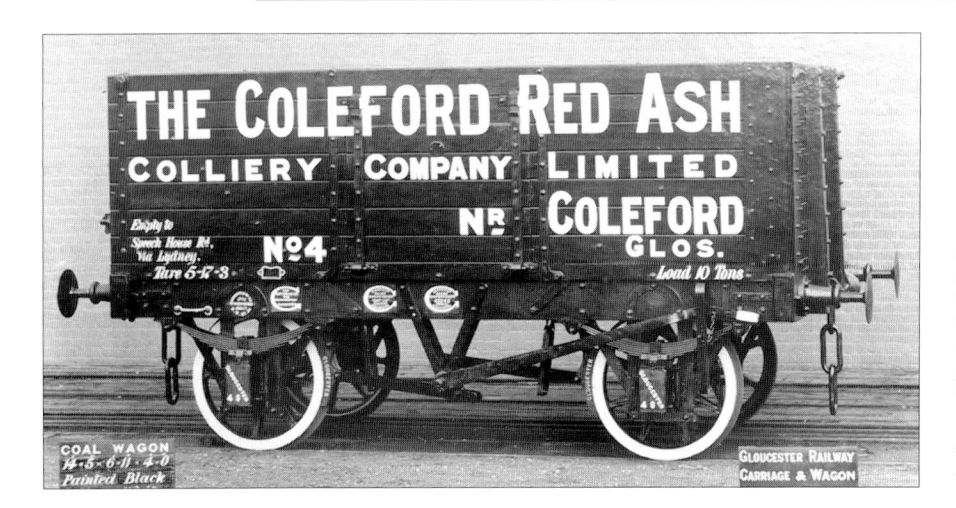

Left: Photographed in August 1905 was wagon No. 4. Below is No. 6 which was photographed in September. How the numbering sequence went is uncertain. It could have been in increments of two, or 1-6 consecutively.
Both GRC&WCo.

THE WAGONS

In July 1905 two new 10-ton wagons were ordered from the Gloucester Wagon Co. on 7 years deferred payments. August saw an order for three more new 10-ton wagons on the same terms. In October 1905 came the final order for one 10-ton wagon. In all cases the Wagon Co. were to keep the wagons in repair.

COLEFORD RED ASH

The Coleford Red Ash Colliery Co. Ltd was incorporated on the 23rd January 1905 to acquire the interests of George Morgan & Sons who were working the Foundry and New Road Levels close to Speech House Road. The subscribers included an E. T. Ward, coal merchant of Stroud. The Morgans had previously traded as the Forest Red Ash Co. In 1909 the concern was up for sale and included a 'self acting incline [which] works the tubs direct to a railway siding'. This was at Wimberry. Coleford Red Ash Colliery Co. was wound up in 1912 but the gales continued to be worked until the 1920s. Part of the workings are today preserved as the Hopewell Colliery Museum.

CLEMENT'S TUMP

In 1908 J. C. Binks & Co. of Forest View House, Bream are recorded as being the owners of Clement's Tump Colliery which was working the Lass of the Mill gale. By 1918 the colliery was in the hands of Thomas Peglar, also of Bream.

THE WAGONS

March 1908 saw a 7-plank wagon photographed at the Gloucester Railway Carriage & Wagon Co. However, an order for the wagon or wagons cannot be traced. Branded *'Empty to Sling Siding, Severn & Wye Rly.'*. Coal would have been brought to the siding for loading using horse and cart. How long the wagon(s) would have been in use is unknown.

Branded *'Empty to Darkhill Siding. S&W&S.B. Ry'* is wagon No. 50 which was painted black with white lettering and is seen here at Gloucester in November 1893. GRC&WCo.

WALLSEND

A rarity is a wagon which worked up the Forest of Dean Central Railway as the collieries at Howbeach were very sporadic in their working. The Wallsend Colliery was at one time worked by Messrs Gollop & Co. The colliery then changed hands several times before at some point in the 1890s Wallsend Limited was formed to purchase the concern. They appear to have worked through to around the end of the First World War.

THE WAGONS

In January 1916 Gloucester let ten secondhand 10-ton wagons on hire for 5 years. The following month saw a further forty secondhand 10 ton wagons let on hire for 5 years and also a repairing contract was taken out on five 10-ton wagons for 7 years at £3 19s. 0d. war rate (£2 12s. 6d. ordinary rate). This latter contract suggests that the colliery may also have had wagons from another builder but had put them with Gloucester for repairs as with their hired wagons.

DARKHILL & ELLWOOD

The Darkhill & Ellwood gale was taken by Noah Howell in 1892 and he began trading with his son as the Darkhill & Ellwood Colliery Co. It was not long before Arthur Latham of the Phoenix Coal Co. became interested and took a share in the colliery. However, the colliery was not a success and the ledger account with the S&W was closed in January 1897.

THE WAGONS

In November 1893 two 10-ton wagons were let over 7 years deferred purchase with the tenants to keep them in repair. One was number 50 so it is likely that the numbering sequence started at this point. Two 10-ton secondhand wagons were also let on temporary hire at the same time. In February 1895 two 8-ton secondhand wagons let on 3 months hire for £8. 0s. 0d. It was probably soon after this date that the colliery ceased work.

Wallsend Collieries wagon No. 1 in a cruel enlargement from a photograph. This is the only known view of a wagon from this concern.

There is also a company letter which mentions a wagon No. 22 in 1916 in trade to Sharpness.

Another very rare view and only recently discovered is this one of a wagon lettered up for Woorgreens Colliery. This is possibly one of the 17 offered for sale in 1913. Interestingly above Woorgreens Colliery appears the name of David Buck who held the mortgage on the colliery – although it has to be said that his exact connection with the concern is a little murky! Photographed at Lydney in August 1909.

WOORGREENS

The Woorgreens gale was awarded on the 27th June 1843 in equal parts to John Davis of Cinderford, James Richard and William Tingle, (both of Littledean). Davis sank a shaft to the coal, which was only about 20 yards beneath the surface, and began to drive an underground roadway. However, this was the limit of his activities and no more work was done until August 1900 when the colliery was sold to two London financiers, Messrs Marshall and Dott.

The new proprietors, trading as the Woorgreen Colliery Co., had great ideas for the concern. However, the two proprietors 'had a difference between them' in May 1901 and by November only Thomas Dott was shown as the proprietor on letter headings. It was not until October 1903 that a siding to the colliery was completed. In January 1904 the Joint Committee felt it desirable to have an additional loop at Woorgreen for the reception of empties. Further problems with the siding arose in July 1904 when some wagons ran away and damaged the gate.

Finance seems to have got the better of Dott though as by May 1908 a Mr D. Buck held a mortgage on the colliery. At first it was not at all clear as to the relationship between Buck and Dott. Initially it was stated that Buck had bought the gale but in September 1909 it was reported that Dott had let the gale to Buck, although at the same time it was stated that Buck was the registered owner. In June 1918 it was noted in Joint Committee minutes that the colliery had been closed for some time. No more work was done and Dott finally surrendered the gale as from the end of May 1938, the siding agreement with the Joint Committee being terminated on the 31st December.

THE WAGONS

In February 1913 Dott was offering to sell seventeen railway wagons lettered 'Woorgreen Colliery' to Henry Crawshay & Co. Ltd for the sum of £425. Crawshays offered £15 per wagon to which Dott, on a postcard to Crawshays, replied '*Thanks for your letter of yesterday and will let the matter drop, your suggestion being quite out of the question*'.

Apart from the photograph above nothing else is known about the wagons.

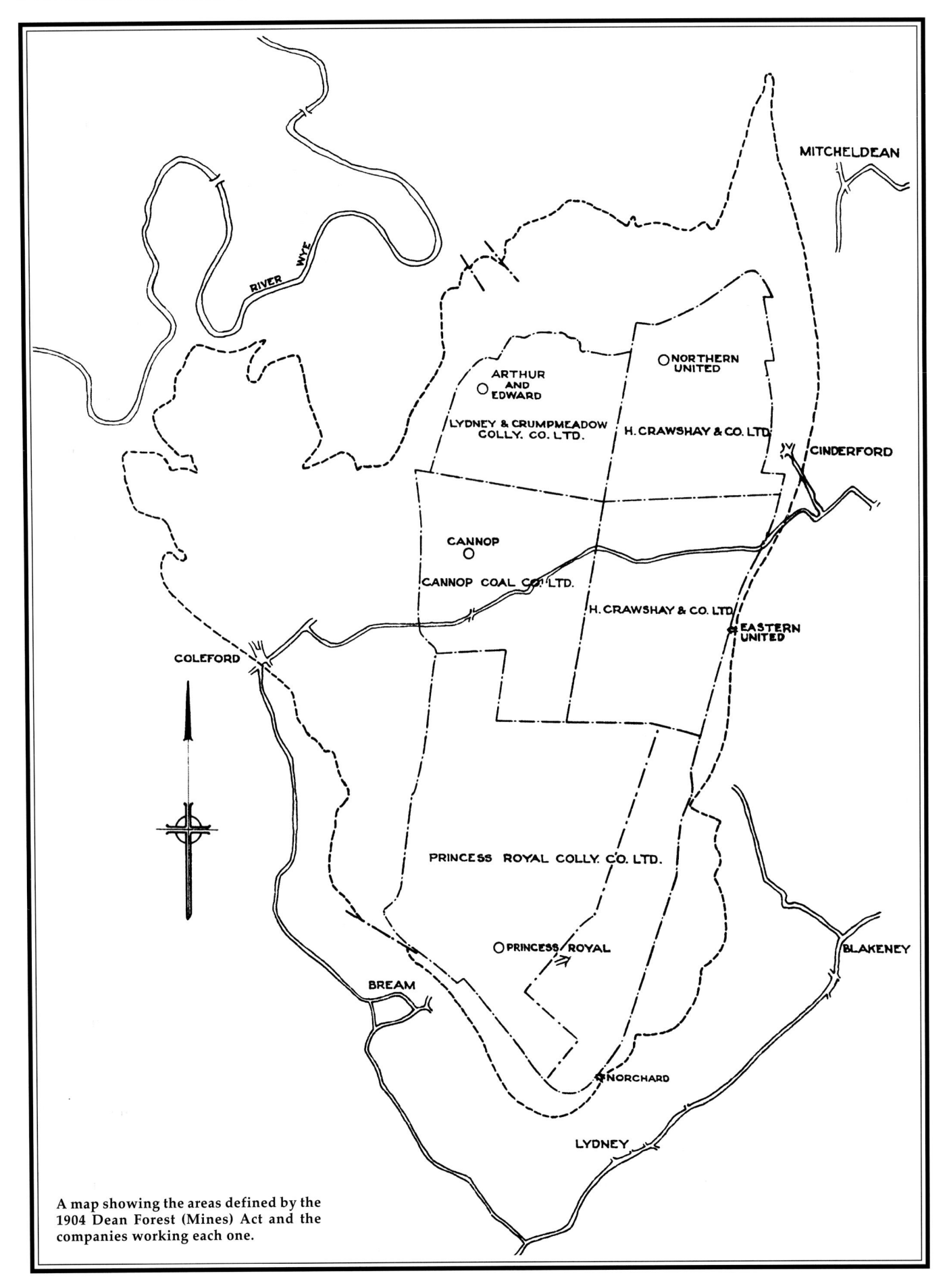

A map showing the areas defined by the 1904 Dean Forest (Mines) Act and the companies working each one.

Part Two
The Deep Pits

FOR the purposes of this work the Deep Pits in the Forest of Dean are taken as those collieries working areas as defined in the 1904 Dean Forest (Mines) Act and working the Coleford High Delf seam and the Trenchard coal as their main output.

The new collieries were not the first to work these seams as originally they were worked around the edge of the basin at the outcrop of the coal. Here the coal was fairly easy to win and whilst sufficient coal could be won by these means there was no incentive for others to try and sink shafts to the lower measures in the centre of the basin. This work, with the depth of the shaft and the amount of water to be dealt with, which would require heavy pumping plant, was beyond the means of the smaller companies. This difficulty of working was compounded by the way that the coal was divided into small areas.

The first attempt to win the deep coals had been made in 1864 at Bowson north of Cinderford but was beaten by the lack of capital, bad engineering and a surfeit of water. The first colliery to successfully work the Coleford High Delf was Hawkwell in 1876 which was owned by Jacob Chivers, closely followed by Haywood Colliery in Cinderford, owned by Edwin Crawshay the son of Henry. Both however, were soon to fail due to lack of capital investment.

It was not until the groups of smaller deep gales were amalgamated together that a worthwhile area of coal to be worked by one concern was created, thereby justifying the investment in deeper shafts and larger pumping plant. The 1904 Act created seven areas which were then sold on behalf of the body of Free Miners, who took out the grants, to the larger colliery companies.

It was these collieries which survived through to the nationalisation of the coal industry in 1947. Their wagon fleets had, however, been taken over as part of the national emergency in October 1939 with the Government paying for repairs and an amount for rental. This enabled wagons to be 'pooled' and therefore spend less time running empty. It also signalled the end of the private owner coal wagon.

There had been a previous proposal to put all of the Forest's colliery wagons under one ownership. In June 1937 it was reported in Crawshay minutes that an approach had been made by Messrs Wagon Repairs Ltd to acquire all Forest wagons and that representatives of the firm had taken particulars of Crawshay's fleet. At this time it amounted to 310 mainline wagons and 70-80 'converted' wagons. Wagon Repairs were prepared to re-hire the wagons to the collieries on simple terms. It was decided by Crawshays not to proceed with the idea and as it did not go ahead it was presumably rejected by the other coal owners as well.

Arthur & Edward Colliery, one of the older concerns given a new lease of life by developments under the 1904 Dean Forest (Mines) Act.

A general view over Norchard Colliery c1910. Prominent in the foreground are the screens with the empty wagon road running in front of them. Standing on this are three Norchard wagons, the left-hand one being in the standard grey livery with white lettering shaded black. The centre wagon, however, appears to be in black and lettered in white **NORCHARD COLLIERY** whilst that on the right is lettered **NORCHARD** and also appears to be in a black livery.

NORCHARD

Norchard Colliery was started prior to 1810 but only worked on a spasmodic basis. In 1890 the Park Iron Mines & Collieries Co. Ltd was set up to re-open the Norchard drift and to work the Tufts Iron Level, both of which were under Lydney Park Estate, owned by the Bathurst family.

In 1896 the concern was taken over by the Park Iron Ore and Coal Company Ltd who worked Norchard until the formation of the Park Colliery Company in June 1912. Extra coal was acquired with the purchase of the Pillowell United gale. Following a flooding of the adjoining Princess Royal Colliery a controlling interest in the Park Colliery Co. was obtained by the Princess Royal Collieries Co. in February 1930.

The colliery finally closed in 1957.

THE WAGONS

The earliest evidence for wagons connected with Norchard can be found in the Western Wagon Co's books. In July 1892 twelve 10-ton wagons were ordered by the Park Iron Mines and Collieries Ltd on seven years redemption hire. In April 1893 a further seventeen wagons were ordered and in July 1894 a further 30 wagons. Of this last order 15 wagons were built by the Yorkshire Wagon Co. and 15 by the British Wagon

Above: An early Park Iron Ore & Coal Co. 5-plank wagon. The fleet number is 100 and the original photograph has wagon 101 standing to the left. The wagon has an oval plate on the left-hand end of the solebar. It could be that this wagon has just been repainted in 1896 into the new owner's livery.

Left: Another early Park Iron Ore & Coal Co. livery. It would appear that the wagon strapping is of a darker shade and thus that the wagon is probably grey with white lettering, ironwork black. The top line of lettering appears to read 'PARK IRON ORE & COAL COMP'. The running number looks like 34 and bottom right reads 'LYDNEY GLOS'.

48

A wagon from the first batch built for Norchard by the Gloucester Railway Carriage & Wagon Co., photographed at the works in May 1902. Painted 'lead color' with white lettering, shaded black and with black ironwork. The oval plate on the solebar is an owner's plate reading 'The Park Iron Ore & Coal Co. Ltd. Owners. Lydney'. *GRC&WCo.*

Co. On all of the orders there are no payments made after January 1895 and in June the company is listed as 'debtors'.

When the Park Iron Ore and Coal Company Ltd was formed to take over the business in 1896 they also took over the Western Wagon Co's agreements and a new one was signed in January for 47 8 and 10-ton wagons. This does not quite tally with the three previously recorded orders which add up to 59 wagons, all of 10-ton capacity. It could well be some of these wagons which are seen on the page opposite.

The first reference to wagons for Norchard in the records of the Gloucester Wagon Co. comes in September 1887 when the Park Iron Ore & Coal Co. purchased six 10-ton wagons on deferred payment over five years at a cost of £10 per wagon per year. In June 1894 it was recorded that the Park Iron Mines & Collieries had put forward a proposal to the Wagon Company for the sale of thirty of the colliery's 10-ton wagons to the Wagon Co. for the sum of £50 each. The wagons were then to be sold back to the colliery on deferred purchase. This was obviously a way for the colliery to raise money and not surprisingly the Wagon Company declined the offer. As already mentioned, there was a change of management in 1896 but it was not until March 1902 that any new wagons were ordered from Gloucester. This is not to say that other wagons were not acquired from other sources, either other wagon builders or from secondhand suppliers such as the Bute Supply Company.

The order placed in 1902 was for ten 10-ton wagons at £58 each, the wagons were also to be kept in repair by the Wagon Co. for seven years. A wagon was photographed in May 1902 from this batch and carries the number 305.

The next record is of thirty secondhand 10-ton wagons being let on hire to the Park Iron Ore & Coal Company for the period of one year at a cost of £8 0s. 0d. per wagon in April 1903. Business was obviously looking up at the colliery. In June a contract for repairing fifty-seven 10-ton wagons over seven years was taken out and another repairing contract was signed in October 1904 for thirty 10-ton wagons over seven years.

The hire contract for thirty secondhand wagons taken out in April 1903 was renewed in January 1905 at a cost of £6 12s. 6d. per wagon, a reduction of 27/6.

Further new wagons were ordered on the 10th January 1906 with an order for thirty 10-ton wagons at £11 0s. 0d. to be paid over seven years. Repairs were to be done by the tenants and therefore a repair contract was taken out at the same time.

In November 1906 ten 10-ton secondhand wagons were hired for the short period of 1¹/₆ years at a cost of £7 10s. 0d.

On the 12th December 1906 another order for new wagons was placed with

Wagon No. 801 was built as part of the order placed in January 1906 for thirty wagons, possibly numbered 801 – 830. *GRC&WCo.*

Gloucester, this time for twenty 10-ton wagons over seven years at £11 3s. 6d. and again on tenant's repair which resulted in a parallel agreement for repairs.

In January 1908 a hire agreement for twenty 10-ton wagons was renewed for a further three years and on the 10th October the 1903 repairing agreement for 57 10-ton wagons was renewed 'temporarily'. That repair agreement was the last to appear in the Gloucester records.

In 1912 the Park Colliery Co. Ltd took over Norchard. This would have resulted in the repainting of the wagon fleet, probably whenever repairs were necessary or at a fixed repainting date in the life of the wagons. Private owners were undoubtedly repainted at regular intervals as being effectively a mobile advert for the colliery they would have been kept in a reasonably good external appearance.

However, after the Park Colliery takeover there only appears one photograph in the Gloucester records of

Left: Part of the order placed in December 1906 and photographed in January 1907 included wagon No. 846. Painted grey, or 'lead color' as Gloucester referred to the shade, with white lettering, shaded black and with black ironwork.

The same wagon later in its life having just had a repaint, possibly at the Gloucester Wagon Co's outstation in Lydney Junction Yard. The wagon painter stands proudly by with the tools of his trade. The lettering is subtly different, the number being slightly larger and a different layout of the *Empty to* instructions.

The only view in the Gloucester collection of a wagon lettered for the Park Colliery Co. Ltd. Also there is no reference to any orders at this date so this might have been just a repaint in the new owner's simplified livery.

a wagon in a simplified livery. What happened thereafter with the wagon fleet is unknown. Possibly no more wagons were acquired or, if they were, they may have come from other wagon builders.

A large proportion of Norchard coal after 1923 was sent direct to the West Gloucester Power Co's generating station which was built alongside the colliery. Where the rest of Norchard's output went is unknown as no order books survive and, to date, no views have been found showing Norchard wagons at other locations.

There is only one mention of a Norchard wagon off in the Severn & Wye letter books, this was Park Iron Mines wagon No. 720 off at Drybrook Rd. on the 29th May 1901.

A 6-plank wagon in black livery when in the ownership of the Park Colliery Co. Ltd. Builder unknown.

Right: A pair of Norchard wagons in the colliery yard, sadly partly obscured by the group of proud Norchard colliers posing for their photograph. The nearest wagon is of interest being a 4-plank wagon, probably of 8-ton capacity and apparently painted black. The second wagon is No. 13 again but now repainted in the grey livery and in the standard lettering style. In the far distance are two **BEDWAS** wagons from South Wales.

Flour Mill Colliery with the new shaft to work the deeper coals furthest from the camera. This site was not directly rail connected and a rope-worked colliery tub route went to the screening plant which was erected alongside the Park Gutter shaft. Here sidings were connected to the Severn & Wye Railway's Oakwood Branch which joined the S&W mainline at Tuft's Junction.

PRINCESS ROYAL

Princess Royal Colliery Co. Ltd worked several gales in the Bream area, notably Park Gutter and Flour Mill. Princess Royal was first galed in 1842. By October 1855 the collieries were in the hands of one Thomas Dyke who wanted to build a tramroad to the Severn & Wye.

In December 1890 the Princess Royal Colliery Co. Ltd was incorporated and the Oakwood Branch was extended to the colliery. The colliery was expanded as a result of the 1904 Dean Forest (Mines) Act. A new, deeper, shaft was sunk at Flour Mill Colliery and in 1913 the shaft at Park Gutter was deepened. The colliery closed in March 1962.

THE WAGONS

The first wagons for the colliery that can be traced come after the formation of the Princess Royal Colliery Co. Ltd. With the expansion of the concern, orders were placed in December 1893 with the Gloucester Wagon Co. supplying fifty new 10-ton wagons on seven years deferred purchase. In February 1894 ten

An enlargement off the view at the top of the opposite page showing the two three-plank dumb-buffered wagons, both with end doors. The use of such wagons seems a little strange as they cannot have had a large capacity and this is the only known view of these low sided wagons engaged in the coal trade from the Forest. Load would have been 8-tons. They have running numbers of 19 and 18. Livery was probably the same as later Princess Royal wagons of red with white lettering, shaded black and with black ironwork.

courtesy Bob Essery

A rake of Princess Royal wagons in the yard at Lydney in 1908. Of particular interest, and thus reproduced on the previous page, are the three-plank dumb-buffered wagons in the centre of the view. The two wagons nearest the camera are both 6-plank wagons, No's 251 and 278, and do not appear to be of Gloucester origin, nor do No's 32, 198, or 191. Finally, under the bridge, is No. 136, a wagon with four deep planks which also features in a photograph overleaf.
courtesy Bob Essery

10-ton wagons were bought from the Western Wagon & Property Co. These had been built by the Standard Wagon Co. (possibly at Bullo Pill, see page 171) at a cost of £43 per wagon and were sold on seven year redemption hire to the colliery at £44 per wagon. In October 1896 trade seems to have demanded extra wagons and to meet this fifty 10-ton secondhand wagons were obtained on weekly hire from the Gloucester Wagon Co. These were ex Speech House Colliery and had been taken back into Gloucester Wagon Co. stock at £2,769 16s. 7d. In January 1897 the hire was changed to purchase over seven years on deferred terms.

Between October 1899 and December 1910 various repairing contracts with the Gloucester Wagon Co. were either taken out or renewed and it was not until July 1912 that a further order for new wagons was placed.

The order, dated the 8th of July 1912 was for one hundred 12-ton wagons on seven years deferred purchase.

In March 1916 a repairing contract was taken out for one hundred & fifteen 10-ton wagons for 7 years and for twenty-three 8-ton wagons for 2$\frac{1}{3}$ years. These 8-ton wagons were described as being 'late Somerset Trading Co.' (see page 117).

The Princess Royal Co. had obviously picked them up cheaply, possibly in lieu of outstanding debt.

Apart from a couple more repairing contracts the colliery does not feature again in the Gloucester books. Wagons do, however, appear frequently in the S&W letter books:
Wagon 186 off Lydney Docks 24.10.1900.
Wagons No's 230 & 252 off at Sharpness 12.7.1913.
Wagons 113 and 268 damaged at Lydney Junction 3.11.16.
3.50 pm Goods Lydney Jct to Princess Royal 9.11.16 Princess Royal wagons 118 and 400 off.

Photographed in December 1893 at Gloucester is wagon No. 62, part of an order for 50 10-ton wagons. Branded *'Empty to Lydney S&W R^y'* the wagon entered service only a few months before the end of the Severn & Wye's independent existence. Painted red, lettered white with black shading and black ironwork.
GRC&WCo.

Right: Wagon No. 136 is seen again running empty back to the colliery, behind 2021 Class 0-6-0 saddle tank No. 2038, at Tuft's Junction. In this view its four-plank construction is clearly seen.
courtesy Mrs Knight

To the left is another view of a four-planker, this time No. 56. Who the producer of these wagons was is unknown but the four wide planks makes them very distinctive. No. 56 is seen at some point during the Second World War, which can be deduced from the white diagonal stripe painted on the wagon side (in this case conveniently using the side strapping). This stripe was useful in dock and industrial areas during the blackout to quickly ascertain which end had the opening door for discharge.

Below: Painted in similar style to No. 56 is No. 80 seen here enlarged out of a view of Norchard Colliery. Unlike 56 this wagon is of standard 6-plank construction. Note the enlarged L at the start of Lydney.

54

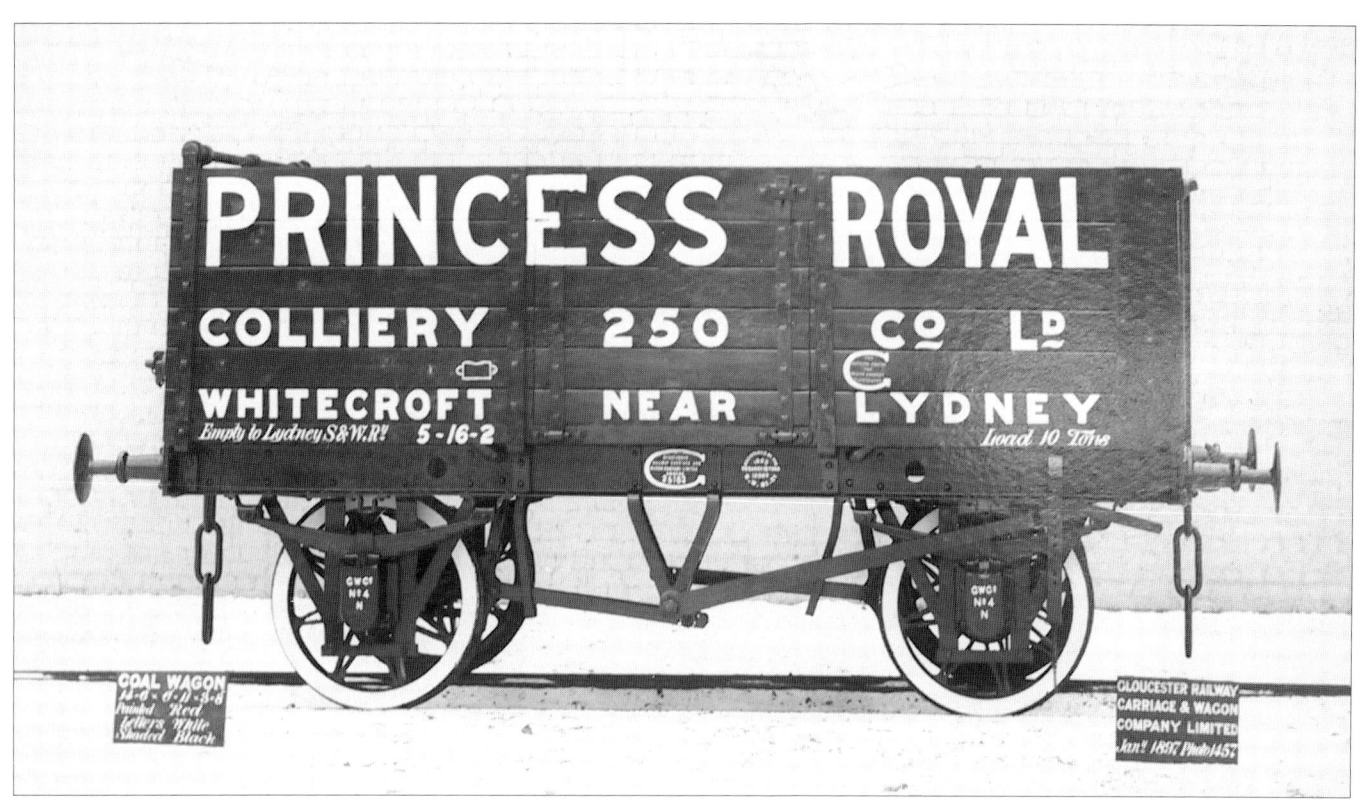

Wagon No. 250 was photographed in January 1897 as part of a batch of fifty. A 10-ton 6-plank wagon with a steel underframe registered with the GWR and with Gloucester builder's and repairer's plates. Note that like the majority of private owner wagons it is provided with brakes on one side only.
GRC&WCo.

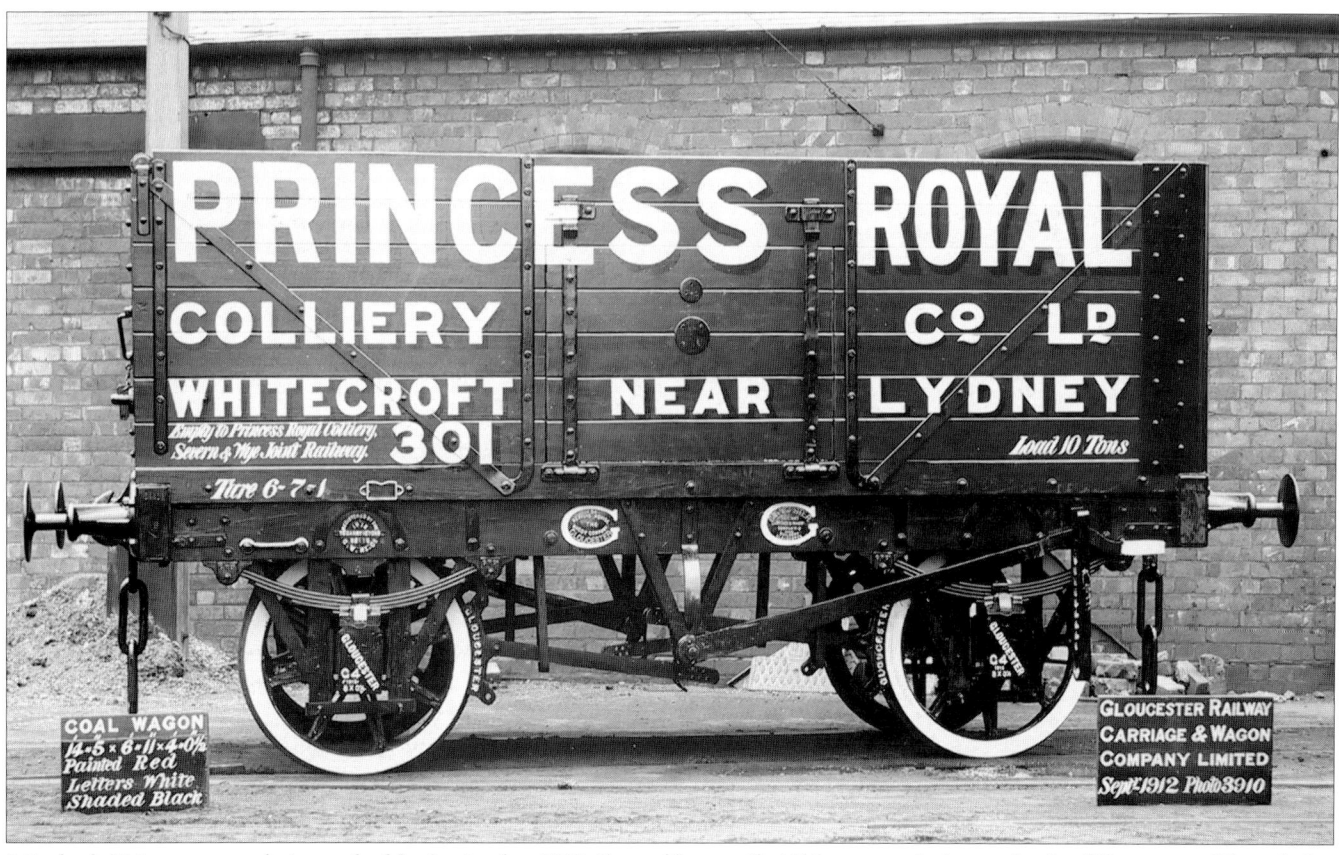

A 7-plank 10-ton wagon photographed in September 1912. It would seem that this was part of an order for 100 wagons although the order book shows the Princess Royal Co. as wanting 12-ton wagons. The wagon also has brake sets on both sides, a regulation brought in by the Board of Trade in 1911, although conversion of old stock was not enforced until 1938. In February 1920 it was reported that it would cost Crawhays £10 per wagon to comply with the regulations – a total outlay of some £4,000 for their wagon fleet. No doubt Princess Royal also faced such expenditure.
GRC&WCo.

THE CANNOP COAL CO. LIMITED

COLEFORD

GLOUCESTERSHIRE

TELEGRAMS:
"CANNOP, COLEFORD"

NAT. TELEPHONE:
017 LYDBROOK

STATION FOR COLLIERY:
"SPEECH HOUSE ROAD."

GOODS AND WAGONS TO:
"CANNOP COLLIERY SIDING
SPEECH HOUSE ROAD,"
G. W. & MID. JOINT RLY.

Feb. 18th 1908.

The colliery soon after production had started. A Cannop wagon is emerging from the screens and running down to the loaded wagon roads.

CANNOP

Cannop Colliery was commenced in 1906 and was producing coal by 1910. It was owned by a north-country syndicate led by Mr M. Maclean. Two new shafts were sunk to a depth of 204 yards to develop the Western United gale. In the 1930s a pneumatic dry cleaning plant was installed which allowed the colliery to output a different grade of coal – virtually dust and used in the paint industry. Wagons loaded with this went out sheeted over. Cannop was one colliery in the Forest which seemed to cut prices whenever possible to win trade from its competitors, something it probably needed to do as it was a very expensive colliery to operate. For every ton of coal won about 10 tons of water were pumped out. In 1928 1,104 million gallons of water were removed from the workings.

The colliery closed in 1960.

A wagon from Cannop's first batch photographed in June 1910. This seven-plank 12-ton wagon was painted in a style that the colliery retained through its lifetime. *GRC&WCo.*

Wagon No. 52, photographed in August 1911, was part of a batch of fifty new wagons ordered in that month. *GRC&WCo.*

In July 1912 wagon No. 101 was recorded at Gloucester. Although at first glance similar to No. 52 there are several subtle changes. This wagon is fitted with brakes either side and also the running number has moved to the left-hand end of the wagon. *GRC&WCo.*

THE WAGONS

With the colliery coming into production an order was placed on the l0th November 1909 with the Gloucester Railway Carriage & Wagon Co. for fifty new 12-ton wagons on 10 years deferred payment. December 1910 saw twenty-five 10-ton secondhand wagons let on hire for 4 months. Fifty more new 12-ton wagons, paid for over 10 years, were ordered in August 1911. In October 1911 thirty 12-ton and ten 10-ton secondhand wagons were hired for 3 years.

In July 1912 one hundred new 12-ton wagons were ordered on 10 years deferred payment. The following month saw the hire for five years of fifty secondhand 10-ton wagons. A further one hundred 12-tonners were ordered in October 1913 on ten years deferred payment.

The wagons hired for 3 years in October 1911 were retained in the Cannop fleet when a further hire agreement~ this time for 5 years was signed in September 1914. The agreement for the hire of fifty wagons signed in August 1912 was renewed in September 1917 for a further 7 year period.

A further fifty secondhand 12-ton wagons were hired in April 1919. The wagons first hired in October 1911 were again kept on the books when the hire period was extended in September 1919 for a further 5 years.

December 1922 saw an increase in the wagon stock owned by the colliery when fifty new 12-ton wagons were purchased over 7 years followed by a further fifty in November 1923 on the same terms. June 1924 saw a further seventy-five new 12-ton wagons bought over 7 years at £30. 18s. 8d. each per annum, a total of £12,750. 0s. 0d.

The final entry for Cannop in the Gloucester order books is dated the 8th March 1926. It was for twenty-five 12-ton wagons on deferred purchase over a 7 year period at £25. 19s. 0d. each per annum, totalling £3,625. 0s. 0d.

It is assumed that after this large increase in the fleet, some of which would have replaced the wagons hired from Gloucester, that Cannop remained self-sufficient in wagons until the requisitioning of wagons in 1939. The majority probably ran between the colliery and Lydney Docks, although some (as seen opposite) did travel further.

Left: A selection of Cannop wagons, all bar No. 259 being from Gloucester Railway Carriage & Wagon Co. officials. No. 209 was photographed in September 1924. No. 259 was captured at the colliery. No. 323 was photographed in October 1913 and No. 495 in September 1923. The series is useful in that it does show differences in the smaller type, especially the 'Empty to' details, and variations in the G plates.

GRC&WCO. & L.E. Copeland

This enlargement from a commercial postcard reveals a rake of Cannop wagons in the goods yard at Upper Lydbrook Station. Quite what wagons from Cannop are doing here is unknown, there was not an industry here which could take at least five wagon loads of Cannop coal. It is possible that the coal had been delivered at the tinplate works further down the valley and then the wagons were tripped back to Upper Lydbrook for marshalling before being worked back to the colliery. Views do exist of Cannop wagons in trains alongside the River Wye on the Ross & Monmouth Railway which connects with the Severn & Wye's Lydbrook Branch at Lydbrook Junction. This would be the shortest route for Cannop coal to and from south Wales. The Cannop wagons themselves are a bit of a mystery as close inspection shows them to have a solid wooden door stop. Stops of this type do not appear on many Gloucester-built wagons and only wagon No. 264, third from right, has any sign of the c shaped builder's plate on the solebar. They may have been some of the wagons on hire from Gloucester, but then they would have even more Gloucester plates, or they might have been wagons sourced from other builders. The wagon on the right belongs to Richard Thomas and is waiting to be taken back to the sidings at Lydbrook Colliery. One other point of interest in this view is the platform shelter above the wagons. This was removed for a period in 1884 to allow horse-drawn coal carts to be brought along the platform and tipped into the wagons below. The practice did not last long, presumably the dust may have upset some intending passengers!

To show how far Forest wagons could travel we have on the extreme left a Cannop wagon in the goods yard at Bugle, Cornwall. Interestingly this wagon also has the solid wooden door stop mounted on the solebar. *collection Roger Carpenter*

As the pit head for Arthur & Edward was set on the side of a fairly narrow valley there was no room for the provision of railway sidings and screens for the colliery, the only space nearby being occupied by the Lydbrook Colliery sidings. It was also the intention of the Lydney & Crump Meadow Co. to sink a new shaft at Mierystock so it made sense to provide the screens and sidings at this point. However, the new shaft was not sunk so the screens remained connected to the pithead by means of an endless rope haulage which can be seen on the embankment to the left. Wagons visible in the sidings belong to the colliery itself and to Renwick, Wilton; Ricketts; and Wm. Cory. Under the screens is a partially indentifiable wagon lettered **E. BA?? & SON LTD**.

ARTHUR & EDWARD

Arthur & Edward was an old working given a new lease of life by the 1904 Dean Forest (Mines) Act. Started around 1840 the colliery was not a great success and changed hands several times. It would appear that little, if any, work was done after 1860. In 1894 the concern was purchased by the New Bowson Colliery Co. who worked the adjoining East Slad Colliery. No work was done and in May 1908 the colliery and its gales were purchased by the Lydney & Crump Meadow Co. Their colliery at Cinderford (page 30) was beginning to run out of coal and so they acquired the new North Western United gale. An easy way to work this was by using the existing shafts at Arthur & Edward and driving dipples (inclined roadways) from pit bottom down some 350 yards. The pit head was some distance from the screens and can be seen on page 47. In 1911 output stood at 4,000 tons of steam coal a week and the daily output was 70 wagons requiring two trains a day.

The colliery closed in December 1959.

Under the screens at Mierystock with two Crump and an E. Jarrett wagon emerging. The Crump wagons show the two livery patterns, that on the left being painted grey, lettered white with black shading and ironwork. A 7-plank wagon, its running number is either 850, 858 or 859, the builder is unknown although there appears to be an oval builder's plate on the solebar. Next is wagon No. 134, which like wagons already seen belonging to other concerns, has four deep planks and is painted black with white lettering, again the builder is unknown. Edgar Jarrett's wagons are dealt with on page 77.

```
SHIPPING PORTS:                                              TELEGRAPHIC ADDRESS: "CRUMP, CINDERFORD."
LYDNEY, SHARPNESS, NEWPORT, CARDIFF, BARRY.                  TELEPHONE No. 81.
                          REGISTERED OFFICE,
```

Mr. Fred Hale
Nailbridge

Cinderford,
GLOS.

Apl 1933

Bought of

The Lydney & Crump Meadow Collieries Co. Ltd.

PROPRIETORS OF THE CELEBRATED

FOREST OF DEAN "COLEFORD HIGHDELF" HOUSE, STEAM AND GAS COALS.

COPY OF ANALYSIS ON APPLICATION.   EMPTIES TO MIREY STOCK SIDING, LYDBROOK—S. & W. RY.

ALL REMITTANCES AND INLAND ORDERS MUST BE SENT DIRECT TO CINDERFORD.

TERMS:—NET CASH.   INLAND, 10TH OF MONTH FOLLOWING DELIVERY.   CARGOES, 30 DAYS AFTER SHIPMENT.

This letterhead for the company is of interest in that it lists as shipping ports for the company 'Lydney, Sharpness, Newport, Cardiff, Barry'. This reveals that it would be quite possible to see a Forest of Dean wagon heading into south Wales loaded with coal for shipping at a Welsh port - truly 'Coals to Newcastle'! As with Lydney the company probably had shipping agents at each of the ports hoping to pick up both regular cargoes and the odd 'spot' load. The Welsh ports had the advantage over both Lydney and Sharpness in terms of the size of vessels that they could accommodate.

Right: A drawing of a Crump wagon prepared for a wagon repair shop belonging to Wagon Repairs Ltd. Of interest is that the notes on the original drawing give a livery of:

Wagon	Light Shade Grey
Letters	White
Shaded	Red Oxide
Ironwork	Black Up

There is evidence of an agreement between the colliery company and Wagon Repairs Ltd for the period 1/3/34 - 28/2/39. A payment of £5 8s. 6d. per wagon per annum was made.
courtesy Robert Tivendale

THE WAGONS

Crump wagons have already been dealt with under Crump Meadow Colliery on page 31. However, a few more figures are pertinent only to Arthur & Edward. In August 1944 an attempt was made to sell the colliery and its assets included 513 wagons. At the time of nationalisation an inventory of the colliery showed that there were the following numbers of mainline wagons:

12-tons	60
10-tons	414 + 29 (443)
8-tons	3 + 1 (4)

Although these wagons were nominally company assets it has to be remembered that since 1939 they would have been in the central pool. How many would have returned on derequisition is unkown.

A rake of Crump wagons on the sidings at Mierystock. That nearest the camera appears to be a 5-plank wagon with a raised end plank and numbered 547.

Above: Two views of a Crump wagon at Clevedon Gas Works. A 7-plank wagon with the running number 824 it makes an interesting comparison with the grey wagon on page 60. In this case the grey looks much darker and shows the difficulty at this distance in time of determining colours. Greys would have varied depending on the mix of constituents made up in the paint shop. *courtesy Roger Carpenter*

Wagon No. 434 is seen at an unknown location. Whilst of similar appearance to 824 above as 434 is of six planks, as opposed to seven, the *CRUMP* lettering reaches right to the top of the wagon. Another variation is the 'No.' in front of the running number. The wagon is branded '*Empty to Mirey Stock Sidings. Near Upper Lydbrook GW & LMS Jt Rly.*' The photograph possibly dates from 1934 as there is a painting/inspection date of 9/34 on the solebar above the left-hand axlebox. The 'mushroom' shaped builder's plate should enable the wagon builder to be identified. The registration plate is to the right of the 'V' hanger and the small oval plate might be a repairer's plate or possibly a wagon hire plate. *courtesy HMRS, Ref. No. AAX611*

A somewhat distressed CRUMP No. 136 seen at Monmouth. This sort of condition would usually be associated with the wartime years when wagons were pooled with little maintenance but in this case the photograph was taken in April 1931. It appears to be a four-plank wagon which has had the top plank replaced, and also the second plank on the right-hand side, without a visit to the paint shop. Livery would appear to be plain black with white lettering. It would appear also that it has brought a load of coal to Monmouth which has just been discharged.

H. C. Casserley, courtesy Paul Karau

Another view of Monmouth Troy with a CRUMP wagon in the yard on the left. This time only the top is visible but it would appear to be a grey wagon, lettered white, shaded black. It is possible that the company's wagons were regular visitors to Monmouth but with no records surviving it is impossible to say.

Finally a snapshot of wagon No. 737 on the dead-end siding below No. 9 tip at Lydney Docks. This siding was often used for the transshipment of bunkering coal for steam coasters coming into Lydney to load coal. It is possible therefore that a load of steam coal has been brought down from Arthur & Edward for just such a purpose.

Eastern United Colliery.

Eastern United was worked by means of adits driven into the hillside and both of the entrances can be seen in this early view of the colliery. Screening plant is still rudimentary, the later screens can be seen in the photograph reproduced on the opposite page. Wagons visible belong to: Messrs Baldwin, a Bristol coal factor who did a lot of business with Eastern; two Lightmoor wagons which were probably in use prior to wagons branded for Eastern being supplied; and a Dean Forest Coal Co. apparently of four-plank construction, with raised ends and no end door. This latter feature would restrict the wagons use as it could not be used for shipping traffic at any of the docks as there would have been no way of tipping the wagon.

EASTERN UNITED

Soon after the passing of the 1904 Mines Act Henry Crawshay & Co. were aware that the coal reserves of their Lightmoor Colliery were going to run out in ten to twenty years time. After much debate it was decided to purchase the newly created Eastern United gale. Work began early in 1909 and in September 1910 it was reported that the first coal had been dispatched from the colliery. This was 250 tons of steam coal for Messrs R. Thomas sent in wagons belonging to E. Jones & Son.

The colliery had some geological difficulties due to faults but was generally successful. Its one ongoing problem was the cramped layout of the colliery sidings.

Despite new development work taking place at the time the colliery closed at the end of January 1960.

THE WAGONS

It is difficult to split the wagons ordered for Eastern United out of the wagons ordered for Henry Crawshay & Co. The colliery co's minutes do give some direct references to wagons for Eastern. It would appear that the question of wagons for the colliery was first addressed in March 1911. However, it reads 'the question of more wagons for Eastern United was raised'. Whether this means more wagons for Henry Crawshay & Co. in general to be used specifically for Eastern is unknown. Certainly in June 1911 it was decided to debit the Eastern United account with 3d. per ton on all Lightmoor wagons used there.

The discussions in March were sparked by a communication from the Lincoln

A wagon built by the Ince Waggon & Ironwork Company, Wigan and lettered up for Eastern United. The oval plate on the left-hand end is possibly the Lincoln Wagon Company owner's plate.   *HMRS Catalogue No. ACA112*

Photographed in January 1914 at Gloucester was wagon No. 354, part of an order for twenty 12-ton wagons placed in that month. The livery was standard for Crawshays of black body, white lettering with red shading. *GRC&WCo.*

Wagon Co. that they could supply 30 wagons on 7 years deferred purchase for £8 16s. per wagon per year to be purchased on completion of the seven years for the sum of 5/- each. It was decided to have the wagons at this price provided that Crawshays could not get better terms elsewhere. The agreement for the purchase was signed in April. Whether the Lincoln Wagon Co. actually built wagons or whether they were 'middle men' in the form of a wagon finance company is unclear. Certainly the Lincoln Wagon Co. of Doncaster ordered wagons from the Ince Waggon & Ironworks Co. of Wigan and it may have been from this source that the wagons were acquired.

In August 1911 the minutes again recorded that the company needed more wagons and in October 1911 quotations for twenty new 10-ton coal wagons were received from several firms. It was decided to order them from the Lincoln Wagon Co. Ltd at £10 13s. per wagon per annum on 7 years redemption lease. The trucks to be lettered and charged to Eastern United.

The first order for Eastern United wagons from the Gloucester Carriage & Wagon Co. was in January 1914 when twenty new 12-ton wagons were let on deferred payment over 7 years at £16 5s. 6d. per wagon per year with the wagon company responsible for repairs.

The wagons which had been purchased in 1911 from the Lincoln Wagon Co. came to the end of their deferred purchase period in 1918 and the Crawshay minutes for February record:

'Secretary reported we had now paid the redemption hire due on 30 wagons hired from the Lincoln Wagon Co. numbers 295 - 324. Had now received our agreement back from them cancelled together with an authority from them to remove their owner plates on the wagons. These wagons were now the property of Henry Crawshay & Co. Ltd and the same was considered most satisfactory.'

Little else is known of Eastern United wagons and few photographs have been seen of them in areas away from the Forest.

Taken at Brixham in the mid-1930s Eastern United wagon No. 353 is caught in the yard next to a Renwick Wilton wagon. Whilst it is the preceding number to the wagon in the official Gloucester view above it does not imply that they were from the same batch. There is some debate as to whether Gloucester photographed the first or last wagon of a batch or even if they just took one out of the middle at a convenient time to be photographed. On close inspection there are subtle differences between the wagons, certainly the axleboxes are different but in the twenty years they could well have been replaced.

G. H. Platt, courtesy Paul Karau

NORTHERN UNITED

In July 1931 Henry Crawshay & Co. purchased the Northern United gale from the Lydney & Crump Meadow Co. Ltd who had done a limited amount of work. Crawshays decided to sink a new shaft and also to reopen the old Hawkwell Colliery shaft. Sinking began in May 1933 and coal was first produced in August 1935. Northern United was to be the last major colliery development in the coalfield.

Northern was also the last of the major collieries to close when the final shift was worked on Christmas Eve 1965.

THE WAGONS

In November 1938 an order for fifty new 12-ton wagons was fulfilled for Crawshays at the Gloucester Railway Carriage & Wagon Co. The wagons were bought on deferred purchase spread over seven years at a cost of £155 per wagon. Once delivered these smart looking wagons would not have run for long before being taken under Government control at the outbreak of World War 2.

The pit head at Northern United during the sinking operation. The whole colliery was set up to be worked by electricity supplied from a power station at Lydney. The screens were built in the far distance.

Wagon No. 597, photographed in November 1938 at Gloucester. The livery was black body, letters white with only the main title shaded red.
GRC&WCo.

Cannop Colliery in the early 1930s. Wagons from several coal factors stand in the empty wagon sidings waiting to pass under the screens. The building work on the right is for a pneumatic coal dry-cleaning plant which the Cannop management hoped would give them the edge over other Forest collieries.

COAL FACTORS

COAL factors acted as middlemen between the colliery and larger customers. As wholesalers they kept large stocks of coal, often held in wagons in yards or at major junctions, and could be good both for the colliery and the customer. In the colliery's case the orders placed by the factor, often for a twelve month period with deliveries in regular instalments, meant that they could plan ahead. At times when other orders were short at least they knew that they had all the factor's orders to supply and this might be sufficient to keep the colliery at work. From the customers end they knew that if for some reason they had a sudden demand for extra coal the factor would be able to supply at short notice from his stocks.

Looking at the Crawshay minutes it is possible to see to a certain degree how a colliery company dealt with its factors. The factor who took the most coal from Lightmoor Colliery was the Dean Forest Coal Co. This was hardly surprising as there were family links between the two concerns and the founder of the Dean Forest Coal Co. worked for Crawshays for many years, even when factoring. However, these strong ties did not always give the Dean Forest Coal Co. an advantage. For example, in July 1908 the Dean Forest Coal Co. wrote to Crawshays asking why they, as the main factors at Lightmoor, were getting a smaller rebate on coal prices than other factors. It would appear that special rebates had been given to the other factors to induce them to bring orders to Lightmoor but such extra discounts had not been given to the Dean Forest Coal Co. To keep the Dean Forest Coal Co. happy, and to keep their trade, it was decided to grant them an extra rebate.

In December 1908 the question of forcing factors to fulfil orders placed was raised as factors had placed firm orders for a certain quantity of coal each month but were then not taking the full amount. It may have been this which led Crawshays to decide in the following year to attempt to sell as much of their new Eastern United coal directly to consumers although advertisements for it would be sent to factors. One disadvantage of selling coal directly was that the colliery would have to have a larger fleet of wagons and this might explain why the Crawshay wagon stock was expanded considerably after this time. Whilst seeming a good idea it does not necessarily appear to have worked as in March 1920 it was reported that although Eastern coal had been going to the open market rather than factors in the last few years many of their customers had disappeared from their list and had apparently gone to factors. Whilst Crawshays did not want to take customers from factors, nor did they want factors to take customers from them but the factors had done so. They thought it ought to be understood that the system of selling should be carried out as it was started. The Company had two factors taking practically the whole supply of Eastern United coal. Not surprisingly these were the Dean Forest Coal Co. and the New Bowson Coal Co.

However, the sales manager was getting numerous enquiries direct from potential customers and cited one just received from the Austin Motor Company as an instance. Six trucks were being sent to Birmingham and if they ordered a further twenty trucks would be sent but this would mean that the factors would have to go short as production was running at full capacity. It was thought that the factors would probably feel aggrieved! Some on Crawshay's Board felt that the factoring system was most objectionable and should be discouraged. Then it was added that the Dean Forest Coal Co. were offering to contract for up to 2,000 tons of through coal and 500 tons of blocks per month from Eastern United but it was agreed that Crawshays could not bind themselves to such large quantities.

Another interesting aspect of factoring is dealt with on page 76 where it can be seen that factors were supplying other factors who then supplied customers – but then there were family links between all of them!

One other area where factors worked together, at least the local ones, was in the mixing of coals for specific orders. In the case of the Forest coalfield, with much being

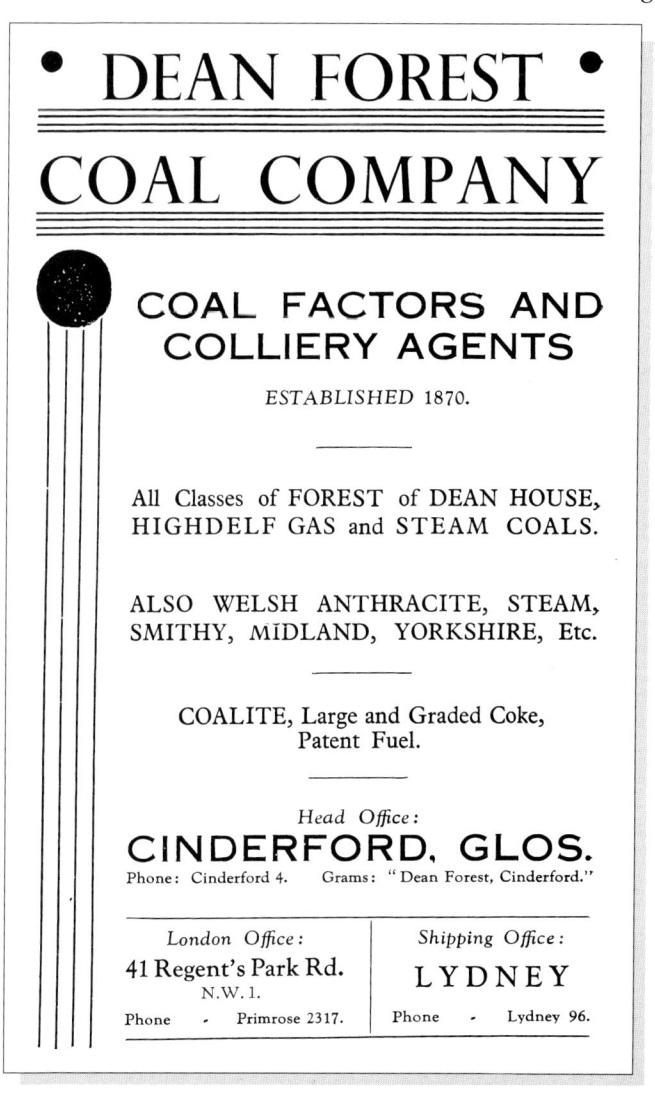

• DEAN FOREST •
COAL COMPANY

COAL FACTORS AND COLLIERY AGENTS

ESTABLISHED 1870.

All Classes of FOREST of DEAN HOUSE, HIGHDELF GAS and STEAM COALS.

ALSO WELSH ANTHRACITE, STEAM, SMITHY, MIDLAND, YORKSHIRE, Etc.

COALITE, Large and Graded Coke, Patent Fuel.

Head Office:
CINDERFORD, GLOS.
Phone: Cinderford 4.   Grams: "Dean Forest, Cinderford."

London Office:	Shipping Office:
41 Regent's Park Rd. N.W.1.	LYDNEY
Phone - Primrose 2317.	Phone - Lydney 96.

Bullo Yard on the South Wales mainline was the junction for the Forest of Dean Branch and here wagons were sorted for destination. In this view all are empties awaiting a trip down the branch to either Eastern United or Northern United, the latter colliery having recently opened at the time of this 1936 photograph. Wagons visible mainly belong to coal factors – Renwick Wilton, Dean Forest Coal Co., and Baldwin of Bristol.
W. A. Camwell

Edgar Jarrett & Co.
LIMITED

BREAM (Forest of Dean)

GLOUCESTERSHIRE

HOUSE, STEAM & GAS

COALS

WELSH ANTHRACITE
AND
SMOKELESS STEAM.

GAS AND FURNACE COKES

Telephone: Parkend 8.   Telegrams: "Jarrett, Bream."

---

shipped from Lydney or Sharpness, it was easy to mix, or blend, coals as it could be done by tipping alternate wagons into a ships hold. It is the minutes of Henry Crawshay & Co. which reveal this practice. In October 1908, for instance, it is recorded that an order for 4,000-5,000 tons of small coal from Lightmoor Colliery was to be shared between Messrs Sully and the Dean Forest Coal Co. on behalf of the Princess Royal Collieries Co. The same occurred in early 1909 (see Appendix One).

Factors were also keen to get business from other factors. A supply of 9,000 tons of coal a year from the Forest had gone down to Torquay Corporation's electricity works for many years in the hands of Lowell Baldwin and Renwick Wilton & Dobson. In 1928 William Cory quoted a higher price and still got the business! This led to some dispute and eventually Cory's took half of the supply through Baldwins and half from Renwicks.

Mention of different grades of coal leads on to the need for factors who required a particular grade, or a coal from a certain coal seam, to have their wagons in the colliery yard in good time for the day on which that coal was being wound and put through the screens. It was the fact that collieries and factors had their own wagon fleets which made life a lot easier in this respect. The railway companies would not have been able to guarantee to get wagons to a certain place at a certain time.

With factors such as Renwick Wilton, Baldwins, Baker & Kernick, Barker & Lovering, Alfred Smith, etc. working to Forest collieries it would mean that Forest factors would be working to other coalfields as well. This was certainly the case with I. W. Baldwin who was a sales agent for a Staffordshire colliery. However, despite trawling through many colliery and coalfield photographs it has to be said that no view can be found of a Forest factor's wagons loading on 'foreign' territory!

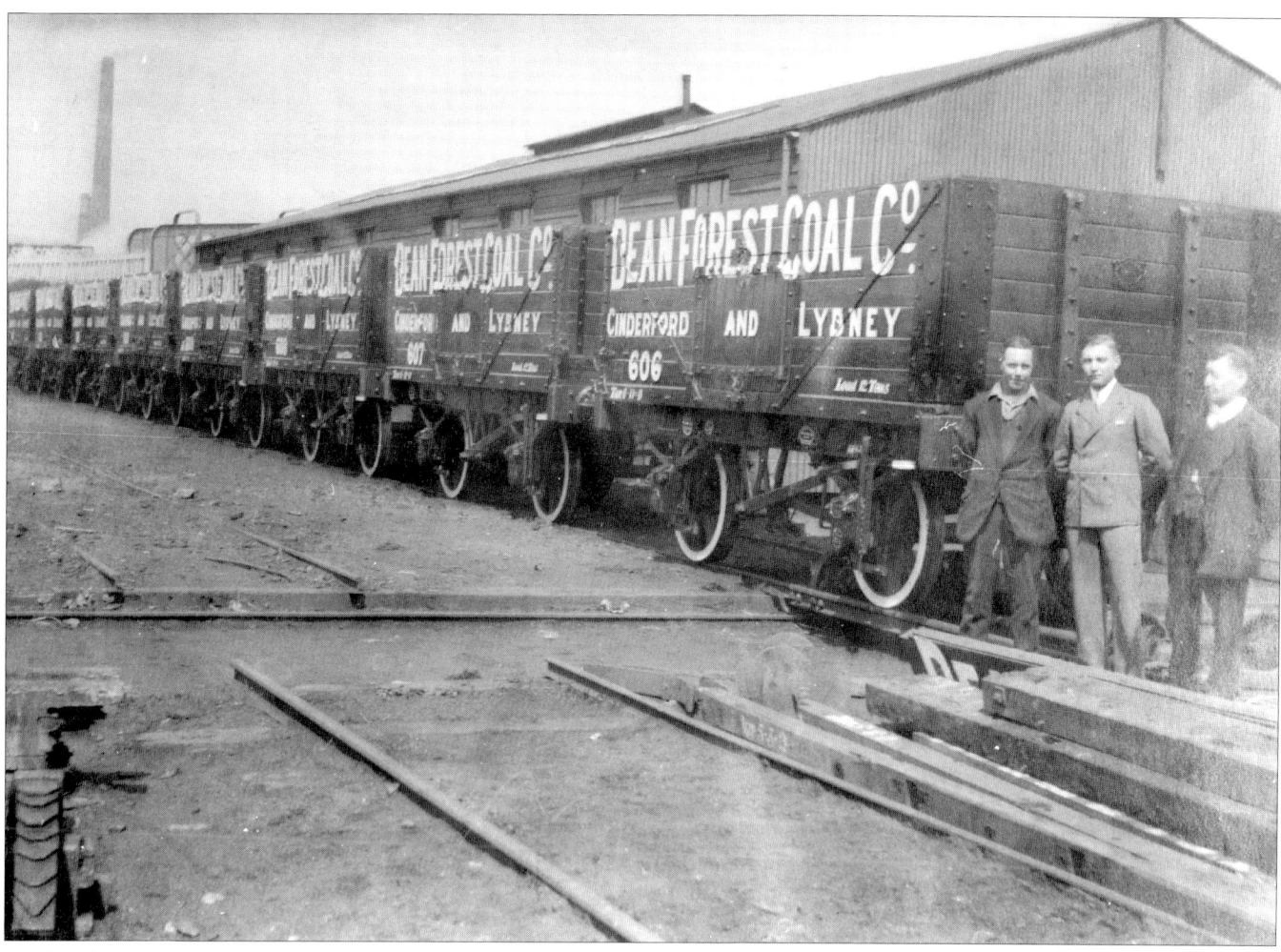

A rake of Dean Forest Coal Co. wagons outside Messrs Wagon Repairs Ltd's works at Lydney Junction. It is unlikely that the wagons were new, possibly they had just been acquired secondhand and had been repainted. Wagon No's appear to go in order starting with 606, then 607 etc. They are unusual for Forest of Dean wagons in that they have 'cupboard' style side doors. They are also all fitted with end doors. Livery would appear to differ from most Dean Forest Coal wagons in being a red body, with white lettering and with black endplates and strapping on the opening end doors but with body-coloured side strapping. Possibly this was a 'new look' first introduced in the 1920s for a batch of new wagons supplied by the Gloucester Railway Carriage & Wagon Co. in 1927 which were outshopped with red bodywork. There are builder's plates on the non-opening ends and also a different shaped plate on the solebar. The solebar plate might well be a 'for repairs advise' plate for Messrs Wagon Repairs Ltd.

DEAN FOREST COAL CO.

Set up in 1870 the Dean Forest Coal Company was formed by an employee of Henry Crawshay & Co. and as such always seems to have had a good working relationship with the colliery company. The founder was George Frederick Morgan who had been Trade Manager for Henry Crawshay & Co. Indeed the relationship may have been deeper as in September 1882 there are two orders in the record books of the Western Wagon Co. that relate to wagons for the Dean Forest Coal Co. One gives 'Henry Crawshay and Fred. Morgan' and the other 'Charlotte Crawshay and Fred. Morgan' as trading as the Dean Forest Coal Co. Charlotte Crawshay is likely to be the wife of Henry's son, Edwin. Later the partnership appears to be with a member of the Haddingham family, probably Stephen Haddingham with whom Morgan had been connected in the

Possibly the earliest view of a Dean Forest Coal Co. wagon was taken at Lydney in July 1908. Although indistinct it shows a four-plank wagon with the main lettering along the top plank. Livery probably black with white lettering, possibly shaded red.

courtesy Bob Essery

Taken from a postcard of Lightmoor Colliery c. 1910-11, two Dean Forest Coal Co. wagons, No's 27 and 310 are caught standing loaded on the sidings alongside the Severn & Wye's Mineral Loop. In the background can be seen the earlier screens at the colliery, still in use and in an area where coal could be stacked on the ground. Lightmoor was unusual in having the space to do this and coal was often stacked to keep the colliery at work in periods of low demand. Wagon 310 appears to be from the same supplier as No. 311 illustrated opposite and has either been through a wagon works recently or is of new construction and probably on its first revenue earning trip. Wagons would not have remained so pristine for long and soon 310 would be looking more like 27 alongside. Wagon 27 was probably the last wagon in the batch bought from the Western Wagon & Property Co. in April 1904 having been built by Edwards & Brown. In the background can be seen a number of Lightmoor Colliery wagons and some more for the Dean Forest Coal Co.

Forest of Dean Iron Co. Ltd, owners of the Parkend iron furnace in the late 1870s – also connected with this venture were the Crawshay family. In May 1910 the partnership between Fred Morgan and Mrs Haddingham was dissolved. Fred Morgan died early in 1912 and the business was carried on by executors until the death of his widow, Ada. The manager during this period was Henry Morgan, George Frederick's son.

The company was still trading in 1935 as witnessed by their advertisement reproduced on page 69 which appeared in *Fine Forest Coal*, produced by the Forest of Dean Colliery Owners Association.

THE WAGONS

The Western Wagon Co. books contain the earliest references to wagons for the Company. The two orders already mentioned in September 1882 were for eight 10-ton wagons, No's 198-205 (possibly WWCo. numbers) which were 'late Parkend Tin Plate Co.' at a cost of £225 and for ten 10-ton wagons No's 303-312 (again possibly WWCo. numbers) bought on five year redemption hire for £200. The Dean Forest Coal Co. would probably have known that the Parkend Tin Plate Co. wagons were available as the Parkend works were leased from Edwin Crawshay (see page 159).

The first mention in the Gloucester Wagon minutes is in August 1883 when a repairing contract was signed for ten 10-ton wagons for a period of $3^{1}/_{4}$ years.

Four months later, in December, a contract for the purchase of 20 8-ton wagons on seven years redemption hire, was signed with the Western Wagon Co. The wagon Co's numbers were 433-452 but here details of the painted numbers are given which were 101-120. The wagons cost £660.

A further repairing contract with Gloucester was signed in February 1887 for twenty 10-ton wagons for 7 years and 39 days. This may have included the original ten wagons contracted for in August 1883. Two months later, in April, a repairs contract was taken out on two 8-ton wagons and thirty-one 10-ton wagons for a 7 year period. Later in the year, in September, a further contract was signed for twenty 8-ton wagons for a 7 year and 16 days period.

The next traceable order for wagons comes in April 1904 when 27 10-ton wagons were bought from the Western Wagon Co. on five years redemption hire. The wagons had been built by Edwards & Brown of Gloucester and bought by the WWCo. at their sale. The painted numbers were 1-27. Wagons 1-20 were bought in by the Western Wagon Co. at £15 per wagon and let out at £6 12s. 6d. per wagon per annum, a total of £33 2s. 6d. per wagon – not a bad profit. Wagons 21-27 may have been newer as they cost £40 each from the same source and were let at £11 11s. 0d. pwpa.

A repair agreement was taken out with the Western Wagon Co. in December 1905 for five 8-ton and five 10-ton wagons.

The Dean Forest Coal Co. ordered its first wagons built by Gloucester in January 1914 when ten 12-ton wagons were purchased on 7 years deferred payment. The following year saw another order for five 10-ton wagons bought for cash at £77 8s. 0d. per wagon in January. A repairing contract for them was taken out at the same time.

A further wagon was obviously added to the fleet in February 1915 as a repairing contract was signed with Gloucester for a single 8-ton wagon for $6^{1}/_{4}$ years at £3 2s. 6d. (late J. E. Bailey). This wagon was obviously acquired secondhand, possibly through Gloucester Carriage & Wagon as they had built wagons for J. E. Bailey of Evesham.

Several repairing contracts were signed through 1915 and '16 which were possibly renewals of earlier contracts. They were for a total of twenty-four 12-ton wagons, one 8-ton and twenty-six 10-ton wagons.

In December 1927 ten 12-ton wagons were bought new for cash at £137 per wagon. Interestingly the official photograph of the wagons is dated November so presumably the date in the order book is retrospective for a 'done deal'.

This was the last order to appear in the books of the Gloucester Wagon Works for the Dean Forest Coal Co.

There is only one reference to a Dean Forest Coal Co.'s wagon in the Severn & Wye letter book and that was when No. 318 was off the road at Lydney Docks on the 12th April 1902.

Wagon No. 311 in the [possibly] later red livery with white lettering shaded black. It is of 4-plank construction with a raised solid end and an end opening door. Builder unknown. It does appear that the enlarged initial letters of the main name only appear on wagons painted red after a certain date. *L. E. Copeland*

A wagon from the first batch of ten ordered from Gloucester in January 1914. Painted black with white lettering. The plates on the solebar left to right are a GWR registration, a Gloucester repairs plate, a Gloucester owner's plate and the builder's plate. *GRC&WCo.*

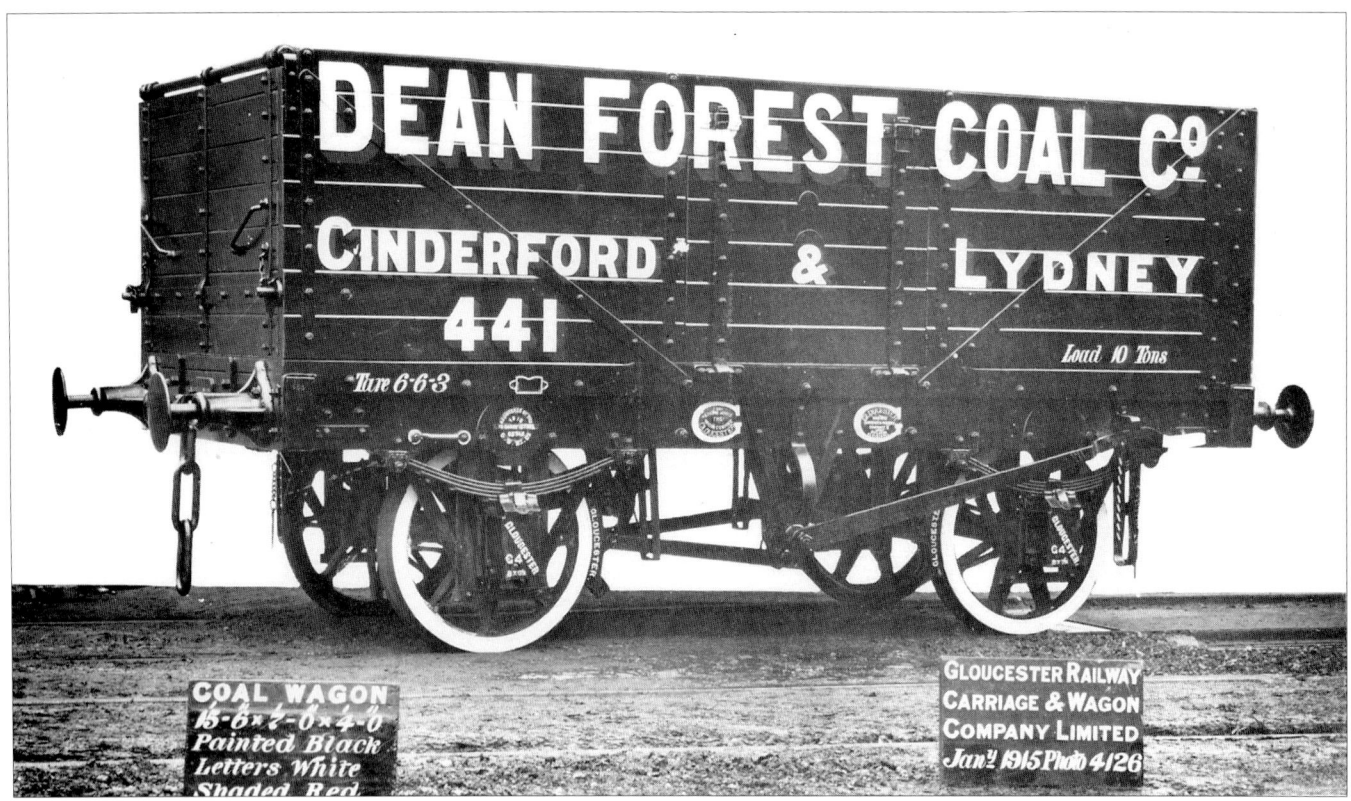

Photographed in January 1915 is wagon No. 441, one of a batch of five bought for cash. The livery is a little more elaborate than on No. 437 on the previous page as the lettering is shaded red. *GRC&WCo.*

One of the final batch of wagons built by Gloucester and supplied in November/December 1927. Painted red with white lettering, shaded black, and with black ironwork, wagon No. 549 is branded *'Empty to Eastern United Coll{y} Ruspidge. GWR'*. The two images on this page show well how care has to be taken when attempting to work out colours for the wagons. At first glance the body colour would appear the same and it is only by careful study of the shading, especially on the right-hand end of this wagon, that a difference can be seen. We must be thankful that the Gloucester Wagon Co. put information boards in front of its wagons. *GRC&WCo.*

Enlarged from a postcard view of Eastern United Colliery is wagon number 23. Of 5-plank construction and with what looks like a steel underframe. It could well have been built by Edwards & Brown and have been bought from the Western Wagon & Property Co. in April 1904 at the same time as No. 27 on page 72. It does have solid ends, both with a raised plank. As such the Dean Forest Coal Co. would have been unable to send the wagon to Lydney, Bullo or Sharpness with loads for shipping as there would have been no way to tip the wagon. Such considerations had to be borne in mind when the wagon was being loaded for dispatch. Presumably the load would be trimmed a little before the wagon left the colliery.

A Dean Forest Coal Co. wagon, probably in the red livery if the enlarged initial letter theory holds, captured on film at Chipping Norton.

A Dean Forest Coal Co. wagon as it appeared in 1944, the location of the photograph being the South Wales mainline at St. Fagans, Cardiff. The condition that the wagons got into during the war with wagon pooling in operation is clearly seen with maintenance and repainting being at a minimum. Livery of the wagon appears to be a black body with plain white lettering. The diagonal strapping on the opening door end was painted white in order to assist wagon tippers during the blackout in picking out the opening end. The view possibly shows the wagon lettered as it would have been immediately pre-war, although the main lettering does appear to have been 'touched-up', possibly because a couple of new planks have been inserted. If this is the case then this wagon shows the only known instance of this lettering style.

J. G. Hubback, courtesy John Hodge

E. P. & R. L. Morgan's wagon No. 154 was part of the October 1922 order for ten wagons. The livery was red with white lettering, shaded black and with black ironwork. The wagon is lettered *'Empty to West Cannock Colliery, Hednesford, L&N.W.Rly'* showing that Edwin was also trading away from the Forest of Dean coalfield. *GRC&WCo.*

E.P. & R.L. MORGAN

E. P. and R. L. Morgan were a husband and wife team. Edwin Percy Morgan worked in the offices at Lightmoor Colliery and his wife was Rose Lillian. It would appear that they started out circa 1913, probably on a fairly small scale to augment Edwin's income, and possibly as coal merchants supplying coal dealers. Other members of the family were already in the coal factoring business as the Dean Forest Coal Company and, by marriage, the New Bowson Coal Co.

Edwin's 'outside interests' came to the attention of his employers in November 1920 – although his coal dealings must have been known about as one relative, Arthur Morgan, was Managing Director of Crawshays! As Edwin Morgan worked in the offices at Lightmoor he was privy to the various orders which came in from the other factors, who their customers were and at what price they were being supplied with coal. Arthur Morgan was tasked to investigate and wrote to the three main factors; Messrs Sully, the Dean Forest Coal Co. and New Bowson, to see if any of them had had dealings with Messrs E. P. & R. L. Morgan. Not surprisingly the latter two companies wrote back to say that they had indeed been supplying them with varying monthly quantities of coal from both Lightmoor and Eastern United collieries. Edwin was told that his coal dealing must stop within six months.

Sullys, having been alerted to the fact now wrote to the Crawshay's Board in March 1921 complaining of competition in the trade by members of Crawshay's staff and Edwin was brought before the Board. He stated that to give up his coal dealing would be ruinous for him. Eventually, in September 1921 it was decided that there would be no objection to Mrs Morgan carrying on the business as long as Edwin passed no information to her and that Edwin would be found a new position within Crawshays where he was not privy to sales information. All of this came about at a time when the business was expanding with extra railway wagons being acquired. It is unknown when trading ceased as at no time do entries appear in trade directories.

THE WAGONS

In March 1913 two new 12-ton wagons were let on deferred payment over 7 years with the Gloucester Wagon Co. keeping them in repair.

In May 1921 ten 10-ton wagons were purchased secondhand over 3 years. In October 1922 ten new 12-ton wagons were bought over 7 years at a total cost of £1430 15s. 0d.

A 7-plank 12-ton wagon supplied to E. P. Morgan in March 1918. *GRC&WCo.*

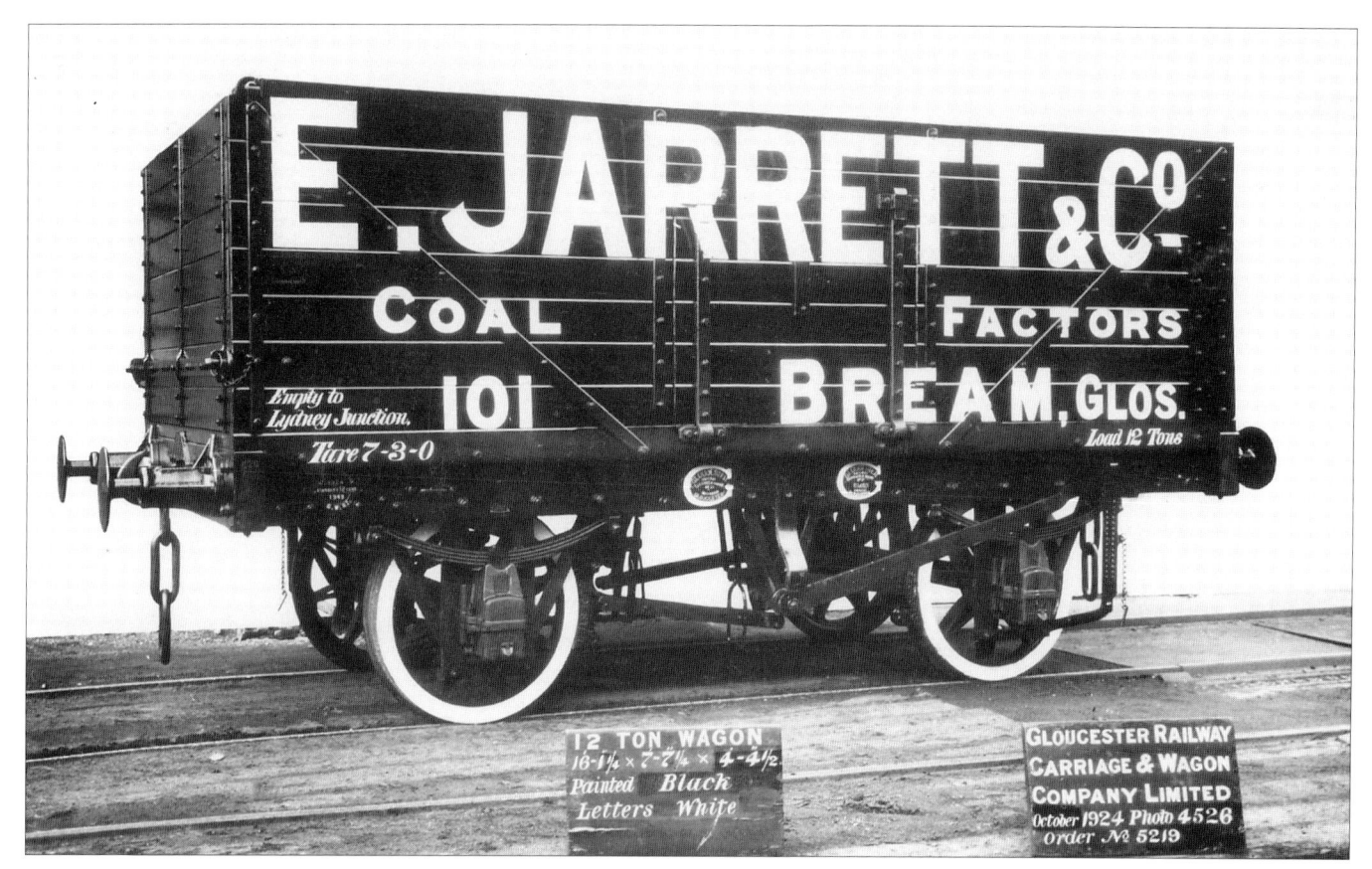

No. 101 was photographed at Gloucester in October 1924 and is a 7-plank 12-ton wagon. Painted black and lettered white it is branded 'Empty to Lydney Junction'.
GRC&WCo.

EDGAR JARRETT & CO.

Edgar Jarrett & Co. were based in Bream which, interestingly, had no rail connection. They appear to have been principal factors for the Princess Royal Colliery which was the nearest large colliery to Bream. Edgar Jarrett was obviously trading by 1884 as in January of that year he bought two wagons from the Gloucester Carriage & Wagon Co. It is possible that they were bought in connection with Jarrett's interests in the Park Iron Mines and Bream Grove Colliery which had been leased by his father in 1881. In 1890 they sold out to the Park Iron Mines and Collieries Co. Ltd (see page 48). Another recent acquisition had been the Dan's Drift Colliery and Edgar Jarrett agreed to remain as manager of this concern.

In this enlargement of a train passing through Lydney Town Station a 5-plank E. Jarrett wagon is next to the locomotive followed by a 6-plank. The two wagons have differing lettering styles, both have E. Jarrett & Co. Ltd along the top planks. In the case of the 5-plank wagon it fills the top two planks whilst on the 6-plank it just runs onto the third plank down. On the fourth plank of this wagon it looks as though the words 'Colliery Agents' are spaced either side of the door while on the 5-plank the same words straddle the third and fourth planks but are centred on the door and fit between the diagonal side strapping. Wagon numbers are bottom left and 'Bream' bottom right. The wagons are likely to have been painted black with plain white lettering. A portion of a wagon painted in a similar style appears in the view of Mierystock screens on page 60.

This 6-plank wagon, No. 74, was seen at Cannop Colliery in the early 1930s.

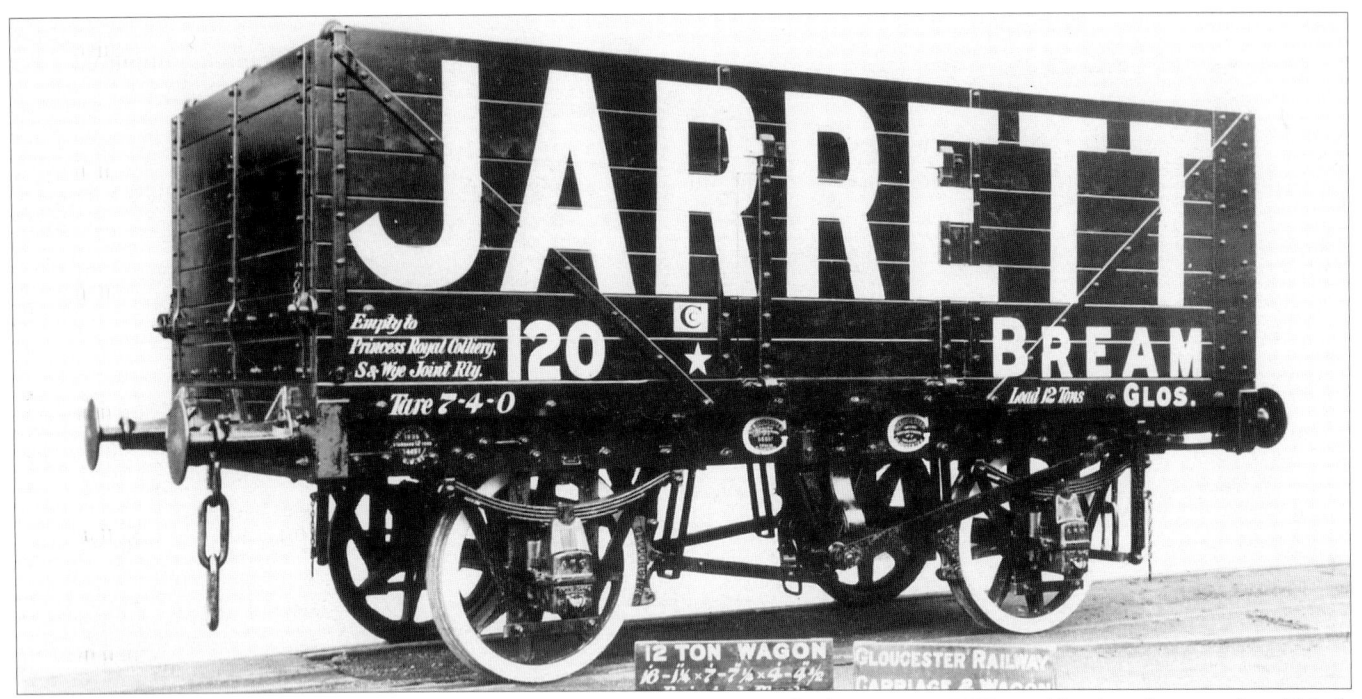

Photographed at Gloucester in January 1935 was wagon No. 120. A 12-ton, 7-plank, wagon to RCH specifications it was painted black with white lettering. Branded 'Empty to Princess Royal Colliery S&Wye Joint Rly.' *GRC&WCo.*

Lettered in a similar style was No. 134 photographed in October 1937. *GRC&WCo.*

Photographed in May 1943 is wagon No. 157. Lettered in wartime, savings were obviously made by having smaller lettering. Note also the steel underframe and the uprated load capacity of 13 tons. *GRC&WCo.*

The company continued trading until recent times as fuel merchants.

THE WAGONS

The first order in the Gloucester books is dated the 8th January 1884 when two new 10-ton wagons were bought for cash at £521 5s. 0d. each.

In May 1895 100 10-ton wagons were purchased on a 7 year redemption contract from the Western Wagon & Property Co.

The next reference at Gloucester comes in November 1912 when a repairing contract was signed for two 10-ton wagons for a period of seven years. A similar contract was taken out in September 1914 for five 10-ton wagons over seven years.

All of the above were done in the name of Edgar Jarrett but when the next order was placed, in August 1924, it was for Edgar Jarrett & Co. It was for ten 12-ton wagons over five years.

There followed other orders from Gloucester, in January 1935 and for ten 12-ton wagons in October 1937. In April 1942, when the wagon fleet would have been under Government control, Jarrett ordered two 12-ton wagons with steel underframes 'to be delivered as soon as possible'. With wartime shortages delivery actually took place in May 1943 – over a year later – and the official photograph reveals that they were rated for a load of 13-tons.

The S&W letter books reveal that on the 13th September 1917 wagon No. 41 was off road in the sidings at Mierystock.

Wagon No. 315 photographed in Lydney Yard in July 1908. Of unknown builder it is a 5-plank wagon of 10-ton capacity. Livery was red, with white lettering, shaded black and with black ironwork. There also appears a letter B on the end between the stanchions. One other view of Lydney Docks shows wagons with NB on the ends, probably New Bowson. Just above the B can be determined an oval builder's plate.
courtesy Bob Essery

Telephone 16.   Telegrams: "Bowson, Cinderford."

THE NEW BOWSON COAL COMPANY

COLLIERY AGENTS, SHIPPERS & CONTRACTORS

Coals obtained from the following principal Collieries

EASTERN UNITED, LIGHTMOOR, PRINCESS ROYAL, CANNOP AND ARTHUR & EDWARD.

CINDERFORD

NEW BOWSON COAL CO.

The New Bowson Coal Co. had a long history, not always as coal factors. A company called the New Bowson Deep Coal Co. Ltd was formed in 1868 to take over work at the New Bowson Colliery north of Cinderford which was one of the first to attempt to reach the deep coals. Closely connected with this were members of the Holden and Illingworth families, both from Yorkshire. It would appear to have gone into liquidation in 1871 and was replaced by the New Bowson Coal Co. circa 1873. They were also working the nearby East Slade Colliery which was certainly far more successful than New Bowson itself. The sidings for the East Slade Colliery were at the end of the Churchway Branch of the Great Western's Forest of Dean Branch. Here was located a set of screens known as the 'wooden house' which was connected to the colliery by a rope-hauled colliery tub route. One contract that the company had was for supplying coal and coke to the Gloucester Wagon Co. during 1873. The colliery manager at East Slade was William Burdess, a family who were to become intimately connected with the New Bowson Coal Co. The East Slade Colliery closed down in 1902 as it was virtually worked out and by 1910 the New Bowson Coal Co. had sold its interests in the deep gales at New Bowson to the Lydney & Crump Meadow Co. who in turn sold them to Henry Crawshay & Co. who developed them as part of Northern United Colliery. The New Bowson Coal Co. also had an interest in Arthur & Edward Colliery which was eventually sold to the Lydney & Crump Meadow Colliery Co. who developed the gale.

It is presumed that after the closure of East Slade the New Bowson Co. concentrated solely on the business of buying and selling coal. In later years the company was in the hands of the Burdess family who continued trading until the 1960s.

THE WAGONS

In May 1872 the New Bowson Coal Co. placed an order with the Gloucester Co. for fifty 10-ton wagons for cash. In November of the same year they bought a further fifty 10-ton wagons for cash which were noted as being 'late James Smith' (probably of

Two more New Bowson wagons in the yard at Lydney are No's 306 and 333. Both are 5-plank wagons with end doors and look to be of identical construction and are probably from the same batch as 315 on the previous page. Note that both the tare and the load details are to be found on the left-hand end, whilst the small italic lettering on the right-hand end appears to read *'Forest of Dean'*.

courtesy Bob Essery

By the date of this official Gloucester photograph, March 1927, the New Bowson Coal Co. were acting as factors and it is believed were 'importing' house coal into the Forest of Dean – hence the branding *'Empty to Netherseal Colly, Gresley, L.M.S.'* Gresley is in Derbyshire, close to Burton-upon-Trent.

GRC&WCo.

80

New Bowson Coal Co's wagons strayed far from the Forest as shown by the one seen on the left of this postcard view of Princetown Station, Devon. Situated high on Dartmoor the area is noted for its prison and an H.M. Office of Works wagon can also be seen behind the water crane. It is unknown who the customer was, or indeed if it was Forest coal which was being supplied.

Stroud, see page 88). These wagons would undoubtedly have been run in connection with the East Slade Colliery.

September 1874 saw the company hiring seven 10-ton wagons, one 8-ton wagon and three 10-ton wagons for a period of one year. More wagons were taken on hire, although this time for only three months, in November 1888 when twenty secondhand 10-ton wagons were taken. A possibly even shorter hire period was in November 1892 when fifty secondhand 10-ton wagons were taken 'temporarily'. In October 1893 the final hire agreement with Gloucester is found for fifty secondhand 10-ton wagons for a period of two years – one is left to wonder if this was a renewal of the November 1892 contract and that the 'temporary' period had turned out to be twelve months.

The only order for the purchase of wagons was in May 1921 when ten secondhand 10-ton wagons were let on deferred purchase over 3 years at £27 2s. 0d. each.

The only reference in the Severn & Wye letters is to wagon No. 310 suffering from a broken coupling on the 22nd April 1907.

New Bowson wagons appear to have always been painted with a red body colour, lettered white with black shading and ironwork and with the initial letters N B on the fixed end of the wagon for a period as seen on wagon No. 315.

Somewhat closer to home is wagon No. 585 standing empty in sidings at Swindon Electricity Works. Two wagons further down is a stablemate whose number cannot be defined, possibly 76. The contract to supply the works with coal from Eastern United Colliery was held for many years by Lowell Baldwin of Bristol but for 1931 it was decided that the contract would be divided between Baldwins and New Bowson, both supplying 100 tons a week.

courtesy Paul Karau

A masterpiece of the signwriter's art but probably difficult to read from a distance, is this 7-plank 10-ton wagon supplied for I. W. Baldwin in October 1906. It can be seen that although he was a Forest of Dean factor he was also acting for other coalfields and was sales agent for the East Cannock Colliery. The wagon was painted black with white lettering. Behind the running number is a diamond which it is believed was painted red. *GRC&WCo.*

I. W. BALDWIN & CO.

As well as acting as a factor at several of the Forest of Dean collieries I. W. (Ivo) Baldwin was also a colliery owner and the sole sales agent for the East Cannock Colliery Co. Within the Forest of Dean he owned the Harrow Hill Colliery between October 1921 and March 1924 and the Addis Hill Colliery between 1931 and 35. Both concerns had sidings on the Forest of Dean Branch and so it is likely that his wagons used them. As a factor it is known that his wagons ran into Lightmoor, Eastern United and Arthur & Edward collieries. It is not known at what date he ceased trading but he was in some difficulties in mid-1935 owing money to Crawshays and offering a car and plant from the colliery in settlement.

THE WAGONS

In October 1906 two new 10-ton wagons were let on deferred payment over 7 years. These were the wagons with the elaborate and extravagant painting style. In April 1908 six 10-ton secondhand wagons were let on 7 years deferred payment with the Wagon Co. carrying out repairs. A repairing contract was signed in November 1913, probably for the two wagons bought in 1906 which were now the property of Baldwin. Those wagons bought in 1908 became the subject of a repair contract for seven years in May 1915. There are no other references to wagons for I. W. Baldwin but it would seem unlikely that he could have traded with only eight wagons so the question is did he have more from another source?

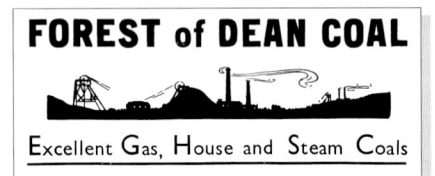

FOREST of DEAN COAL

Excellent Gas, House and Steam Coals

Comparing well with Yorkshire and the Midlands, for the two former, and taking first place, as regards the latter.

We testify thus after an experience of over 20 years of the Coals named, taking price and quality into account.

The Grades of coal offered are Large, Cobbles, Nuts, in House Coals and Large, Through and Through 3" and 2" rough small in Steam Coals.

::   Prices on Application   ::

Prompt Loading of Wagons with every care and attention.

I. W. BALDWIN & CO.
Sole Proprietor:
IVO W. BALDWIN, J.P., MINING AND CONSULTING ENGINEER
OAKLEIGH, DRYBROOK, Glos.

Wagon No. 22, photographed in January 1910, was finished in a much simpler form of signwriting. It was also painted in a different fashion with a chocolate brown body, white lettering shaded black and with black ironwork. *GRC&WCo.*

An 8-ton 5-plank wagon photographed at Gloucester in December 1895. There is no mention in the order book for the wagon under the Phoenix Coal Co., however, in November an order appears from the Kerne Bridge Coal Co. for four 8-ton wagons. It is known that the Phoenix Coal Co. had a depot at Kerne Bridge so possibly the Kerne Bridge Coal Co. was another of Latham's interests. *GRC&WCo.*

PHOENIX COAL CO.

The Phœnix Coal Co. was run by the Rev. Arthur Latham who had been a Baptist minister in Lydbrook. However, he appears to have become interested in the coal business and eventually gave up ministering. Quite when the Phoenix Coal Co. was formed is unknown, it may have been taken over as a going concern by Latham or he could have renamed an existing coal business which was acquired and revitalised which would explain the company name. Certainly a ledger account was opened with the S&W in January 1897.

What is known is that Latham had interests in several small collieries in the Forest whilst still a Baptist minister. In May 1898 Latham submitted a proposal to Henry Crawshay & Co. to transfer all his trade to them. He gave various properties as security and the proposal was accepted. It was probably the time at which Latham went full-time into the coal business as in September 1899 it was reported locally that A. W. Latham had resigned the pastorate of the Baptist Church, Lydbrook after 16 years, due to increased commercial interests.

In March 1900 he moved from Lydbrook to Ross where he set up the head office of the coal company. The company had depots at Monmouth and Kerne Bridge on the Ross-Monmouth line and at Mitcheldean Road on the Hereford, Ross, Gloucester line.

Wagon No. 60 photographed at Gloucester in February 1897. With the branding '*Empty to Coleford Junction*' it was probably used in conjunction with one of Latham's collieries alongside the Coleford Branch of the Severn & Wye. *GRC&WCo.*

83

The company, as coal factors and merchants continued trading after the death of Latham in April 1915. A note has been found which possibly links the Phœnix Coal Co. with Frank Step Hockaday and Thomas Carlyle Deakin, the latter being the son of the owner of Parkend Colliery. The company was trading right through to the Second World War and beyond with offices in Ross.

THE WAGONS

The first order under the Phœnix Coal Co. appears in the GRC&WCo. books on the 6th December 1887 when they took twenty-four secondhand 8-ton wagons on hire at daily and tonnage rates of 1d. per ton per day.

The company also had some wagons from the North Central Wagon Co. but it is not known if they were bought or hired. All were 8-ton wagons with the numbers 150, 160, 170, 180, 190, and 200. Originally dumb-buffered they were 'converted' by the fitment of self-contained sprung buffers in 1896 and registered by the GWR as converted wagons.

In January 1897 two new 10-ton wagons were let on seven years deferred purchase from the GRC&WCo. with the wagon co. to keep them in repair. A repairs contract was signed in May 1899 for four 8-ton and two 10-ton wagons for seven years.

In September 1901 two secondhand wagons were let on seven years deferred purchase. These were both 10-ton wagons.

October 1906 saw a further repairs contract, this time for one 6-ton, two 8-ton and one 10-ton wagon for a period of $4^{1}/_{2}$ years. In May 1913 four 8-ton wagons and two 10-ton wagons were put on a repairing contract.

Other mentions of wagons occur in the Severn & Wye letter books:

On the 5th January 1904 wagon No. 140 damaged at Foxes Bridge Colliery. Wagon No. 87 was damaged at Lydney Jct. on the 16th February 1906. On the 11th February 1907 wagon No. 390 was off road at Serridge Jcn. and on the 17th November 1917 wagon No. 475 was off road at New Fancy Colliery.

From the wagon numbers given it would seem that Phoenix had a fairly sizeable fleet. However, this could be misleading as in the early years wagon numbers may have increased in intervals of ten (as witnessed by the wagons from the North Central Wagon Co. and the Gloucester official photos). Later purchases might have filled in odd numbers. Certainly there is no photographic evidence to contradict the increase in tens theory. In the early years the wagons were painted black with white lettering but by the early 1930s at least some of the wagons were appearing with red shading to the lettering.

Two views of wagon No. 50 at New Fancy Colliery. A 6-plank wagon with non-opening ends it would not have been used for traffic to Lydney Docks. Livery appears to be black with white lettering, although in the lower view there is just a hint that the lettering could be shaded. If this is the case then the shading would probably have been red.

Photographed at Monmouth in 1931 is 5-plank wagon No. 520, painted black with white lettering shaded red.

A Sully & Co. Ltd wagon in Lydney Yard in 1908. Still running with dumb-buffers it would soon have to be 'converted' to meet Railway Clearing House standards by having sprung buffers fitted. Possibly this had been foreseen as the wagon is fitted with 'detachable' dead buffers. Sully & Co. were centred on Bridgwater but bought into Parkend Colliery and maintained a shipping office at Lydney which this example is lettered up for. The colour scheme was black body with white lettering and in common with all Sully wagons had the mark of a white cross on the side door. Possibly built in the mid-1880s by the Gloucester Wagon Co. but it has picked up one 'foreign' axlebox. *courtesy Bob Essery*

SULLY & CO.

As ship owners the Sully family had been handling coal in the West Country since the end of the eighteenth century. By the early 1800s they had set up in Bridgwater, Somerset. By 1840 Thomas Sully was trading in coal from both Lydney and South Wales and in 1845 went into partnership with his younger brother James Wood Sully. In 1860 they became Sully & Co.

Previous to this, however, they had taken an interest in Parkend Colliery (page 18) as partners in the Parkend Coal Co. with J. Trotter and Thomas Nicholson. In 1857 they bought the colliery outright and by 1860 Sully had bought out the other partners. Thomas Sully died in 1861 and James became sole owner. In 1876 he handed on Sully & Co. to his three sons but retained the colliery. Two years later he formed the Parkend Coal Co. Ltd to buy the colliery and remained the largest shareholder with Sully & Co. as the selling agents. The colliery closed down in 1880 and was sold off to be successfully reopened.

Although Sully & Co. did not now own a colliery to supply coal to their interests in Bridgwater, they had become established in Lydney as shippers and factors and took offices, a wharf and a coal tip at the docks there. John Sully was manager between 1877 and 1880 after which Mr James Shepherd acted as Shipping Agent for Sully & Co. at Lydney for the next 20 years. The firm then owned 300 railway wagons, twenty sailing vessels and two steamboats which traded continuously with coal to Bridgwater and many other ports in the West of England and Ireland.

SULLY & CO. LTD.

COAL PROPRIETORS AND
STEAMSHIP OWNERS

ESTABLISHED 1826

Agents for all

FOREST OF DEAN

HOUSE, STEAM & GAS COALS

ANTHRACITE COALS

GAS, FOUNDRY AND
FURNACE COKE.

LYDNEY, GLOS.

TELEPHONE - LYDNEY 8.
TELEGRAMS - "SULLY, LYDNEY."

Head Office:
BRIDGWATER

TELEPHONE - BRIDGWATER 20.
TELEGRAMS "COAL, BRIDGWATER."

The letterhead used for the Lydney office which shows that the date used for the establishment of the company, 1826, went back to Thomas's time and predated the founding of Sully & Co. by some 34 years. The letter was in connection with coal to be shipped to Combe Martin, Devon.
courtesy Combe Martin museum

In 1886 the Severn Tunnel opened which formed a more direct route from South Wales. This was a blow to the shipping trade via Bridgwater and the quantity of coal carried by sea considerably reduced. This necessitated an altered policy and the sailing vessels were gradually sold whilst the number of railway wagons was increased to over 600 and repairing works were established at Bridgwater and later at Lydney.

The change of gauge on the GWR in 1892 facilitated the entry of coal from the Midlands to the West of England and this again altered Sully's operation and they immediately entered into arrangements for supplies from these coalfields.

1894 saw Sully & Co. become a private limited company. In 1899, Mr J. Norman Sully, eldest son of Mr John Sully, was appointed manager at Lydney on the retirement of Shepherd.

By 1926 increased railway rates and dock charges, which seriously affected the transport of coal by water, meant that practically the whole of Sully's coal was railborne from the collieries to its destination and that Bridgwater as a port for the distribution of coal in the west had almost ceased to exist. Sully's continued to run ships, however, until 1966 which was six years beyond the last coal shipped from Lydney.

THE WAGONS
Little is known of the broad gauge wagons owned by the company or whether any definition was made between 'Lydney' and 'Bridgwater' wagons. Certainly later photographs of standard gauge wagons show them to have been branded for the separate branches (see next page). After 1872 the company would have had to run both standard gauge and broad gauge wagons following the conversion of the South Wales Railway in 1872. The lines in the West Country were not to be converted for a further twenty years.

Some details of Sully's wagon purchases are known and the writer is indebted to Richard Kelham for the following information.
91-100 came from the Bridgwater Engineering Co. in 1875.
101-150 were built by the Gloucester Wagon Co. in 1878.
231-250 supplied by the Midland Wagon Co. in 1876.
251-270 were built by the Gloucester Wagon Co. in 1881.
281-300 built by the Gloucester Wagon Co. in 1880.
301-310, built by the Gloucester Wagon Co. in 1886.
470-476 were built by the Gloucester Wagon Co. in 1898.
960-963 Derbyshire C&WCo. [?] 1937.
What is not known is whether all of these were for the Bridgwater operation although wagon No. 232 seen at Culmstock was in the batch supplied by the Midland Wagon Co.

The Severn & Wye letter books show that on the 4th November 1900 wagon 139 was off the road at Lydney Docks. More specifically on the 28th November 1901

Wagon No. 206 seen in the sidings at Lydney Dock awaiting shipping, probably into one of the fleet of vessels owned by the company such as the Parkend.   *courtesy Bob Essery*

A view of the upper basin at Lydney, c1895, with a rake of Sully wagons on the right. In May 1883 it was recorded in Severn & Wye Railway minutes that 'Messrs. Sully & Co. rent a wharf and house at the Upper Basin at £285 p.a. and according to terms have to keep it in repair. Messrs. Sully & Co. to pay £30 towards the present necessary repairs.' It was the practice at this time for companies to rent their own tips. Later they became general user. In August 1888 Sully & Co's wharfage was again discussed at a Severn & Wye Board meeting: 'This firm rent a private wharf at Lydney Basin part of the arrangement being that in case of deep draught or high wind rendering it difficult to bring vessels up the canal they should be allowed to load free of extra charge at the Lower Dock but otherwise the charge is $1^{1}/_{2}$d per ton. The General Manager, at a meeting with Mr Sully on the 4th July agreed to extend the free loading at the Lower Dock to vessels pressed for time to avoid being neaped outside Bridgwater, but Messrs. Sully now desire it to be extended to cases in which it is important to load a second vessel at night so as to leave with Messrs. Sully's private steam tug in the morning.' The settling of the matter was left to the General Manager.

collection Alan Corlett

A pair of Sully wagons at Culmstock on the Culm Valley Branch in Devon. Side by side we have a wagon from each of the Sully branches, Lydney and Bridgwater. One immediate difference is that the wagon branded for Bridgwater does not have an end door. This would have precluded it from traffic to Lydney Docks where all coal was shipped from tips necessitating an end door. Wagon No. 232 which was built by the Midland Wagon Co. in 1876 is a 6-plank wagon with end door. It varies from other wagons seen as it has the wording **SULLY & COMP**^{Y}, all other examples seen have '**& C**^{O}.' It is also possible that it has been repainted in that the word **LYDNEY** stands out and the second plank up on the right-hand end appears a different shade – possibly the word **BRIDGWATER** has been painted out. Perhaps there was some interchange of the wagons.

wagons No. 198 and No. 185 were off the road at tip No. 8 in the docks.

On the 16th January 1903 an unidentified wagon was damaged at Moseley Green. There is a reference on the 13th April 1905 to Messrs Sully & Co's wagon 185 but no further details. On the 13th August 1906 wagon No. 256 was off the road at Princess Royal Colliery and on the 21st wagon No. 109 was damaged at Cinderford.

A glimpse of a slightly different livery on wagon No. 196 seen at Cannop Colliery in the 1930s. The cross appears to be still painted on the side door but the word 'Lydney' has moved to the right-hand side.

Photographed in September 1908 is wagon No. 131. Built by the Gloucester Wagon Co. c.1880 (early pattern builder's plate on solebar) it is fitted with detachable dead buffers. The **G** plate on the side is probably a repairer's plate. The wagon was obviously used full time on traffic from Trafalgar Colliery with a return '*Empty to Bullo Pill*'. A similar wagon, No. 253 is seen on the left, again lettered up for Trafalgar Colliery. This one has dead buffers as a direct continuation of the solebars.

JAMES SMITH

Little is known at present about James Smith. He was certainly in business by 1870 as in January of that year he ordered twenty wagons from the Cheltenham & Swansea Wagon Co. and other orders with the same company later in the year suggest that he already had a fleet of wagons. He can be found in an 1876 trade directory listed as 'James Smith, coal merchant, Port house, Chalford Road, Stroud'. By 1885 his address was given as 'Woodhouse, Rodborough, Stroud'. A lot of his trade in the Forest appears to have been with Trafalgar Colliery – indeed he was a director of the Trafalgar

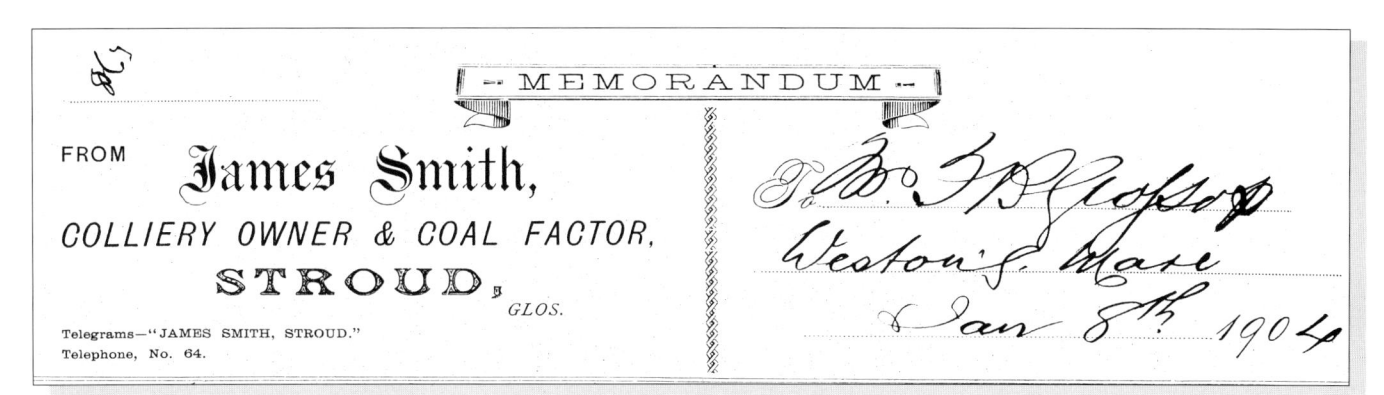

> **MEMORANDUM**
>
> FROM **James Smith,**
> COLLIERY OWNER & COAL FACTOR,
> **STROUD,** GLOS.
>
> Telegrams—"JAMES SMITH, STROUD."
> Telephone, No. 64.
>
> To Mr F B Glossop
> Weston S Mare
> Jan 8th 1904

Colliery Co. Ltd. Smith must have bought a large shareholding, probably in 1883 although most shares were held by members of the Brain family.

He may also have been the 'Mr. Smith, coal factor' connected with Simeon Holmes in working the Nags Head Colliery (see page 41).

Details of one of Smith's regular trades have survived as a bundle of papers in the Gloucester Records Office (D5385/1). These are a series of delivery notes, or vouchers, to an F. B. Glossop of Weston-super-Mare who may have been a coal merchant, he certainly had at least one wagon of his own. The notes date between 1891 and 1904 and show regular deliveries of one wagon load. There are also some letters between the two parties, one of which reveals that all was not smooth in business. In 1890 Glossop had sent his own wagon to load at Trafalgar Colliery on the account of Messrs Read (possibly Reads of Salisbury who also appear to have acted as factors and who were also dealing with Trafalgar Colliery). In reply Smith wrote '*he* [Read] *certainly cannot do better for you than I can and I do not like to lose trucks that have always worked ... especially when they belong to one of my oldest friends like you – why is it?*'.

In August 1877 Smith took out a rental on a coal tip at the lower basin at Lydney Docks, probably in connection with his shipping of coal to the Bridgwater River.

In 1932 there is a mention of a 'Mr. Smith, coal merchant, Stroud' taking coal from Thatch Colliery near Coleford. If this was James Smith then it would appear that he may have scaled down his business as Thatch was a fairly small concern. Smith was still trading in 1935 but he fails to appear in a trade directory for 1939. At present, the date at which his business finished is unknown.

Wagon No. 819 photographed at Lydney in September 1908, clearly built at Gloucester. There has obviously been some dispute over the tare as the painted weight of 5-18-0 has been chalked out and 5-17-2 chalked on. This would of course alter the tonnage charges when the wagon was weighed loaded. Unlike wagon No. 131 seen on the previous page (and which was actually in the same rake of wagons) the '*Empty to*' branding this time is Lydney Junction. As Smith mainly traded to Trafalgar he had the two alternative routes for his empty wagons, *via* Lydney Junction and the Severn & Wye line or over the Great Western's Forest of Dean Branch *via* Bullo. He also had the same options for his loaded wagons, including a choice of shipping port – Lydney or Bullo. In April 1888 it was reported in the Severn & Wye Railway Minutes that James Smith had applied for a rebate of 2d. per ton on his rates as the difference in carriage charges between Bullo and Lydney was 4d. He stated that owing to competition from other traders if the reduction could not be made then all his traffic would have to be shipped *via* Bullo. It was decided that the reduction would be made over the summer months, April to September, on coal shipped to the Bridgwater River. He fell foul of the Severn & Wye again in July when it was pointed out that not all of his traffic to south western stations was being routed over the Severn Bridge *as promised*. Some was obviously going *via* Gloucester.

[Delivery note reproduction:]

STROUD,
GLOUCESTERSHIRE.

Nov 4th 189 9

Bought of JAMES SMITH.

☞ All Trucks must be emptied and *returned* within 24 hours of their arrival. If detained over that time demurrage will be charged.

Per G. W. R. to _Weston S Mare_ Station, agreeable to order.

	Trafalgar Coal.	NO. OF TRUCK	TONS.	CWTS.	PRICE.	£	s.	d.
Rubbles		207	9	0				

A delivery note for 9 tons of Trafalgar rubbles delivered by James Smith to F. B. Glossop of Weston-super-Mare in truck No. 207. The Gloucester Records Office hold a run of these notes at dates between 1891 and 1904 showing that the trade was fairly regular, usually one truckload at a time. Most went in Smith's own wagons but some in Trafalgar Colliery wagons and some in Glossop's own wagon (which was always No. 1, suggesting that it might have been his only wagon) for which he opened a S&W Ledger Account in July 1897.

THE WAGONS

The earliest order so far found is with the Cheltenham & Swansea Wagon Co. for twenty wagons in January 1870 on three years redemption hire. In June his offer of £2 10s. 0d. per wagon per year for repairing 'his last twenty wagons' for two years was accepted. This seems to suggest that Smith had already had some wagons from the company or its predecessors and this is borne out by a further agreement in October for 'repairing 32 wagons' for which Smith offered £150 per annum.

The order books of the Gloucester Wagon Co. are littered with orders for wagons from Smith. He hired 130 10-ton wagons in February 1872 and in May had 42 wagons converted, presumably from broad to standard gauge, for cash and also took out a repairs agreement on them to run for fourteen years. On the 12th November fifty of Smith's wagons were transferred to the New Bowson Coal Co. From 1872 through to 1875 and beyond he was having broad gauge wagons converted. In December 1907 James Smith hired 40 secondhand 10-ton wagons for a period of 3 years.

From the Severn & Wye letter books we find that on the 22nd November 1901 James Smith's wagon No. 68 was off the road at Lydney Docks. On the 6th October 1903 wagon No. 173 was off at Lydney Jct. (S&W). On the 16th August 1904 wagon No. 118 was off at Lydney Jct. On the 9th March 1907 it was reported that the middle bearer was broken on wagon No. 252. The 15th June 1910 found wagon No. 169 off at Cinderford Old Station.

Wagon numbers which appear on the Glossop delivery notes are:
4, 7, 8, 9, 11, 30, 32, 35, 37, 40, 41, 42, 47, 76, 77, 79, 80, 81, 82, 83, 84, 85, 87, 91, 92, 99, 101, 103, 104, 105, 107, 109, 110, 113, 114, 116, 117, 119, 122, 123, 127, 129, 130, 132, 135, 141, 142, 143, 144, 145, 146, 147, 163, 164, 165, 169, 170, 172, 175, 176, 178, 180, 182, 184, 185, 187, 188, 189, 190, 194, 195, 197, 198, 199, 200, 202, 203, 204, 206, 207, 208, 209, 210, 211, 213, 215, 217, 218, 220, 251, 252, 253, 254, 259, 260, 276, 322, 973. Several of these made more than one journey. If his numbering system was consecutive then the fleet was large but 937 does rather stand out on its own at the end, although the photographs show wagons with numbers in the 6 and 800s.

Strangely, although Smith had so many wagons from the Gloucester Wagon Co. it would appear that none of them were photographed officially. This is possibly because many of them were on hire.

Above: This wagon, captured on film in Lydney Yard in August 1909, is included here as it is branded for the use of James Smith. However, it is believed that the wagon is an example of a short-term hire from Gloucester. The lettering on this wagon reads on the left-hand side:
Gloucester Wagon Co. Gloucester
The next line is indistinct but possibly reads: *Stroud to Gloucester* then:
Empty to Princess Royal Coll.
of [?] *James Smith*
Tare 4-1-2
The right-hand side reads:
For Coal Traffic Only
No. 21
Being branded 'Empty to Princess Royal' shows that Smith was dealing with other collieries than Trafalgar in the Forest.

A pair of Smith's wagons in the Fetterhill Sidings off the Severn & Wye's Coleford Branch. Both wagons are fitted with dumb buffers and No. 172 carries what could be a Gloucester Carriage & Wagon Co. repairs plate. The wagons are both lettered for Trafalgar Colliery and No. 172 is branded *'Empty to Bullo Pill'*. It is unknown whether they were collecting coal from one of the small collieries, such as Dark Hill, situated here, or delivering coal for use at the Darkhill Fire Brick Works on the far side of the road. The latter is the most likely with the coal having been brought from Trafalgar. This photograph is the only known view of the brick works which were started in the mid-1850s. They were connected with the St. Vincent Colliery gale owned by James Grindell in which the clay was found. It was in 1855 that a licence for the digging of clay was granted to Grindell and Philip Wanklyn. The siding on which the wagons stand was an extension to the existing siding allowed by the S&W in 1875 for the use of Wanklyn & Grindell. By 1901 the works were owned by James Cole and appear to have ceased production by the First World War.

courtesy Robin Simmons

Probably from the same batch as 819 on page 89 is No. 824, again seen at Lydney.

courtesy Bob Essery

This dumb-buffered wagon for Read & Son of Salisbury was photographed in October 1878. It appears to be painted with either a grey or red body with white lettering and black ironwork. It is branded *'Empty to Trafalgar Colliery Bilson'*. *GRC&WCo.*

READ & SON

With an office at 42 Fisherton Street, Salisbury, the business was in existence by 1867 when they had broad gauge wagons from the Swansea Wagon Co. Reads appear to have acted as factors, rather like James Smith, and were also taking coal from Trafalgar Colliery. From the wagon evidence it is possible that Read, or a relative, went into partnership with Westmoreland for a period in the 1880s. Later wagons produced for Reads, such as one photographed by Gloucester in December 1904, are lettered again for Read & Son. Reads were still getting coal from the Forest in 1907, both from Trafalgar Colliery and also from Lightmoor. They are recorded in Crawshay's minutes as attempting to get the best deal possible stating that if Crawshay's wanted to get their business they had to match the 9d. per ton rebate that they got all year round from Trafalgar. It was decided to do so to encourage Reads to take as much coal as possible. They were obviously a firm to be taken seriously. The company was still trading in 1926 and probably through to the 1940s.

THE WAGONS

In October 1867 Messrs Read & Son took six wagons on five-year redemption hire from the Cheltenham & Swansea Wagon Co. Ltd, together with a repairing contract for twenty wagons. In June 1868 they took a further twenty wagons from the same supplier. It is likely that all of these wagons were built as broad gauge.

In May 1869 a repairing agreement was signed with Reads by the C&SWCo. for the repair of six narrow gauge wagons, this is the last mention of them in the available records of the Swansea Wagon Co.

It would appear that Reads then switched their wagon buying to the Gloucester Wagon Co. and many orders appear in their books. In July 1885 an order was placed for 166 six, seven, eight, and ten-ton wagons, all secondhand and to be kept in repair by Reads. It is also recorded in the company minutes that 'Mr. George Read (Read & Son) was to be advanced £4,000 upon 166 wagons, the sum to be repaid over 5 years at an interest rate of 6%' and by way of guarantee Read deposited deeds of freehold land in Salisbury. His wagons were to have Gloucester owners plates attached for the period in question.

The Seven & Wye letter books reveal that wagon No. 172 was damaged at Lydney Jct. on the 30th August 1901.

This elderly wagon was photographed in August 1899 with the left-hand board proclaiming it to be 36 years old 'the Wheel bosses are dated 1863'. It was apparently built as part of an order dated August 1862 for the Chester district. It carries a GWR registration plate for 1865. Presumably it is going out on hire to Read & Son. *GRC&WCo.*

92

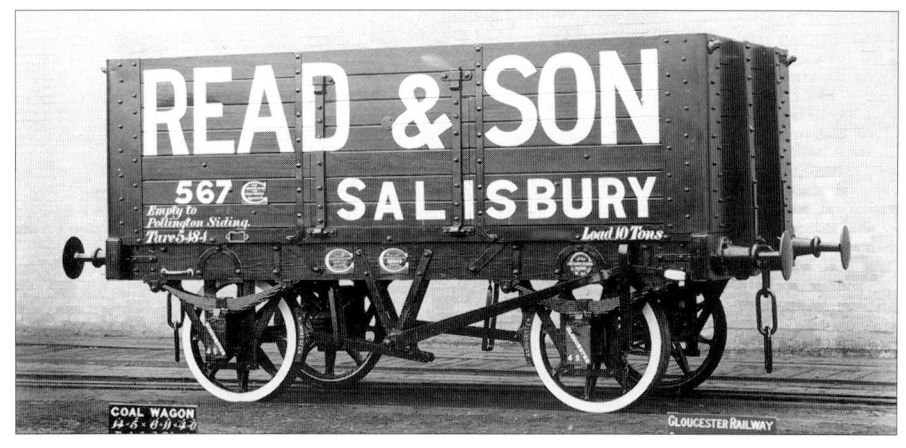

Photographed at Gloucester in October 1902 is wagon No. 567 displaying a larger style of main lettering. Painted black with white lettering. *GRC&WCo.*

Photographed in August 1903 although an earlier wagon as witnessed by the GWR diamond shaped reconstructed plate. *GRC&WCo.*

December 1904 saw wagon No. 614 built by Gloucester. *GRC&WCo.*

Possibly by 1884 Read had gone into partnership as this wagon for Read & Westmoreland may testify. However, with no other evidence to hand it could well have been a separate company. As with the wagon at the top of the page this one is branded '*Empty to Trafalgar Colliery Forest of Dean*' *GRC&WCo.*

ALFRED J. SMITH

In 1874 Alfred J. Smith, an accountant aged 31, of Totterdown was taken on by Richard Charles Ring, a coal merchant of Bristol and it would seem that at some point they ended up in partnership. This was dissolved in 1884 by mutual consent and Smith announced that he was to start trading on his own account. He took premises at 47 Queen Square, Bristol as a 'shipper of steam, house & mining coals and contractor for freight' and stating that he had been 'for more than 20 years actively engaged in the trade'. The business later moved to 9 Queen Square. In 1893 he purchased the Newport Coal & Coke Co., under which name he traded until 1897 when he turned the business into a limited company.

In November 1912 Alfred J. Smith Ltd was incorporated to purchase the existing business of coal, coke and general fuel shipper and merchant, shipowner and broker, colliery owner and freight contractor at 9 Queen Sq. Bristol. There was also a branch at Coleford and various

The screens at Cannop Colliery *circa* 1910/12, together with an enlargement therefrom which shows an Alfred J. Smith wagon being loaded. The wagon behind is likely to be one belonging to James & Emanuel. On the extreme left of the full view stands a W. Sawyer & Co. of Cheltenham (see page 114) and just discernible in the left foreground a wagon with small italic script lettering. This may well be an example of a short-term hire wagon as with the aid of huge amounts of magnification the top line of lettering can just be made out as '*A. J. Smith*'.

A tantalising glimpse of a wagon which can be identified as belonging to Alfred Smith from the partial name 'Alfre' and the part address '9, Queen Sq'. The lower line probably reads 'Welsh Steam Coal'. Unfortunately the central and right-hand portions of the wagon have to be left to the imagination. What the photograph does show is that Alfred Smith was trading into the Forest in September 1908.

Alfred J. Smith, Ltd.
COAL FACTORS & FREIGHT CONTRACTORS

Distributors for West of England for Princess Royal Celebrated Highdelf Coals.

---

9 QUEEN SQUARE, BRISTOL

Telephone: 23011 Private Branch Exchange.   Telegrams: "Carbon, Bristol."

BRANCH DEPOTS:
PYLLE HILL, G.W.R. ..
CANON'S MARSH ..
WAPPING WHARF ..   } BRISTOL
LAWRENCE HILL ..
ST. PHILIP'S, L.M.S. ..
ST. PHILIP'S BRIDGE WHARF ..

BRADFORD-ON-AVON,   TROWBRIDGE,   CLEVEDON, WESTON-S-MARE.

Telegraphic Address,
"CARBON, BRISTOL".

TELEPHONE Nº 39.

Alfred J. Smith,
SHIPPER OF STEAM, HOUSE & MINING COALS,
and Contractor for Freights,

OFFICES, 47, Queen Square,
DEPÔT, Bristol Wharf,
Sᵗ PHILIP'S BRIDGE.

Bristol, 189

branches and depots in Newport; Bradford-on-Avon and Weston-super-Mare. Behind the new limited company was Alfred Sidney Livingstone Smith, possibly a son of Alfred.

A. J. Smith owned collieries in the Forest. Between August 1910 and February 1913 he held a share in Cross Knave Colliery near Coleford and in 1918 is listed as owning Glyncarn Colliery, Coleford. The directors of the company also took over a retail branch of the Princess Royal Colliery Co. in Bristol in 1919 and in 1920 formed it into a limited company called Coal Agencies Ltd.

Other businesses were taken over at various times including Pearces and Summer & Co. who appear to have been coal merchants in Bristol.

Alfred Smith senior died in 1920 aged 77, at the time he was living at 'High Grove', Wells Road, Bristol.

In January 1949 the company was wound up voluntarily with the business being taken over by Coal Agencies Ltd 'the directors and shareholders of the two company's [being] the same'.

THE WAGONS

It is not known where Smith sourced his wagons from in the early years. In 1912 on the formation of Alfred J. Smith Ltd the fleet appears to have consisted of 18 wagons.

In July 1938 ten 12-ton wagons to the 1923 RCH specifications were ordered from Gloucester.

It is also impossible to determine livery from the two photographs available. All that can be said is that his wagons prove very elusive. There is an illustration of a seven-plank wagon built in 1943 by the Gloucester Wagon Co. in Montague, *Private Owner Wagons from the Gloucester Railway Carriage & Wagon Company Ltd*, OPC, page 145 but it is lettered in wartime style.

One of A. J. Smith's vessels, the *Emperor*, built as a sailing vessel in 1906 at Chepstow. She was fitted with an engine in 1915 – in which condition she is seen here in the Tidal Basin of Lydney Dock – and in 1941 was fitted with an 80hp Ruston & Hornsby engine. *Emperor* could carry between 140 and 145 tons of coal in her single hold. She was the only motor vessel in Smith's fleet, the others being steam ships or sailing vessels. Vessels known to have been in the Smith fleet included *Calcaria*, *Iron Duke*, *John*, *William* (sail), *Devonia*, *Seaforth*, *Margaret*, *Tel El Kebir*, *Carbon*, *Regina* (sail), *George* (sail), *Effort*, *Ellen* (sail), *Superb* (sail), *Perseverance* (sail), *Happy go Lucky* (sail), *Good Intent*, *Swift*, *Henry*, *Queen*, *Secret*, *Galley* (trow), *Henry* (barge), *Spry* (trow), *Duke of Wellington*, *Eliza* (trow), *Marquis*, and *County of Lancaster*. In 1949 Smith was advertising the *Calorie*, *Radstock*, *Collin*, *Elemore*, *GFB*, *Roma*, *Tanny*, *Emperor* and the *Alma* (sail) for sale.

Wagon No. 215, photographed at Gloucester in September 1907, appears to have an oval owners plate, possibly for Thomas Silvey (see also page 98). Painted black, lettered white. *GRC&WCo.*

THOMAS SILVEY

In 1870 Thomas Silvey left his job as an inspector for The Gloucester Wagon Works to found a coal factoring business in Bristol, based in St. Phillip's. Coal was supplied to many Bristol businesses including George's Brewery and Fry's, Carson's and Cadbury's chocolate factories. They also conducted a domestic delivery service. As with Alfred Smith, Silvey also owned some ships including the *Yarrah* which was the last vessel to load coal at Lydney Docks in late 1960. The company still trades today in the oil delivery business.

THE WAGONS

Some were supplied by Gloucester and these were painted black with white lettering. Some, however, appear to have been given a body colour of either grey or red as witnessed by the one view of such a wagon at Cannop Colliery reproduced opposite. One order for Silvey was placed with Gloucester in December 1935 with thirty 12-ton wagons to RCH specifications to be delivered in February 1936. It is believed that prior to nationalisation the company were operating about 100 wagons. Some of these were acquired secondhand from unknown sources.

Photographed in December 1905 at Gloucester was wagon No. 76. Again it was lettered in white on a black body. *GRC&WCo.*

Thomas Silvey & Co.

COAL MERCHANTS

AND

SHIPOWNERS

PRINCIPAL AGENTS FOR

CANNOP COLLIERY

Producing the celebrated Highdelf Steam, Manufacturing and Gas Coals. Dry Cleaned and Sized Coals for Mechanical Stokers a speciality. Also Screened Large and Nuts for Household purposes.

CARGOES TO ANY PORT

TRUCKLOADS TO ANY STATION

MIDLAND ROAD, BRISTOL

Telephone : 25445 (3 lines).

Established over 60 years.

The official Gloucester portrait of wagon No. 522 taken in August 1924. The wagon is branded *'Empty to Cannop Colliery Sidings, Speech House Road, G.W&Mid. Joint Rly.'* It was registered with the LMS.
GRC&WCo.

No. 264 at Cannop Colliery in the early 1930s. The wagon was supplied by the Gloucester Carriage & Wagon Co. Three more Silvey wagons can be seen behind.

A painting variation for Thomas Silvey is seen here at Cannop. The livery is either a grey or red body with white lettering shaded black and with black ironwork. A 7-plank wagon, its running number appears to be 602.

A 5-plank 8-ton capacity wagon supplied to F. H. Silvey by the Gloucester Wagon Co. in 1905 and photographed at Gloucester in August. It was registered with the Midland Railway, No. 46042 and also carries a Gloucester repairs plate and an oval owners plate showing the wagon to be owned by F. H. Silvey of Fishponds. The livery was 'chocolate' with white lettering shaded black and with black ironwork. *GRC&WCo.*

F. H. SILVEY

F. H. Silvey was an off shoot of Thomas Silvey & Co. and was set up after the founder's sons, Frank and Gilbert, separated from their father's business circa 1900. In 1935 their address was New Station Road, Fishponds, with city offices listed as Montpelier railway station which was located in the north of Bristol on the Clifton Extension line. After an independent life F. H. Silvey was bought back by Thomas Silvey Ltd in 1970.

THE WAGONS

As with Thomas Silvey, many wagons were supplied by the Gloucester Wagon Co. Orders for which wagons were photographed were fulfilled in 1905, 1909, 1911, and 1924.

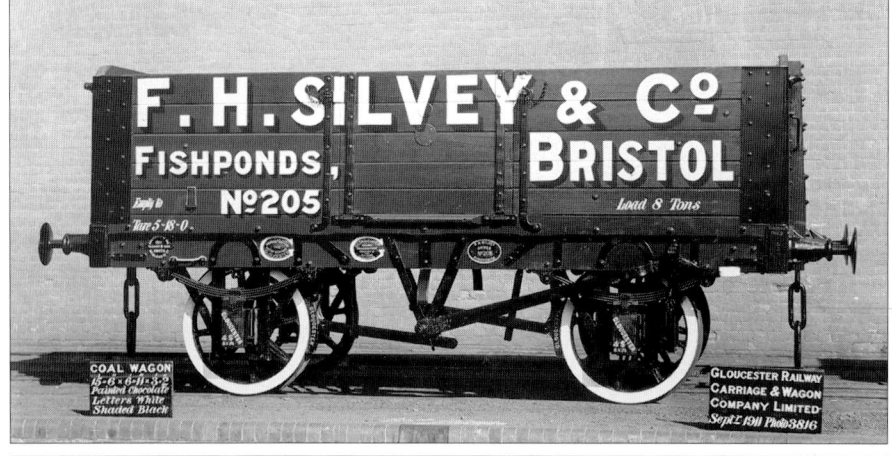

Top Right: Wagon No. 205, another 5-plank, was photographed in September 1911. No. 204 had been photographed in January 1909 and was in an identical lettering style. Both were painted 'chocolate' with white lettering and black shading and ironwork. *GRC&WCo.*

Bottom Right: No. 218, photographed in February 1924 was a larger example, being of 7-plank construction and 10-ton capacity. Whilst the lettering layout was similar the wagon was painted 'dark lead colour'. Note that it also has a Silvey owners plate, a feature that seems to appear on all Silvey wagons. *GRC&WCo.*

Wagon No. 1733 apparently fresh out of the paintshop in 1936 according to the painter's mark on the solebar above the nearest axlebox. The small oval plate on the solebar could well be a finance company owner's plate. It is unlikely to be a Wagon Repairs 'for repairs advise' plate as the small italic writing on the solebar appears to read *'For repairs advise Head Office, Redcliffe Hill, Bristol'*. The wagon is registered with the GWR.

Two Baldwin wagons in the yard at Eastern United Colliery. The furthest is No. 1743 but the running number of the nearest wagon is obscured by the group which includes Lowell Baldwin himself – the tall figure, third from the left. The photograph was taken during a visit to the colliery to discuss future orders etc. Quite why the side door of the wagon is open and the load partially discharged whilst still in the colliery yard is not at all clear. It is as if the wagon is being used for local coal sales in which case if it was factored by Baldwin's then it must have been one of the shortest of rail journeys!

LOWELL BALDWIN

Lowell Baldwin of Bristol was a family business, started soon after the First World War. In 1921 it was made into a limited company with a capital of £40,000. Head office was at 6 Redcliffe Hill, Bristol. A 1935 trade directory gives their address as 6 and 8 Redcliffe Hill with depots at Redcliffe Railway Wharf, Barton Road, St. Phillips, Gaol Siding and Wapping Wharf. Frustratingly, further details of the business are unknown.

THE WAGONS

Where Baldwin's early wagons came from is unknown. Some were acquired from the Gloucester Railway Carriage & Wagon Co. with fifty 12-ton wagons ordered in November 1935 to be delivered in January 1936. This was followed in June with an order for another twenty-five similar wagons.

The wagons were, in the main, painted black with white lettering although some were lettered in pale blue. There are also photographs of Baldwin wagons fitted with coke rails painted a light grey. Fifty 12-ton coke wagons came from Gloucester in late 1934.

Above: A pristine No. 2032 at Cannop Colliery about to pass under the screens after Thomas Silvey's No. 529. The latter is similar in lettering style to 522 on page 97 apart from not having 'No.' in front of the running number.

Left: Two Baldwin wagons passing under the screens at Eastern United, that on the right being No. 1428. The wagon on the extreme left belongs to Barker & Lovering of Cardiff.

A 20-ton steel mineral wagon belonging to Lowell Baldwin in the empty wagon sidings at Eastern United Colliery *circa* 1935. Wagons such as these were developed from locomotive coal wagons on the Great Western Railway. In the mid-1920s Sir Felix Pole, the GWR Chairman, realised that such wagons if used for the movement of coal in South Wales would considerably reduce siding congestion. In that area thousands of 10 and 12-ton wagons shuttled back and forth between the collieries and the docks and the introduction of 20-ton capacity wagons would reduce the number of wagons and the overall train weights thereby giving further savings. However, for such a scheme to work there had to be cooperation from the colliery companies as their screens and sidings had to be capable of dealing with such wagons and also at the docks the coal tips had to be such as to lift a 20-ton wagon. To win users over Pole introduced a rebate scheme on the haulage costs and later had to give further incentives in terms of reduced dock charges. To further tempt the traders the Great Western themselves built a batch of wagons which they then sold on redemption hire principles. One such wagon is illustrated in *A History of GWR Goods Wagons* by Atkins *et al.*, on hire to Frederick Bendle a coal merchant from Frome, Somerset and branded '*Empty to Cannop Coll. Speech House Road, S&W Jt.*' Later most of the large wagon building companies started to produce their own 20-ton steel mineral wagons and in this illustration we may have one such wagon, built by the Gloucester Carriage & Wagon Co. with whom an order for five wagons was placed in January 1931 by Baldwins. Unfortunately the running number cannot be discerned. Life cannot have been easy with 20-ton wagons at Eastern as the screens were fairly cramped as were both the empty and loaded roads and a slightly longer wagon could make a lot of difference. It is certainly not picking up coal for shipment at Lydney or Sharpness as the coal tips at both ports could not handle such wagons.

A selection of Dunkerton wagons, all seen at Cannop Colliery in the early 1930s. On the left is wagon No. 1102 built by Charles Roberts in 1911. *Top right* is wagon No. 2094 and, *bottom right*, No. 304.

DUNKERTON COAL FACTORS

Dunkerton Coal Factors was formed in 1921 as an offshoot of Dunkerton Colliery, Somerset. The colliery had opened in 1907 but by 1921 was running out of coal and closed in 1925. As coal factors they are known to have traded out of Cannop Colliery and Lightmoor.

THE WAGONS

The wagons are comprehensively covered by Richard Kelham: 'The Collieries of the Cam Valley', *British Railway Journal* No. 9, Autumn 1985. Some were provided by Charles Roberts, Wakefield, and others by the GRC&WCo. Livery was grey body with white lettering, shaded black and with black ironwork.

THE
Dunkerton Coal Factors
LIMITED
DUNKERTON, BATH
Also at Exeter, Hereford, Poole, Plymouth and Salisbury.

Sales Agents for
FOREST OF DEAN COALS
drawn from the well-known Collieries
CANNOP, EASTERN UNITED, Etc.

GAS, HOUSE AND INDUSTRIAL COALS.

Write for prices.   Phone: Radstock 60 & 61.

CLUTTON

As with Dunkerton Coal Factors the Clutton concern started life as a colliery operator in Somerset. The colliery was located in the village of the same name on the GWR's Bristol & North Somerset line and only about five miles west of Dunkerton. Coal winning seems to have ended c1921, after which, presumably, they continued trading as coal factors.

THE WAGONS

The livery appears to be a black body with white lettering. In the bottom right corner the word appears to be Bristol but unfortunately the small lettering running through the large Clutton cannot be deciphered apart from 'coal' being the first word.

A very cruel enlargement of a Clutton wagon at Eastern United Colliery in 1926.

A wagon produced by Gloucester in 1912, painted black and lettered white.   *GRC&WCo.*

RENWICK, WILTON

Renwick, Wilton began trading in the 1890s and appear to have become a limited company in late 1902/early 1903. From beginnings in the West Country they went on to become one of the largest coal factoring firms in the country. In the 1920s they were joined by Mr Dobson to form Renwick, Wilton & Dobson Ltd. Although it is known that they traded out of the Forest photographs of their wagons in the area are rare.

THE WAGONS

Being such a large concern the wagon fleet was vast. Many were acquired from Gloucester but the books have not been studied in detail for orders from this company. Renwick, Wilton probably deserve an article or book to themselves.

Two views which show Renwick, Wilton & Dobson Ltd wagons with differing lettering styles. That on the left, of wagon 674, was taken at Bullo and below can be seen 77 and 151

FOREST OF DEAN COALS

Renwick, Wilton & Dobson
LIMITED

CONTRACTORS

FOR

FOREST OF DEAN

GAS, HOUSE & STEAM

COALS

♦

FIRST-CLASS VALUE AND SERVICE

♦

OFFICES AT

BRISTOL - Cheese Lane
Telephone: Bristol 20632.

CHELTENHAM - Promenade
Telephone: Cheltenham 3674.

NEWBURY - 6 Fir Tree Lane
Telephone: Newbury 698.

Also at
TORQUAY, BIRMINGHAM, SWANSEA, LONDON, NEWCASTLE, DARTMOUTH, Etc.

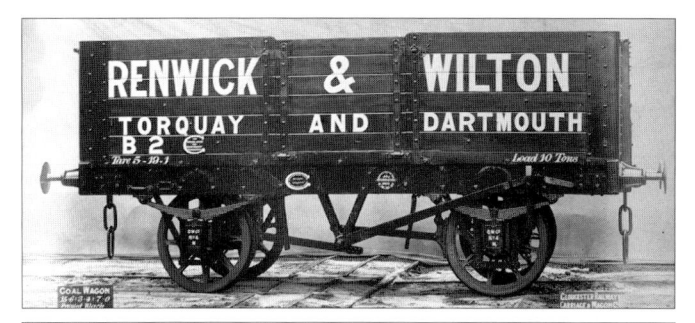

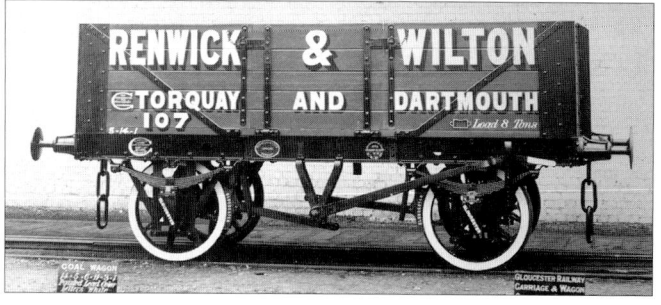

Wagon B2, photographed in July 1892, M12 in March 1893, No. 33 in December 1894 and No. 107 in August 1899 are early examples of Renwick & Wilton wagons. All were painted black with white lettering apart from 107 which was 'lead colour' and had black shaded white lettering and black ironwork. The significance of the numbering system on the first two wagons is unknown. Note that the last three wagons have steel underframes.
GRC&WCo.

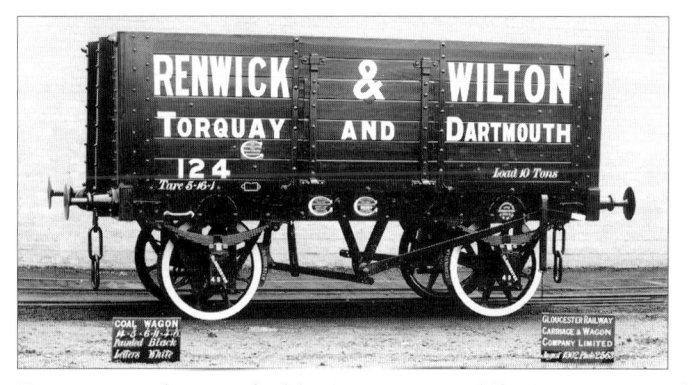

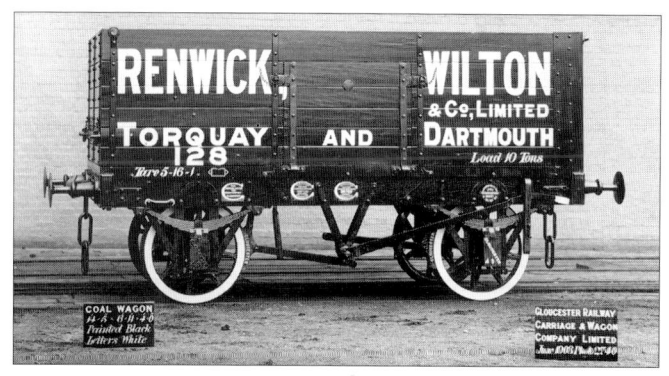

No. 124 was photographed in August 1902 whilst No. 128 was taken in January 1903. The significance is that between these dates Renwick & Wilton have become a limited company. Little changed in the layout of the lettering apart from the place names moving down one plank to allow space for the '& Co, Limited' and the removal of the '&' and its substitution with a ',' after 'Renwick'. Painting has reverted back to a black body with plain white lettering. The formation of the limited company was the start of an expansion for the business marked by the number of wagon orders placed with Gloucester. Two batches of wagons were completed in June 1903 with wagons No's 143 and 153 being photographed, both identically lettered to No. 128 above. However, the batch which included No. 128 were fitted with end doors.
GRC&WCo.

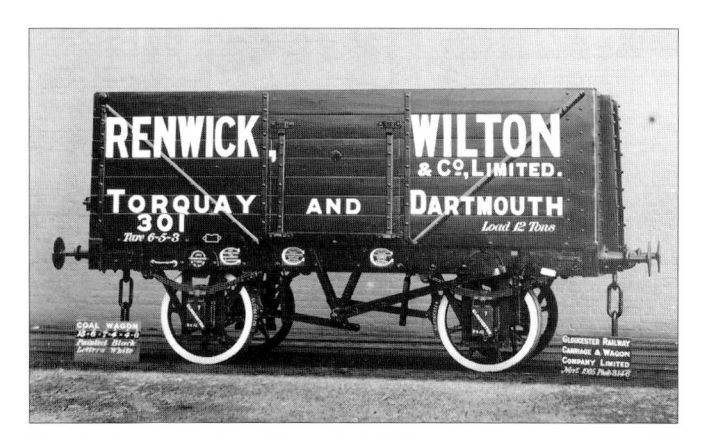

Two further examples of Renwick, Wilton wagons to round off the coverage. No. 301 was photographed in November 1905 whilst No. 521 was taken in January 1909. Both are 12-ton wagons and both orders were for wagons with side and end doors. The 1909 order varies in the positioning of the lettering and also in the fact that the body colour for the wagons was 'purple brown' and the white lettering was shaded black. Ironwork was also black.
GRC&WCo.

BARKER & LOVERING

John Lovering was born in 1887 in Bristol and moved to Cardiff in 1906. Here he became a partner in Barker & Lovering, coal factors. In 1936 the company entered into the ship-owning business when they purchased the first diesel powered vessel on the Severn, the *Calyx*. She was just the right size to work into Lydney and taking 290 tons was perfect for the trade to southern Ireland. John Lovering died in 1946 and the business was taken on by his sons, Robert and Thomas, and continued until 1959 when it was taken over.

In 1925 they were doing business with Henry Crawshay & Co., when it was reported in the minutes that 'Messrs Barker & Lovering were somewhat of a speculative firm doing £1,500 - £2,000 a month business with us. They had usually paid on the 15th of the month following delivery but for August account they had taken the full 30 days credit. As a protective measure he had offered them a special discount of $1/4$% for payment on the 15th of the month following delivery and they had apparently elected to take advantage of this for they had paid their September account on October 15th'. Speculative or not, the company were big customers for Forest of Dean coal.

A lot of the coal went to industrial customers in south Wales, especially steelworks and at one time the company was taking 5,000 tons a week for this trade from Cannop Colliery.

The company also supplied housecoal to many coal merchants throughout the country and in Ireland. As already mentioned they went into the shipping business in 1936 with the purchase of the *Calyx* and soon added to the fleet the motor vessels *Teasel* and the *Cornel*.

The best image of a Barker & Lovering wagon in the Forest is this rather fuzzy enlargement from a view taken at Cannop Colliery in the mid 1930s. The running number appears to be 268.

Having new vessels the *Calyx*, which had been purchased secondhand, was sold in 1938. Other vessels owned were the *Fennel*, *Empire Punch* and *Petertown*.

Another arm of the company was a wagon repair business in Newport where not only their own fleet was maintained but also repairs to other owners' wagons were carried out.

THE WAGONS

At its maximum the company were running 300 wagons. These were all acquired secondhand from a variety of sources. One hundred 12-ton wagons came from E. H. Bennett and are remembered as being wagons that the company were proud of.

Like all factors the wagons were requisitioned at the start of the Second World War, never to return to the company. It would appear that the company did quite well out of the deal in terms of the compensation given for the wagons.

Lettering was BARKER & LOVERING occupying the top three planks. On the fifth plank was COLLIERY AGENTS then bottom left the number and bottom right, CARDIFF.

Another partial view of a Barker & Lovering wagon having just passed through Eastern United screens, a second wagon from the company can just be discerned under the screens in the background.

Barker & Lovering

Specializing in—

FOREST OF DEAN COAL

for—

Export and Coastwise Cargoes
Pulverized Fuel Plant
Gas Producer Plant

Dowlais Chambers, CARDIFF

A Baker & Kernick wagon seen after the Second World War when in the general wagon pool. The number, preceeded by a P denotes a previously privately-owned wagon. *courtesy Paul Karau*

BAKER & KERNICK

Another Cardiff factor was Messrs Baker & Kernick Ltd. In June 1925 it was reported that Messrs Baker & Kernick's liability to Crawshays was £4,622. There was no payment overdue from them and in fact in response to a request they had recently paid an amount of £1,000 on account. In May 1936 they were contracting with Crawshays for 2,000 tons a month for shipment to Ireland.

THE WAGONS

In 1942 ten 12-ton wagons were ordered from Gloucester otherwise nothing else is known.

FOREST OF DEAN AND
HIGHDELF COALS
by
RAIL
or SEA
Ask . . .

BAKER and KERNICK Ltd.

to quote you for

GAS, HOUSE and STEAM
:: COALS ::

We charter ships and personally superintend all our own shipments
:: at Lydney Docks ::

ADDRESS:
DOCKS - LYDNEY
Phone: Lydney 113.   Grams: "Bakernick, Lydney."

HEAD OFFICE:
BUTE DOCKS, CARDIFF
Phone: Grams:
Cardiff 4708 (3 lines).   "Bakernick, Cardiff."

Bunker Coals—Welsh Coal By-Products

TREVOR POWELL

Listed as a coal factor in an 1876 trade directory, Trevor Powell had offices in Cookson Terrace, Lydney. His main trading address was in Gloucester at 23 Commercial Road where he also operated a coal merchants business.

THE WAGONS

In October 1875 Trevor Powell is recorded in Gloucester minutes as hiring 28 10-ton wagons for 3 years 'late himself' which suggests a re-hiring. From then on there are several other orders in the Gloucester books but only the one official photograph.

From the Severn & Wye letter books: T. Powell's wagon No. 4 damaged at Moseley Green the 27th June 1899. On the 17th March 1904 wagon No. 44 was damaged at Lydney Docks.

Top right: Photographed in November 1905 was wagon No. 57. Branded 'Empty to Foxes Bridge Colly, Forest of Dean'. GRC&WCo.

Bottom right: An Osman Trevor Powell wagon, No. 34, on the Foxes Bridge sidings at Bilson.

105

Coal merchant activity can be seen bottom right in this view of Newnham Yard with a wagon belonging to an unidentifiable merchant **A. E. ?? COAL ??**. **No. 1** is being unloaded into a cart whose horse can be seen patiently waiting. Another part filled cart stands behind the horse. This has very short shafts so it might be a donkey cart or even a hand cart. The Mark Whitwill wagon has probably collected coke from the local gas works. Whitwills are dealt with on page 118. *J.E. Kite collection*

COAL MERCHANTS

THE next level down from the wholesaler was the merchant, although wholesalers could also act as merchants. Most railway stations would have had at least one merchant operating out of the goods yard and some of the larger merchants might have depots at several stations in a given area. Within the station yard the merchant might have an office and also some stacking ground for coal so that he could keep a small stockpile. He might also have a yard within the village or town where again coal could be stored and his means of delivery garaged or stabled.

The merchant would also supply the last level in the supply of coal, the coal dealer. These were the individuals who would hawk coal around the district, probably by handbarrow, in the hope of selling a small amount here and there to those who did not require, or could not afford, regular supplies from a merchant.

Most merchants would receive their supplies through coal factors and in factors' wagons. These would need to be unloaded as quickly as possible to avoid paying the railway company siding rental or 'demurrage'. Others might have their own wagons but were unlikely to deal direct with the collieries and would take coal on the account of a factor. An example of this was F. B. Glossop, coal merchant, of Weston-super-Mare taking coal from Trafalgar Colliery on the account of James Smith of Stroud. Usually the coal was sent in Smith's wagons, but occasionally Glossop's own wagon was used and sometimes, possibly because of a shortage of Smith's wagons or because of sudden extra demand, the collieries wagons. It would be cheaper for the merchant if his own wagons were sent as otherwise he would have to pay a hire charge for the colliery wagons but offset against this would have to be the cost of maintaining his own wagons.

Within the Forest of Dean it would be feasible for merchants to collect their coal directly from the collieries. This was known as 'land' or 'country' sales and could explain why there are no photographs known of coal merchant operations in station yards in the area. Of course coal would also be brought in from other coalfields, the merchant would source his supplies wherever the cheapest price could be obtained. The Forest of Dean was always up against coalfields in the Midlands such as Leicestershire.

By the same token merchants from other areas would pick up coal from the Forest when the price was right, even if there was a closer coalfield. Hence a lot of Bristol merchants obtained coal from the Dean even when the South Gloucestershire and Somerset coalfields were nearer.

FOREST MERCHANTS

A look through trade directories soon reveals that there were not many Forest coal merchants who had railway wagons, those who had and are covered elsewhere in the book do not appear in the list below. These merchants are taken from directories of a range of dates. Of course, not all merchants may be listed anyway - they could have decided not to pay for an entry in the directory.

1876
Charles Bailey, Newnham
Dunning Brothers, Coleford
Wm Dykins, Cookson Terrace, Lydney
Henry Harris, The Cross, Lydney
George Holford, Cookson Terrace
Jas Meek, John Breeze, Mitcheldean
Stephens & Co., Cookson Terrace
1885
William Mills, Station Yard, Coleford
Charles Roberts, Coleford
1889
E. Jones & Son, Lydney Basin
1894
John Bailey, Newnham
Theophilus Cooper, Rock House, Coleford
E. Jones, Lydney Basin
Charles Reece, Coalway Road, Coleford
Henry Shapcott, Newnham
Henry Thomas & Son, Bath Place, Lydney

1897
John Bailey, Newnham
David Camm, Primrose Hill, Lydney
Theophilus Cooper, Rock House, Coleford
Charles Reece, Coalway Road, Coleford
Charles Roberts, High Street, Coleford
Henry Shapcott, Newnham
William Trigg, Bullo
1910
James Morgan, Cinderford
1923
Joseph Bailey, Newnham
1927
Joseph Bailey, Newnham
1931
Joseph Bailey
Wm Knight, 3 Mt Pleasant, Tutnall, Lydney
1935
Joseph Bailey, Newnham
Bream & Parkend Coal Co. (F. B. Hirst)
Wm Knight, 3 Mt Pleasant, Tutnall, Lydney
1939
Bream & Parkend Coal Co. (F. B. Hirst)
Ernest William Gittings, Parkend
Hail & Son, Mitcheldean
James & Son, Littledean Hill Road, Cinderford
Wm Knight, 3 Mt Pleasant, Tutnall, Lydney
Patrick John Perkins, Milkwall.

Wagon No. 9, photographed at Gloucester in April 1901, was purchased secondhand. From the registration plate it can be seen that it was originally registered by the London, Brighton & South Coast Railway in 1899. *GRC&WCo.*

THE LYDNEY COAL CO.

The Lydney Coal Co. was in existence prior to 1894 as a trade directory for that year gives William J. Jones as manager. A directory for 1897 lists Frank C. Gosling as manager and in September 1898 Alfred Thomas and John Pritchard took over a wharf, office and coal weighing machine formerly leased by Gosling as manager of the Lydney Coal Co. in the yard north of Lydney Town Station. John Pritchard was given as manager from 1901 through 1914 in trade directories but by 1919 the manager was Mansfield Collins with an address in Albert Street, Lydney. When the company ceased trading is unknown. They were still listed in 1923 but not 1927.

THE WAGONS

There are numerous references to wagons for the Lydney Coal Co. in Gloucester records. In November 1894 one new 10-ton wagon was let on 7 years deferred purchase with the wagon co. keeping it in repair. The following November saw another 10-ton wagon acquired on the same basis. In September 1898 a secondhand 8-ton wagon was hired for the period of one year and one month, a hire which was renewed in October 1899 for a three year period. In April 1901 one secondhand 10-ton wagon was let on deferred purchase over 7 years.

After this the only references in the Gloucester books are for repairing contracts:
11 December 1901: one 10-ton wagon for 7 years. 10 December 1902: one 10-ton wagon for 7 years. April 1908: one 10-ton wagon for 7 years. December 1908: one 10-ton wagon for 7 years £2 12s. 6d. with 7/6 in advance. December 1909: one 10-ton wagon for 7 years. May 1915: one 10-ton wagon for 7 years. December 1915: one 10-ton wagon for 7 years. December 1916: one 10-ton wagon for 7 years.

No. 10 is again a secondhand wagon, purchased over seven years by the Lydney Coal Co. in November 1894. The builder's plate suggests that the wagon had been built the previous year. However, again, traces of shading can be seen on the lettering. The painting slate on the left says 'Painted Black. Lettered White'; was this wagon a repaint of a previous Lydney Coal Co. livery? Certainly the shading is not perfect, witness the **D** in Lydney. *GRC&WCo.*

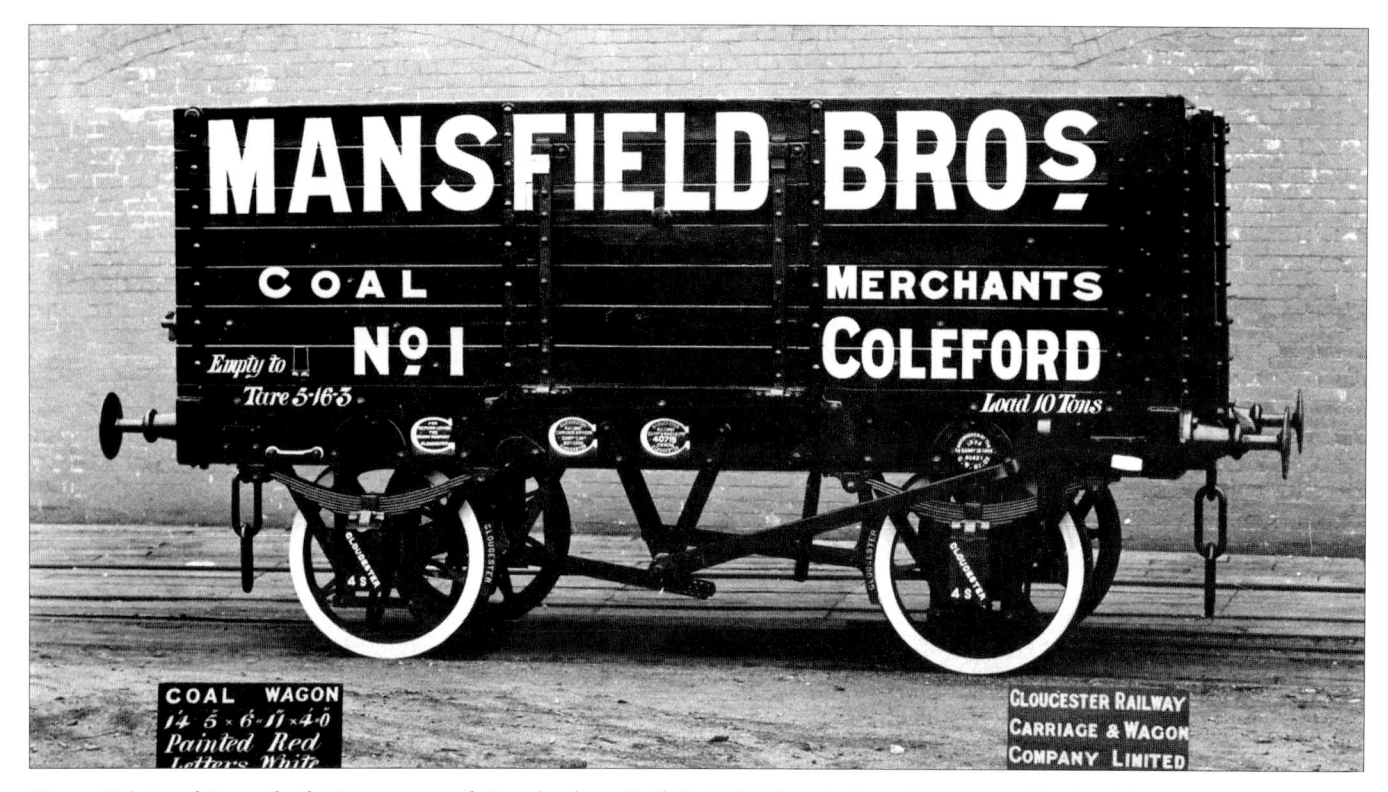

Wagon No's 1 and 2 were both 10-ton wagons lettered as here. Built in 1903. The painting scheme was red body with white lettering shaded black and with black ironwork.
GRC&WCo.

MANSFIELD BROS

Mansfields appear to have started trading c. 1910. A trade directory for that year lists them in Coleford as 'coal merchants and carriers'. Behind the business was George Mansfield who later was also the railway carting agent at Coleford.

It is presumed that Mansfields got their coal from within the Forest of Dean coalfield but which colliery, or collieries, were used is unknown. They were still trading in 1939.

THE WAGONS

The first two wagons were acquired in 1903 and were a pair of 10-ton wagons. In October 1910 an 8-ton wagon was acquired new on 7 years deferred purchase with the Gloucester Wagon Co. to keep it in repair. At the same time that the 8-ton wagon was purchased a repairing contract was signed for the two 10-ton wagons. This was for a period of seven years and it was renewed in November 1917, together with one for the 8-tonner.

No. 3 was a five-plank 8-ton capacity wagon, painted in the same style as No's 1 and 2.
GRC&WCo.

TERRETT TAYLOR

Thomas Terrett Taylor & Sons had an ironmongers and builders business in Coleford. Members of the Terrett family had been trading in the town as ironmongers since at least the 1830s.

THE WAGONS

Only one reference to any wagons can be found in the Gloucester records when in December 1897 Terrett Taylor & Sons purchased one 10-ton wagon on 7 years deferred purchase. It was this wagon which was photographed at Gloucester in December 1897. Numbered 3 it may have been the only wagon they possessed.

Wagon No. 3, photographed in December 1897 was painted 'dark lead' colour and lettered in white with black shading and ironwork. It is branded *'Empty to Wimberry Sidings Speech House R^d'* so it looks as though they got their coal on a regular basis from Wimberry Colliery or one of the smaller pits or levels served by the Wimberry tramroad. *GRC&WCo.*

W. H. JAMES

One of the most elusive merchants is William H. James of Cinderford. James worked at Lightmoor Colliery and was known as 'Dr. James' because of his position as a first-aid man there. He operated a coal merchants business firstly from Haywood Wharf, Cinderford and after August 1900 from the station yard at the new Cinderford station. James retired from Lightmoor in February 1927 having worked for Crawshays for 57 years.

THE WAGONS

Sadly, only tantalising glimpses of his wagons have been found. He apparently had both 8 and 10-ton wagons. They seem to have been painted black with either **WILLIAM H. JAMES** on a curve or just **W. JAMES**. The numbers are unknown as is the smaller lettering but it could well have followed the style of his letterhead.

Left. It is just possible to make out the **WILLIAM H. JAMES** on a curve in this view of one of his wagons at Eastern United taken from the view on page 64. Across the side door appears to be written **COLLIERY AGENT** whilst **CINDERFORD** is probably the indistinct writing on the right-hand side. Frustratingly, the wagon number cannot be seen. The wagon is of 4-plank construction.
Below. Even more fragmentary is this top left-hand corner of one of his wagons, again at Eastern United. The **WILLIAM H.** can be seen and again it looks to be a 4-plank wagon.

NON-FOREST

A. E. MOODY

A 5-plank 8-ton wagon built by Gloucester for Albert E. Moody of Sharpness. The order was placed in early August and the completed wagon was photographed in September 1907. The wagon has the 'full-house' of Gloucester plates on the solebar; builders, owners – as the wagon was let on seven years deferred payment, and a 'For Repairs Advise' as Moody took out a repairing contract as part of the price. The wagon was registered by the Midland Railway. It is likely that this was the only wagon run by Moody as there are no further orders in the Gloucester records. The wagon was painted 'purple brown' with white lettering and black shading and ironwork. The 'Empty to' reads 'Oldminster Sidings, Sharpness'.

H. J. MABBETT

Mabbett had offices in Canonbury Street, Berkeley according to a 1905 directory. This 8-ton wagon was built in October 1895 and was bought new from Gloucester on five years deferred purchase. Painted 'chocolate brown' with white letters, shaded black and with black ironwork. Mabbett may well have ceased trading in 1913 as it is recorded in the Gloucester minutes that in October a secondhand 8-ton wagon had been let on hire to the Berkeley Farmers Association Ltd for 7$^{1}/_{2}$ months and that it was 'late John Mabbett'.

F. J. HOLPIN

A 7-plank 12-ton wagon to the standard Railway Clearing House design built for F. J. Holpin of Berkeley Road. This was the junction station between the Severn & Wye lines and the Midland Railway Birmingham-Bristol mainline. The wagon was ordered in December 1933, photographed in January 1934 and delivered on the 3rd February. It was registered by the LMS. Painted black with white lettering.

R. E. ALDRIDGE

In 1936 Robert E. Aldridge of Berkeley ordered two 12-ton wagons, numbered 1 and 2, and both were registered with the LMS. The 'Empty to' branding reads 'Cannop Colliery Sidings, Speech House Road, GW&LMS Joint Railway'.

This is the only wagon that can be said to have worked into the Forest of Dean with any certainty. However, with the ease of access over the Severn Bridge to the coalfield all of these merchants probably at some point collected coal from the Dean. An alternative source of supply would have been the Bristol coalfield just down the Midland Railway mainline and, of course, the Midlands coalfields.

111

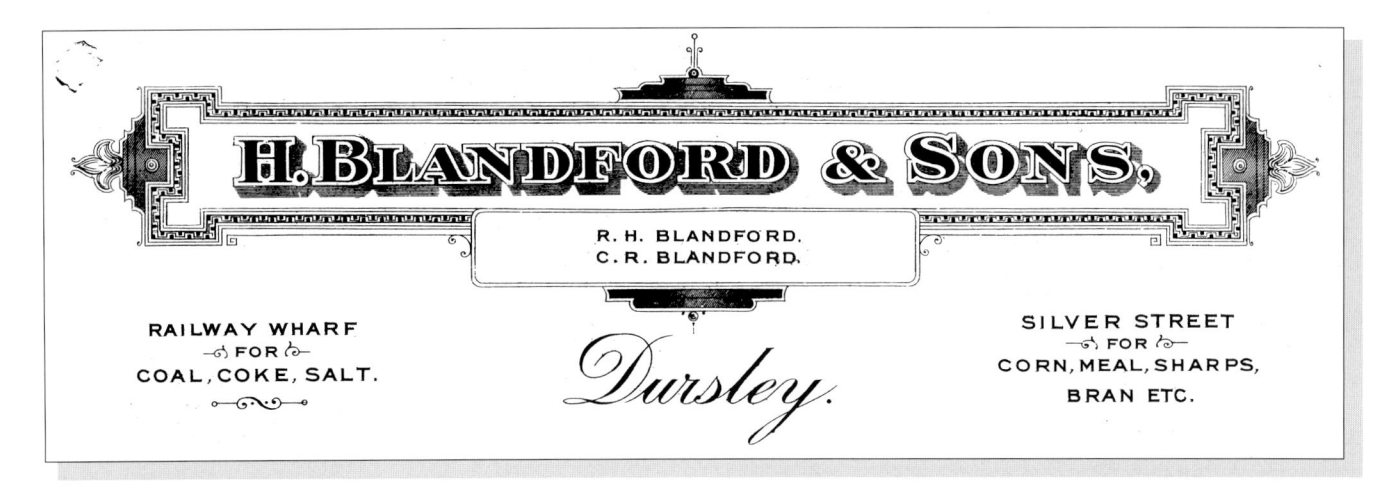

One of two wagons photographed in June 1884, No'd 4 and 6.
GRC&WCo.

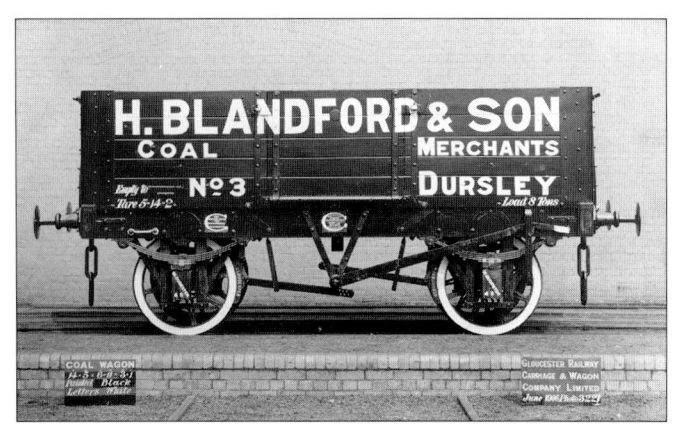

Photographed at Gloucester in June 1906 was wagon No. 3, probably a replacement for one of his earlier wagons. *GRC&WCo.*

H. BLANDFORD

Henry Blandford was born in 1841 and was in business as a coal merchant by 1876, initially as Henry Blandford but by 1906 '& Son' had been added. Henry died in 1907 and the business was then run by his son Ryland Harris Blandford. On his enlistment at the start of the First World War a brother, George, returned to run the business until his return. Ryland died in 1931 after which George again carried on the business with the help of another brother, Charles. In 1926 their offices were in Hill Road, Dursley but by 1933 they had moved to Silver Street. At both dates coal could be obtained from the Railway Wharf at Dursley Station which was at the end of the Midland Railway branch from Coaley Junction, the next station north of Berkeley Road on the Midland's Gloucester-Bristol line. Thus there would have been easy access to the Forest coalfield via Berkeley Road and the Severn Bridge.

Blandford was ordering from Lightmoor Colliery in 1915, possibly 10 tons (or one wagon load) per month from April to June.

THE WAGONS

Blandford appears to have got all his wagons from Gloucester. In May 1877 he hired two 10-ton wagons for a period of three years. Wagons were also supplied in 1884, 1906, 1914 and 1926. Most appear to have been painted black with white lettering though at least one rebuilt in 1926 was finished in grey with white lettering shaded black.

The Severn & Wye letter books record that on the 3rd July 1906 Henry Blandford's wagon No. 6 was off the road at Lydney Jct.

No. 2 was photographed in March 1914. *GRC&WCo.*

This wagon, photographed in February 1926 is described on the board as a 'rebuilt 8-ton wagon'. Inspection of the solebar plates indicate that it was registered by the GWR in 1902 and is thus likely to have been built in that year. The furthest right plate, shaped like a mushroom, is a Wagon Repairs Limited 'Repairs by' plate. The colour of the wagon had also changed. All previous Blandford wagons were black, this one is grey with white lettering shaded black and with black ironwork. *GRC&WCo.*

DICKINSON, PROSSER & COX

Coal merchants from Stroud and Chalford. The business may have started as J. Dickenson in Stroud although note the different spelling. A wagon was supplied to them in 1894. In 1924 wagons were being built for Dickinson & Cox so it is possible that the business went through several changes. However, none of this is, as yet, confirmed.

From the evidence of the upper photograph, taken at Lydney in 1908, it is difficult to work out the livery but the lettering does appear to be shaded. The builder of the wagon is unknown but on the original print what may be an oval builder's plate is on the end of the wagon three planks down. Also of interest is what would seem to be a plate with small lettering on the left-hand side of the side door – sadly it is unreadable. Gloucester-built wagons were painted 'lead colour' with white lettering, shaded black and with black ironwork as shown in the official view of No. 21 taken in October 1903.

PATES & Co.

Pates were trading in Cheltenham by 1893 in St. George's Road. They also had a depot at Fosse Cross Station on the Midland & South Western Junction Railway.

The upper wagon, photographed in December 1893 shows Pates at the Central Wharf which was at St. James Station on the GWR. The wagon is painted red with white lettering, shaded black and with black ironwork.

The lower illustration is of a wagon photographed in September 1906, by which date the company is trading from the more grandly titled 'College Coal Exchange'. This wagon was branded *'Empty to Woorgreens Colliery, Forest of Dean.'* (see page 45). It was painted 'bright red', with white lettering and black shading and ironwork. The Woorgreens Colliery connection is the only evidence of this company's wagons working into the Forest.

Wagon No. 18 was photographed at Gloucester in November 1905 and differs in having the main lettering on the top two planks only and being branded for Moira Colliery in Leicestershire.

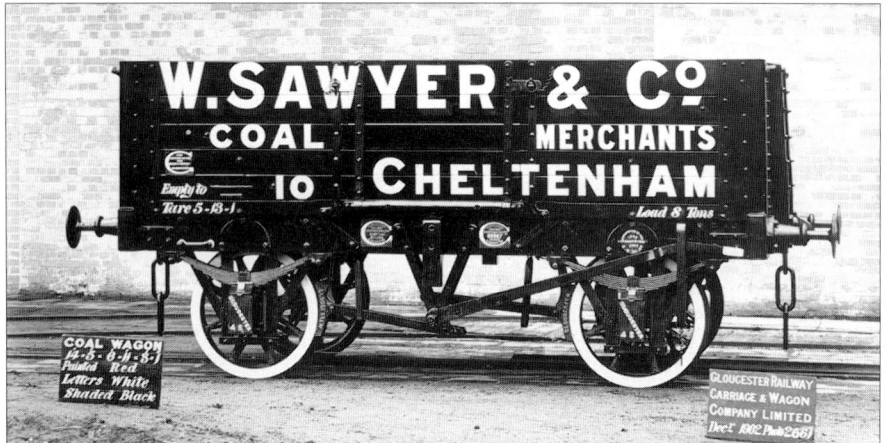

W. SAWYER & Co.

Another Cheltenham coal merchant, Sawyer is listed in a 1906 trade directory at the Great Western Central Wharf, St James's Square and 10 Clarence Street. By 1927 the latter address had changed to 19 Promenade, Cheltenham.

He was certainly in business before 1906 as the upper wagon seen here was photographed at Gloucester in November 1900. It is painted 'lead colour' with white lettering and black shading and ironwork. The second illustration of wagon No. 10 shows a similar lettering layout on another 5-plank wagon but this time the wagon was painted red, with white lettering shaded black and was photographed in December 1902.

Sawyer was getting coal at one time from Cannop Colliery as a photograph of *c.*1910 shows one of his wagons about to pass under the screens (see extreme left of upper illustration on page 94).

GRC&WCo.

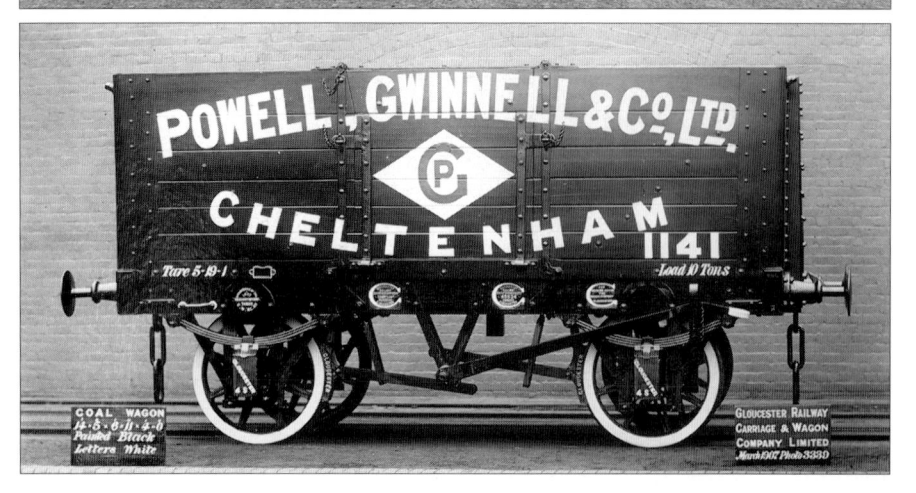

POWELL, GWINNELL & Co. Ltd

Powell, Gwinnell of Cheltenham are known to have been supplied with coal by Crawshays. However, the orders which do survive are placed via a factor.

The two wagons illustrated here are virtually identical in terms of lettering layout but No. 1121 has outside strapping. It was photographed in October 1905 whilst No. 1141 was captured in March 1907. A 1906 trade directory gives their address as Promenade Coal Exchange, 34 Promenade, Cheltenham and they also had a depot at Clevedon, Somerset. They are not listed in 1935.

GRC&WCo.

ALEXANDER CRANE

A coal merchant from Gloucester. In 1910 a trade directory shows Crane to be in Great Western Road, Gloucester and by 1914 his address was 3 Whitfield Street, Gloucester. He seems to disappear from directories between 1923 and 1927.

The upper photograph is taken at Lydney Docks in 1909. The wagon appears to have an end door which suggests that it could be due to tip coal into either a barge or small trow for shipment to Gloucester or maybe the Stroudwater Canal. Also, being sandwiched between two Princess Royal Colliery wagons suggests that his coal might have been obtained from that source. Unfortunately the wagon number cannot be determined but it is of 6-plank construction.

Centre is an official Gloucester Wagon view of wagon No. 115 which has a similar lettering layout and was photographed in March 1911, painted black with white lettering

No. 102, photographed in August 1902, is a 6-plank wagon, painted 'brown' with white lettering shaded black and with black ironwork. No. 103, dating from February 1903, was also in the brown livery but was a 5-plank 8-ton wagon.

Top: courtesy Paul Karau
Rest: GRC&WCo.

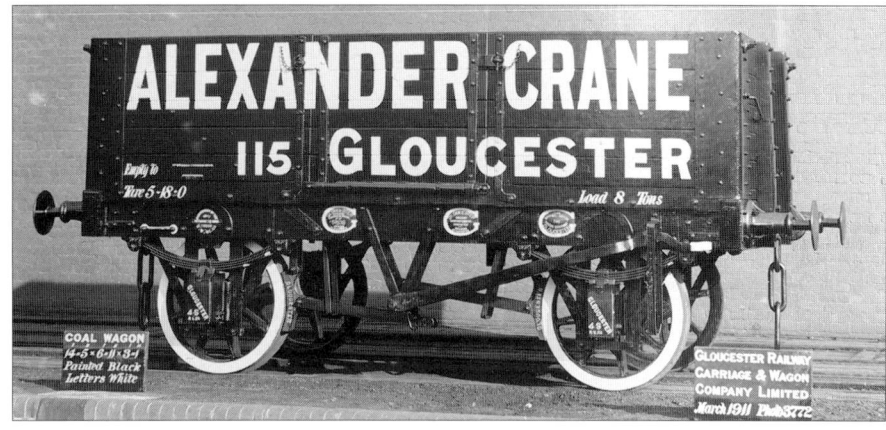

E. T. WARD & SON

The Severn & Wye letter books reveal that on the 21st September 1899 wagon No. 3 belonging to E. Ward was off the road and damaged at Serridge. One possibility for E. Ward is E. T. Ward, a coal merchant from Stroud with an address in 1935 in Gloucester Road. There is also a possible link to the Coleford Red Ash Colliery Co. (see page 43). His wagon No. 4 is seen here photographed at Gloucester in January 1905. It is painted black with white lettering shaded red.

GRC&WCo.

115

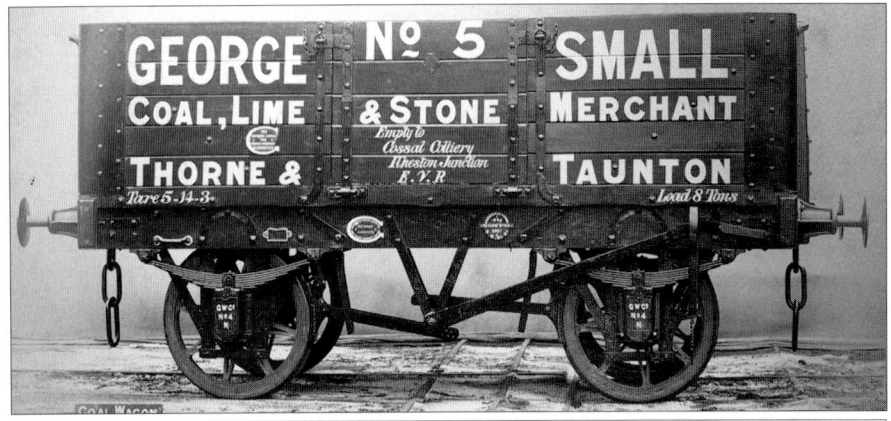

SOMERSET

G. SMALL & SON

They were coal, corn, forage, seed, manure, poultry food, and salt merchants, millers and lime burners of 45 & 46 High Street, Taunton and 58 Station Road and Town Mills. One of their wagons appears at Foxes Bridge Colliery, page 32 and seems to be lettered Small and Son rather than George Small though the number is in the same place above the side door. It can be presumed that the business started out as George Small and then with an addition to his family between 1892 and 1897 the 'and Son' was appended. Later still the 'Son' changed to 'Sons'.

The upper wagon, painted 'red' and lettered in white was photographed in July 1892. No. 8, in the middle, was photographed in November 1897 and is painted 'chocolate' with white lettering shaded black and with black ironwork. Note the steel underframe. Finally, at the bottom, wagon No. 13 seen in August 1900 was given the same colour scheme as No. 8.

all GRC&WCo.

Two different liveried wagons for Small & Son. No. 17 on the left was photographed in October 1904, a seven-plank wagon it was painted 'dark lead' colour, lettered white, with black shading and ironwork. The lettering on the side door provides a good advertisement for Small's business. By September 1907 the Small family had obviously had an addition as the wagon on the right is now lettered **'& SONS'**. Again it is painted 'dark lead' with black shaded white lettering. It is also fitted with a lift-up plank above the side door to make access easier. This hinged up and over to the right.

GRC&WCo.

116

WILLIAM THOMAS

Two of their wagons appear in a view of Foxes Bridge Colliery as seen on page 33. A puzzle occurs in the Gloucester photographs as wagon No. 1 is photographed in September 1897 with dumb buffers and then a wagon No. 1 is photographed again in January 1888 as seen here – according to the orders he had two secondhand wagons on one years hire in December 1887! He did have earlier wagons but so far they remain a mystery as well. Wagons painted black with white lettering. William Thomas was listed in a trade directory for 1935 as a brick & tile manufacturer, Station Yard, Wellington. *GRC&WCo.*

RADSTOCK COAL CO.

Recorded as taking coal from Lightmoor Colliery in 1911 in buyer's trucks. The Radstock Coal Company was formed in 1868 by William Beacham who also ran the Radstock Wagon Company. It was eventually taken over by his son Frank Beauchamp.

courtesy Richard Kelham

SOMERSET TRADING Co.

The company had outlets throughout Somerset with its head office in Bridgwater at 25 West Quay. They were brick and tile manufacturers, timber, cement, slate, manure, cake, corn, salt and coal & coke merchants. Still trading in 1935. The wagon, photographed in June 1904 was painted 'bright red' with white letters, shaded black and with black ironwork. Branded 'Empty to Trafalgar Colliery'. *GRC&WCo.*

HARTNELL & SON

A Taunton coal merchant with offices in St Augustine Street. The wagon seen here was built in 1930 by Charles Roberts of Wakefield and is branded 'Empty to New Fancy Colliery Lydney'. The wagon is painted black, lettered white and shaded red. They also had a 12-ton wagon built by Gloucester which was delivered in January 1934. Hartnells were absorbed by another Taunton coal merchant, Goodlands, in 1938. Goodlands also traded into the Forest. *courtesy HMRS*

BRISTOL

TWINING

A Bristol coal merchant, Lewellin Twining had offices at 91 Alma Road, Clifton and a wharf at Clifton Down Station in 1902 and was at the same addresses in 1935.

Wagon No. 150 illustrated here was built by the Gloucester Railway Carriage & Wagon Co. and photographed in November 1897, as was No. 156 below. The wagons were painted 'lead colour' with white lettering and black shading and ironwork.

Wagons appear in early views of the sidings at Bilson which come down from Crump Meadow Colliery and at Cannop Colliery in the mid 1930s where wagon No. 174 was found waiting to pass through the screens.

MARK WHITWILL & SON

Taken from the circa 1905 view of Newnham on page 106 is this enlargement of a coke wagon belonging to Mark Whitwill & Son of Bristol. It is probably collecting coke from the gasworks at Newnham rather than delivering. When Mark Whitwill began trading is unknown but in July 1912 he joined with William Henry Cole to form Whitwill Cole & Co. Ltd. Mark Whitwill snr. died in December 1921. The company also had interests in shipping and formed strong links with some Dutch concerns. The company was still trading up until 1954 when it appears to have been reformed as a Dutch registered company.

Nothing can be found concerning Mark Whitwill & Son's wagons apart from in October 1924 an agreement was taken out by Whitwill Cole & Co. Ltd with the Lincoln Wagon Co. for the redemption hire of 10 wagons.

Painting details are unknown, body probably black with white lettering. The device on the side door seems to have varied wagon to wagon and in limited company days was often a diagonal cross.

S. STONE & CO.

Two for the price of one caught in the empty wagon roads at Eastern United Colliery in 1935. The S. Stone wagon, No. 76, was an almost new 12-tonner having been built by the Butterley Wagon Co. in October 1924. Samuel Stone was a coal merchant from Bristol with offices in 1935 at 210 Easton Road and a depot at Lawrence Hill Station, Bristol, on the London, Midland & Scottish Railway. Stone was trading prior to 1902. Livery of wagons, unknown.

H. PEPLER & SON

Another Bristol coal merchant, this time with depots at 12 Lodore Road, Fishponds and 370 Fishponds Road, Eastville. No details of the wagons are known.

WILTSHIRE
WILLIAM DUCK

A wagon photographed in August 1907 for a Stratton, Wiltshire, coal & coke merchant and branded '*Empty to Crump Meadow Colly, Cinderford, Glos.*'. He may not have lasted in business for long as in October 1910 Gloucester minutes record a secondhand wagon let on deferred purchase to the Lydney & Crump Meadow Collieries Co. over four years 'late William Duck'.

The wagon is lettered 'To Stratton Station' which was situated on the Highworth Branch.

A good example of where a photograph alone could be misleading as the letter shading appears lighter than the wagon body. However, the board says: painted 'dark red', letters white, shaded black.

GRC&WCo.

G. DAVIS

Another Wiltshire coal merchant, this time with a depot at Swindon Town Station on the Midland & South Western Junction Railway was G. Davis. This 8-ton 5-plank wagon was photographed by Gloucester in October 1901. It was painted black with white lettering and is branded '*Empty to Foxes Bridge Colliery, Lydney.*'

GRC&WCo.

MORTIMORE

Another Wiltshire trader, Mortimores were established in Chippenham in 1840 as coal, salt and hay merchants. It is believed that the livery was red and the 'M' 'M' on the ends was distinctive. The wagon here is seen in the Crump Meadow Colliery sidings at Bilson. It appears to be of 4-plank construction and is numbered 23. It was coupled to No. 34 which exhibits a differing lettering style. However, the postcards form a panorama and the quality is much poorer of this wagon as this is from a printed card, the photographic version has yet to be found!

The two enlargements below give other details of Mortimore wagons, that on the right taken in Chippenham Yard shows the two 'M's on the end quite clearly.

both courtesy Richard Kelham

OTHERS

C. & G. AYRES

A Reading coal merchant who was taking coal from Lightmoor and Eastern United Collieries between 1911 and 1914. From the orders it would appear to be about one wagon load per month from Eastern United and one per week for a period from Lightmoor. Eastern United coal was going to Reading and was probably for an industrial customer taking boiler coal. The housecoal from Lightmoor was delivered to Loudwater. (See Appendix for orders.) The wagon illustrated here was built by the Gloucester Wagon Co. and photographed in December 1903. It was painted 'dark red' with white lettering shaded black and with black ironwork.
GRC&WCo.

ALBERT USHER

Little is known of this London merchant. Albert Usher & Co. later became a limited company. Offices were in King William Street, London Bridge, EC4. The wagon is seen here at Lydney in 1908. Its number appears to be 519. *courtesy Paul Karau*

RALLS & SON

Going further afield is a wagon from a Dorset concern. This 8-ton five-plank wagon was built by the Gloucester Wagon Co. in 1905 for Ralls & Son of Bridport. It is branded *'Empty to Trafalgar Colliery'* so presumably worked regular trips to the Forest of Dean for coal. The wagon is painted 'lead colour' with white lettering and black shading and ironwork.

In 1875 a Thomas Ralls was at the railway station Bridport and in 1895 a Richard Ralls was listed. A trade directory for 1915 gives Ralls & Son (late) Somerset Trading Co. Ltd, coal, oil cake, cement, slate, timber & brick & tile merchants & manufacturers, lath renderers & insurance agents, Railway Station, St. Andrews Road and West Bay. In 1939 they were listed as a branch of Burt, Boulton & Haywood Ltd. *GRC&WCo.*

SPENCER ABBOTT

Spencer Abbott was a Birmingham concern with offices in London and Liverpool. A wagon from this company can be seen in the view of the empty wagon roads at Eastern United Colliery in 1935 in the lower illustration on page 100. *courtesy HMRS*

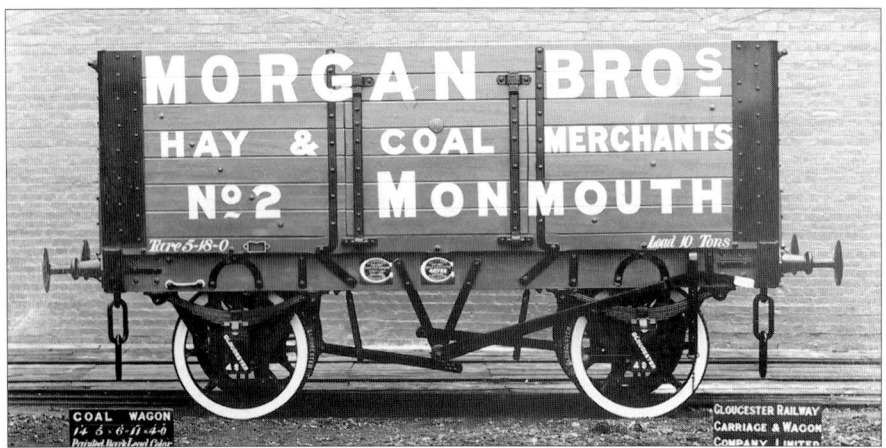

WYE VALLEY
MORGAN BROS

Messrs Morgan Bros were coal merchants with depots at Monmouth Troy Station and at Kerne Bridge which was on the line between Monmouth and Ross. Their advertisement stated 'Forest Coal always in stock'.

The only illustration of a wagon found which actually mentions the Kerne Bridge depot is that at the top of the page of wagon No. 16 photographed at Gloucester in December 1905. It was coupled to No. 18 which was identical. They are both 'converted' wagons which have had self-contained sprung buffers fitted in place of dead buffers and carry the diamond-shaped GWR converted plate. The square Gloucester plate between the V hanger is a builders & owners plate. Strangely the boards in front of the wagons do not give the usual livery details which is unfortunate as they are different from any other Morgan Bros wagons! They could be brown wagons with white lettering, shaded black and with black ironwork or alternately the body colour could be red.

Wagon No. 2 was photographed in October 1903 and was painted 'dark lead colour' with plain white lettering. Wagon No. 6 was actually earlier than No. 2 being photographed in June 1901. An order had been placed with Gloucester Wagon Co. in January for two new 10-ton wagons at £139 to be paid for in cash. No. 6 was painted 'slate colour' with red lettering. There does appear to be a tonal difference between the colour of the lettering and the ironwork so it can be assumed that all ironwork was black. However, it is very difficult to tell red and black apart on old photographic emulsions. Wagon No. 6 also appears in use in the Morgan Bros advertisement.

Wagon No. 14 was photographed at Gloucester in November 1904 when two new wagons were let on 5 years deferred payment. Two other secondhand wagons had been hired for a period of one year in October 1902 which may have been converted into a purchase in October 1903.
all left, GRC&WCo.

122

JOHN YATES

Another Monmouth coal merchant, probably with a depot at Troy Station.
GRC&WCo.

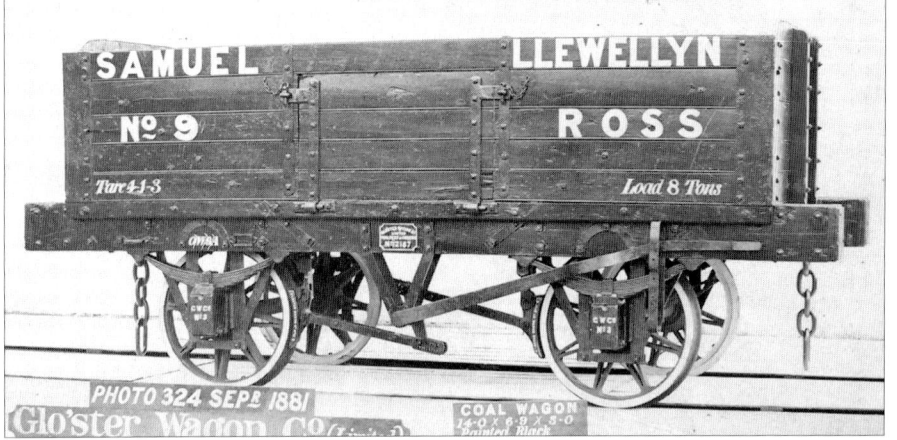

SAMUEL LLEWELLYN

A Ross coal merchant with a depot at the station and also with another at Monmouth. The business was in existence through to at least the 1960s. The Severn & Wye letter books mention that on the 25th September 1897 wagon No. 32 belonging to S. Llewellyn and running on account of Macpherson & Co. was somewhere on the system. This is likely to have been one of Samuel Llewellyn's wagons. The wagon seen here was photographed at Gloucester in September 1881 and painted black with white lettering. *GRC&WCo.*

WEBB, HALL & WEBB

Another Ross coal merchant with a base at the railway station. The wagon was painted blue with white lettering shaded black and with black ironwork. In July 1913 two new 10-ton wagons were bought from Gloucester for £165 cash. In May 1915 two 8-ton wagons were bought on deferred payment, one over $5^{1}/_{2}$ and the other $3^{3}/_{4}$ years. In January 1919 one secondhand 8-ton wagon was had on hire and may have been bought in November 1920 for cash.

GRC&WCo.

JOHN HOLLINS

At the southern end of lines through the Wye Valley is a wagon for a Chepstow coal merchant, John Hollins. The wagon was photographed at Gloucester in June 1896 and was painted black with white lettering. Wagon No. 5 was photographed in the previous November and was identical in layout.

GRC&WCo.

WELSH TRADERS

Wm MORRIS

Wagon No. 34 belonging to William Morris of Newport was photographed at Lydney in July 1908. The Severn & Wye letter books also record that on the 21st April 1917 his wagon No. 2166 was off the road at Sharpness South. Morris is recorded as having wagons from the Western Wagon Co. and the Bolton Wagon Works as seen lower right.

From the wagon numbers Morris may have had a sizeable fleet and could have been acting as a coal factor. No details of liveries carried are known.

Top: courtesy Paul Karau
Lower: courtesy HMRS

VICTOR GREY & Co.

Photographed at Gloucester in July 1911 was this wagon painted 'bright red', lettered white with black shading and ironwork. Victor Grey & Co. of Swansea were getting coal from Crawshays for delivery to Landore, Gorseinon and Briton Ferry.

GRC&WCo.

LEADBETER

Another Newport merchant, Leadbeter was certainly getting coal from Foxes Bridge Colliery as on the 26th April 1901 his wagon No. 13 is recorded as being off the road there. One of his wagons also appears in the view of Foxes Bridge reproduced on page 32.

Wagons were painted grey as shown by wagon No. 105 photographed in September 1901. Wagon No. 211 was photographed at Gloucester in January 1905 and was painted 'bright red' with white lettering, shaded black and with black ironwork and a different layout of lettering.

GRC&WCo.

JAMES & EMANUEL

Yet another Newport merchant a James & Emanuel wagon appears in a view of Cannop Colliery reproduced on page 94 and hiding behind the Alfred Smith wagon. James & Emanuel traded from Dock Street, Newport, first from No. 66, then 90. They were also colliery owners with pits at Aberbeeg and Crumlin. In March 1884 twenty-five 10-ton wagons were supplied by the Swansea Wagon Co. The photograph of wagon No. 451 was taken at Gloucester in July 1942. Livery at this time was black body with white lettering but it is impossible to define what the earlier livery was if different.

GRC&WCo.

BEDWAS

Seen at the end of a siding at Norchard Colliery are two Bedwas wagons. These were owned by the Bedwas Navigation Colliery Co. who had their own colliery at Bedwas, Monmouthshire.

GRAHAM ROBERTS & Co.

A very cruel enlargement off a postcard view of Upper Lydbrook Station reveals a couple of wagons belonging to Graham Roberts & Co. They acted as sales agents for the Lydbrook Colliery for a period.

The wagon standing next to the GW Iron Mink belongs to William Perch & Co. Ltd of Swansea. The emblem on the side door being the giveaway as to its identity.

BUDD & Co.

The first mention of wagons for Messrs Budd & Co. in the Forest comes on the 14th July 1900 when the S&W letter books show that their wagons No's 46 & 90 were off the road at Lydney S&W.

The Crawshay orders reveal that Budd & Co. were taking coal from Lightmoor Colliery during the period 1914-16 for foreign shipment from Newport Docks.

Wagon No. 336 was photographed at Gloucester in May 1902 and was painted 'lead colour' with white lettering shaded black and with black ironwork.

GRC&WCo.

INDUSTRIAL USERS

ANOTHER category of user was industrial concerns, corporations and utilities. Some contracted directly with the colliery, certainly various concerns traded with Henry Crawshay & Co. on a direct order basis, others went through coal factors. Occasionally a colliery concern would appear to have 'targetted' a company in the hope of getting an order without having to go through a factor thus giving larger profits. It would mean, however, that unless the concern had its own wagons then colliery company wagons would be tied up in supplying the contract. From the end user point of view, ordering through factors could ensure a more stable supply as they held coal stocks and could deliver as and when required.

Utilities, such as gasworks, had a regular order and needed to know that they were receiving a 'standard' quality of coal, probably all from one particular coal seam. Any variation could affect the quality of gas produced. Coal for the smaller gasworks, would be taken in factors' wagons, larger ones had their own fleets.

Corporations, such as Gloucester, took coal to supply their municipal electricity or gas works. They often had their own wagons.

PURIFIED FLOCK & BEDDING Co. Ltd

The Purified Flock & Bedding Co. Ltd operated at Spring Mills, Nailsworth. The company was in existence in 1904 and the Harris family bought into the concern in 1906. It continued trading until 1970.

Wagon No. 20 was photographed in February 1912 and is branded '*Empty to Princess Royal Colliery Co.*' It was painted black with white lettering. A valuation of the company in 1919 includes 'one railway wagon, £100'. This suggests that the wagon numbers started and ended at 20! *photograph GRC&WCo.*

Wm PLAYNE

William Playne & Co. were manufacturers of superfine woollen cloth at Longfords Mill, Minchinhampton. The mill operated between 1759 and 1990 so well within the time span for private owners!

A wagon appears in a view of Upper Lydbrook Station (below) and could well have been collecting coal from either Lydbrook Colliery or Arthur & Edward Colliery, probably for use in the boilers at the mill.

Wagons were painted 'purple brown', lettered white with black shading and ironwork. No. 1 was photographed in November 1901 and was of 5-plank construction and 8-ton capacity whilst No. 2, photographed in January 1902, was a larger 7-plank wagon of 10-ton capacity.
wagon photographs, GRC&WCo.

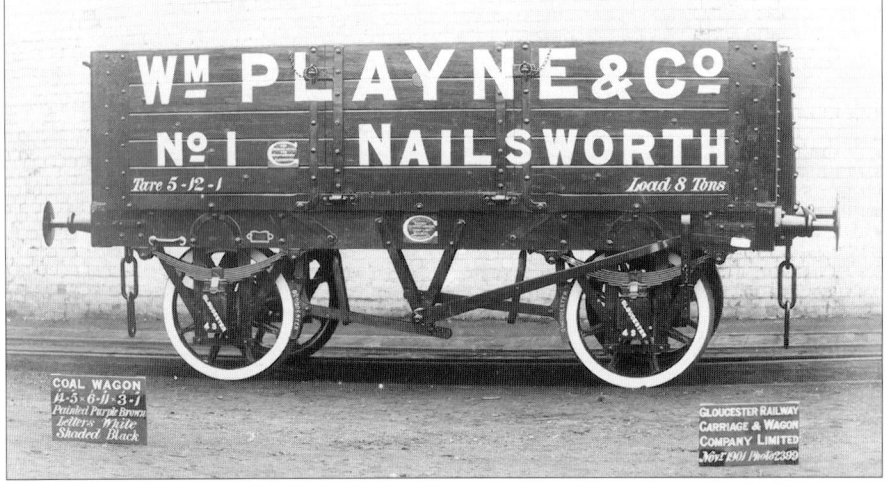

HILLIER'S BACON CURING Co. Ltd

With a head office at Newmarket, Nailsworth and other premises at Parsonage Street, Dursley they advertised finest Wiltshire bacon, matured hams and sausages. Coal from the Forest, as with the other wagons on this page, would have gone via the Severn Bridge and the Midland Railway branch to Nailsworth. Established in 1819 the company was still trading in 1935.

Wagon colour would appear to be grey or red, lettered white, shaded black.
courtesy Paul Karau

E. A. CHAMBERLAIN

Chamberlains were a leatherboard producer. They were latterly involved in the production of leatherboard for interior trim for motor vehicles.

Photographed in November 1901 at Gloucester was wagon No. 3 which was painted black with white lettering. No. 6, photographed in September 1914, was painted in similar style apart from the addition of Ltd. which involved the reduction in size of all of the main lettering apart from the initials. Some of the wagons, probably in the late 1920s-early '30s were lettered '*Empty to Princess Royal Colliery, Lydney*'. *GRC&WCo.*

STROUD GAS LIGHT

Hidden amongst the girderwork at Cannop Colliery can just be glimpsed a wagon of the Stroud Gas Light & Coke Co. The gasworks at Stroud were established in 1833 but until 1924 all coal was delivered by canal. A siding was put in during 1924 off the LMS Stroud Branch and thereafter coal could be delivered by rail. Wagons would have had an end door as a hoist was used to tip the wagons at the gasworks. Livery and builder unknown.

SAMUEL JEFFERIES

A 1905 trade directory lists Samuel Jefferies as 'brick manufacturers, patent brick making machinery manufacturers & coal merchants at Dudbridge and at Hayward's Field; Imperial works Stonehouse and Woodchester'. He was getting coal from Henry Crawshay & Co. in June 1912.

The upper wagon, photographed in July 1893 was painted 'red' with white lettering and black shading and ironwork. Wagon No. 14 was photographed in July 1926 and was a 'rebuilt' wagon hence the small oval plate. The large oval plate shows Samuel Jefferies to be the owner. Livery is not recorded.

GRC&WCo.

STONEHOUSE BRICK & TILE Co. Ltd

A 10-ton wagon probably used for the transportation of bricks and tiles which were the staple product of this company. They had sidings off the GWR Swindon-Gloucester line at Stonehouse. A 1905 trade directory gives the company as producing 'facing bricks, roofing and flooring tiles, building, terra cotta etc.'

Recorded in 1910-1911 as getting coal from Eastern United Colliery 'in buyers trucks' so they may have had some coal wagons as well. Livery was 'red' with white lettering. *GRC&WCo.*

S. J. MORELAND & SONS

The famous manufacturers of matches with a works in Bristol Road, Gloucester, this wagon certainly made a statement. Photographed in November 1906 after rebuilding from a dumb-buffered wagon. It carries the diamond-shaped GWR converted registration plate and Gloucester pattern self contained sprung buffers. Livery details are hazy. None are recorded on the boards. Some say a black body, grey band and ends, others a blue body with red ends and band. Branded *'When empty to Princess Royal Colliery Co. Ltd. Whitecroft Nr. Lydney'*. *GRC&WCo.*

JOHN STEPHENS, SON & Co. Ltd

The wagon side clearly defines Stephens area of business. Trade directories for 1905 and 1935 give the business address as St. Catherine St, Gloucester. Coal was obtained from Eastern United Colliery. Wagon No. 26 was photographed in November 1901 and painted black with white lettering. *GRC&WCo.*

GLOUCESTER GASLIGHT COMPANY

The gasworks were at Hempstead with company offices in Eastgate Street. Wagons 20, 14 and 22 are seen here at Bullo Pill in 1936. Coal was possibly being obtained from Eastern United Colliery. At one time it is known that coal was taken from Norchard.

The official Gloucester photographs show wagon No. 51 in March 1923 and No. 37 in June 1924. Both are branded *'When loaded to Gasworks Sidings, Hempstead, Gloucester, M.R.'* No. 37 has a board giving empty to details of *'Empty to Rothervale Collieries, Treeton nr Rotherham'*. Gloucester Gas Light Co. were obviously going far afield to get the quality of coal it required. Other companies known to have supplied the works included Gas Coal Collieries Ltd, who had a colliery at Llanharran; the Ruabon Coal & Coke Co. Ltd; Hardwick Colliery Co. Ltd; J & M Gunn & Co.; and Wilson Carter & Pearson Ltd.

upper: *W. A. Camwell*
lower: *both GRC&WCo.*

GLOUCESTER CORPORATION

20-ton, all steel wagons for the Electricity Department of Gloucester Corporation. The works opened in July 1900. Wagons No's 2, 1 and 3 are seen here in Bilson Yard in July 1948 as non-pool wagons awaiting tripping to Northern United Colliery for loading. Note the girders across the top of the wagons to prevent foreign bodies or large lumps of coal getting into the load when passing through the screens or in transit.

L. E. Copeland

BOROUGH OF CHELTENHAM ELECTRICITY DEPT

Another municipal utility wagon for the Borough of Cheltenham whose works were erected in Arle Road in 1894. Wagon No. 1 was photographed in April 1909. It was painted 'dark chocolate' with white lettering. Coal was obtained from Norchard Colliery. *GRC&WCo.*

H. C. Casserley

SOUTH HEREFORDSHIRE AGRICULTURAL CO-OP

Very little is known of this enterprise. They had an office in St. John's Street in Coleford and the wagons suggest that they had also had depots in Ross, and Monmouth. Coal was probably supplied to farmers both for housecoal purposes and for use in stationary engines at threshing and other times. Wagons No's 4 and 3 were photographed in the goods yard at Monmouth in 1931. S.H.A.C.S. were still in business into the 1980s. Builder and livery of wagons unknown.

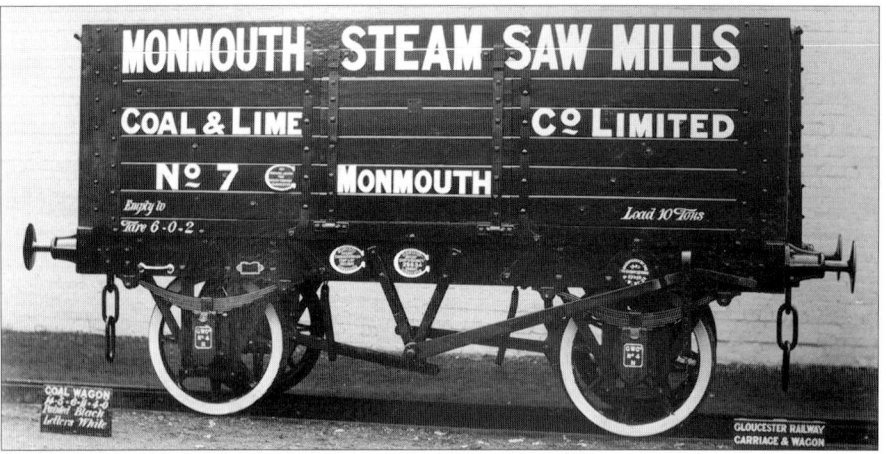

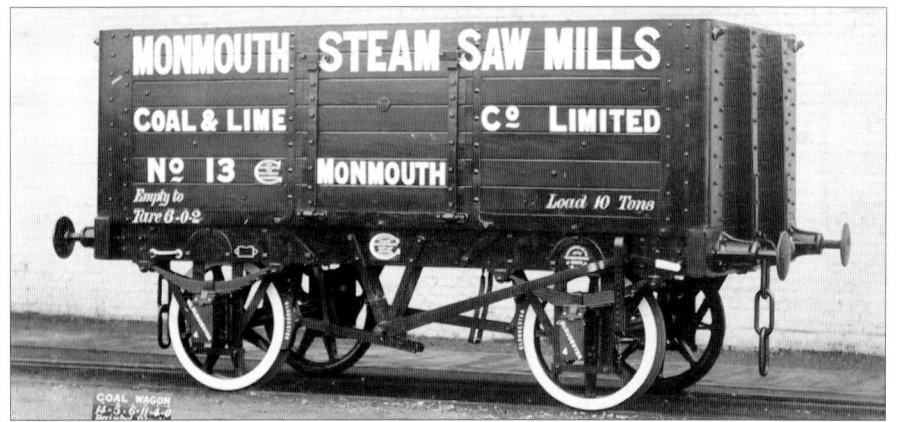

MONMOUTH STEAM SAW MILLS Co. Ltd

The Steam Saw Mills was located at May Hill, Monmouth with a siding provided off the Ross & Monmouth Railway sometime in the late 1870s. As well as operating the saw mill they were coal and lime merchants and also dealt in coke, probably the by-product of the adjoining Monmouth gasworks.

Wagon No. 1 was photographed in April 1895 in a livery of 'lead colour' with white lettering shaded black and with black ironwork. It was ordered in March as part of a batch of six 10-ton wagons bought on seven years deferred purchase. No. 7, photographed in January 1897 was the first of another batch of six, new, 10-ton wagons ordered the previous month. In January 1899 four 10-ton wagons were bought new for cash costing £244, and a repairing contract for them was taken out at the same time. The 1895 batch of wagons were repaired by the Wagon Co. during the period of deferred purchase but when this came to an end in 1902 a repairing contract was taken out on them. The same applied to the 1897 batch with a contract being signed in February 1904. In February 1912 two new 10-ton wagons were bought for £137 cash and also three secondhand 8-ton wagons were hired for a one year period. These latter three wagons were re-hired in April 1914 to the Whitecliff Lime & Stone Co. (late Monmouth Steam Saw Mills).

The saw mill was still in business in 1938.

all GRC&WCo.

A further source of possible wagons in the Forest comes from the S&W Joint Committee's Minute Books which record Ledger Accounts opened. These were where charges for wagons were recorded, both for use of the line and for siding charges. Traders mentioned elsewhere have been omitted, those known to have had wagons are in bold.

14 July 1896
Granted to:
W. Tompkins, Fawley
Geo. Thomas, Coleford
J. Grist & Co., Dudbridge
Benjamin & Co., Bath

21 October 1896
William Calway, Sharpness
Knight & Lansley, Gloucester

19 January 1897
The Lydbrook Iron Mines Company, Coleford
Bedminster Coal Co., Bristol
Palmer & Sawdye, Exeter

20 July 1897
William Wyatt, Taunton
Joseph George Yard, Clevedon
Hewlett & Co., Worle
Henry W. Turner, Ilminster
H. J. Sainsbury & W. E. Sainsbury trading as Sainsbury Brothers, Devizes
R. T. Richards, Axbridge
J. S. Walker, Weston-super-Mare
A. G. Haywood, Montpelier
William Clarke, Corsham

Photographed in September 1898. Painted black, lettered white. *GRC&WCo.*

A Palmer & Sawdye wagon photographed in June 1902. Painted 'lead colour' with white lettering, shaded black and with black ironwork. *GRC&WCo.*

Left & Below: A selection of wagons for F. G. Mullis. Wagon No. 28 was photographed in October 1903 and was painted black with white lettering.
Wagon No. 31 was painted in similar style but on a five-plank wagon and was photographed in August 1906.
Finally, a much later wagon, No. 64 was photographed in September 1924 and was finished 'lead colour' with plain white lettering.
all GRC&WCo.

Two wagons for J. D. Pounsbery of Bristol. No. 1, painted green with cream lettering shaded red and with black ironwork, would certainly have looked different when first outshopped in February 1896. By the date of wagon No. 4, November 1902, the livery had changed to plain black with white lettering. Pounsbery was not trading in 1935. *GRC&WCo.*

Painted 'lead colour' with white lettering and black shading and ironwork, this wagon for David Lansley of Gloucester was photographed in April 1898. *GRC&WCo.*

Peter Buchanan, George Thomas Stephens & Emanuel Gardiner trading as the Dark Hill Dean Forest Stone Company
Henry Butt & Co., Weston-super-Mare
Edgar Richard Quant, Tiverton Junction
Montieth & Alford, Bridport
William Murray, Dorchester
F. G. Mullis, Clifton, Bristol
Charles Reynolds trading as West of England Trading Co., Cullompton
Robert Lewis, Lawrence Hill
Frank L. Harvey, Weston-super-Mare
James C. Bird and Thomas B. Bird trading as Bird Brothers, Bristol
Samuel Stradling, Weston-super-Mare
Thomas R. Davidson and Thomas Aitken trading as T. Aitken & Co., Guildford
David T. Lansley, Gloucester
Arthur S. Hill, Dorchester
George Strawbridge, Colyton, Devon
William Cecil Gethen, Hereford
T. C. & C. Graham, Newport
James Sanders & William Montjoy trading as Sanders & Montjoy, South Molton
G. W. Talbot & Son, Reading
J. D. Pounsbery, Bristol
Adam Wragg, Seend

It was explained that most of the above accounts, opened between January and July 1897 were because the carriage was formerly collected by the GWR who then paid the Joint Committee for conveyance to and from Bilson Junction. This reveals that the wagons were being transferred between Trafalgar Colliery and the Forest of Dean Branch at Bilson.

22 October 1897
John Knight trading as John Knight & Co., Gloucester Docks
Thos. Simmons & Walter Tom Simmons trading as T. Simmons & Co., Reading

Photographed in October 1894, wagon No. 14 was painted 'red', lettered white, shaded black. *GRC&WCo.*

A wagon for the South Wales Coal Company of Hereford which was run in 1898 by Herbert Percy Morris. Photographed in October 1911 the wagon was painted 'lead colour' with white lettering, shaded red, and with black ironwork. Note the hinged top planks above the side door. It would appear that the wagon was bought for cash as it already has an oval owner's plate on the solebar. *GRC&WCo.*

133

26 January 1898
T. Bazzard, colliery agents and brick & tile merchant, Swindon

20 April 1898
Wilderness Brick & Stone Co. Ltd
Berkeley Farmers Association

25 July 1898
Lovie & Co., Cardiff
E. Jenner Davis, trading as Cirencester Brick & Tile Co., Stonehouse
Herbert Percy Morris trading as the **South Wales Coal Co.**, Hereford
Bedlington and T. D. Rowland trading as B. Rowland & Co., Cardiff

18 October 1898
Ernest Henry Dyke trading as H. E. Dyke & Co., Wincanton
E. H. Davies trading as Messrs Ralph, Preece, Davies & Co., Hereford

25 January 1899
Charles Parsons, Dorchester
C. Herris Spear, Tiverton
George Williams & Co. Newport
Park Coal Co., Cardiff

24 April 1899
Stephens, Phillips & Co., Basingstoke
Thomas Hill, Wellington
Webb Brothers, Cheltenham
F. T. Burgess, Wick

30 October 1899
John Lysaght, Newport

22 January 1900
R. H. Clare, Burnham

24 April 1900
G. Norris, Leamington
Jno. Carpenter & Sons, Twerton
E. Gregory & Sons, Berkeley

16 July 1900
The Bunker Coal Co., Newport
Chas Lewis & Co., Cardiff

22 October 1900
G. E. Dowding, Patchway
A. H. Natt [Nott?], Cheltenham

22 April 1901
T. B. & S. Batchelor & Co., timber merchants, Newport
Frederick Biss, coal merchants, Patchway
Bradbury, Son & Co. Ltd, coal factors, Southampton
Graham Brothers, coal factors, Newport
George Player, colliery agent, Teignmouth
David Thomas & Sons, colliery agents, Llanelly

17 July 1901
Direct Coal Supply, Yeovil
Huntley & Cochran, Bristol
W. J. Mills, Bristol

A wagon for Webb Brothers painted **'WEBBS' COALS'** photographed in July 1904, painted black with white lettering. *GRC&WCo.*

Photographed in December 1891, this wagon for H. A. Gwinnell was painted black with white lettering. It is unknown if this Gwinnell later formed part of Powell, Gwinnell & Co. Ltd. *GRC&WCo.*

G. Bryer Ash had a head office in Weymouth with branches at Bournemouth and Bath. A ledger account was opened in early 1902. This wagon, however, dates from 1923 and was painted black with white lettering. *GRC&WCo.*

134

21 October 1901
Workman Brothers, flour mills, Coaley Junction

20 January 1902
H. A. Gwinnell & Co., Cheltenham
Messrs Limites, London
J. P. Thomas, steel manufacturer, Coleford

21 April 1902
Geo. B. Ash, Weymouth
The Central Coal Co., Bristol

21 July 1902
Messrs Meggitt & Jones, timber merchants, Barry
The Old Radnor Trading Co., Kington
Benjamin Paget, Bristol

20 October 1902
Cox, Long & Co., London
Mills & Pollard, Lawrence Hill
H. Newsum, Sons & Co. Ltd, Gainsborough
The Pontithel Chemical Co., Three Cocks
Strawbridge Bros, Colyton

26 January 1903
W. L. Buchanan, Gloucester
Pepler, Edwards & Co., Stapleton Road, Bristol
John Griffiths, coal exporter, Neath
Poole Bros, Bristol

20 April 1903
Cardiff Grain Co.
Happerfield & Willans, Newport

Commencing business in 1875 the Old Radnor Trading Co. had quarries at Dolyhir near Kington, Radnorshire. The wagons would have brought stone into the Forest, possibly for road building. *Mike Lloyd Collection*

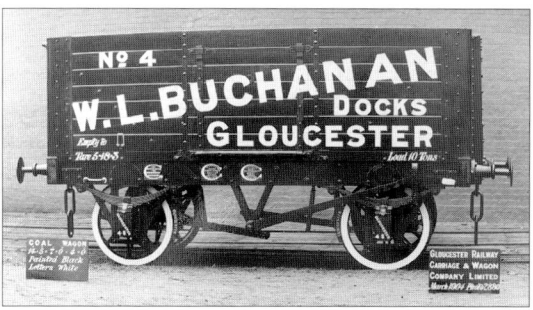

Two wagons for Wilfred Laurence Buchanan, lettered in an identical style. No. 3 was photographed in November 1902 and No. 4 in March 1904. Both were black with white lettering. He was based in the Docks at Gloucester. By 1935 they were trading as Buchanan & Co.
both GRC&WCo.

19 January 1904
Dudley & Gibson, coal merchants, Bristol
The Western Navigation Coal Co., Newport

22 April 1904
Geo T. Whitfield, Tuffley

18 July 1904
Hewlett & Co. Ltd, coal factors, Worle
H. Jordan & Co., Cheltenham

18 October 1904
Critchlow & Sheppard, Cheltenham

24 January 1905
The Earl Waldegraves Collieries, Radstock
Matthew Grist, Merrett's Mills, Woodchester

24 July 1905
Edward J. Cole, coal factor, Cirencester
James McKelvie and Company, colliery agents, Haymarket, Edinburgh

16 October 1905
Messrs Ward & Co., Exeter
The Western Navigation Coal Co., Newport

23 January 1906
A. W. Travis, colliery proprietor, Cardiff
S. Fussell, coal merchant, Durham Down, Bristol

11 April 1906
Eveson Coal & Coke Co., Birmingham
James Brothers & Co., Cardiff
W. Alfred Phillips, Cardiff

23 October 1906
T. H. Burdess, colliery agent, Cinderford

25 January 1907
Wm Perch, colliery proprietors, Cardiff

23 April 1907
Frederick Biss & Co. Ltd, Patchway
Benjamin Paget & Sons, Nelson St, Bristol
Jonathan Williams & Company, Dock St, Newport
J. J. Farthing, Cardiff

25 September 1907
C. & T. Harris, Calne
A. H. Kelly, 57 Dock Street, Newport

21 January 1908
Lansley & Cullis, Gloucester
J. M. Lock, coal contractor, Dorchester
Messrs Le Ray Pullin & Co., Cardiff

24 April 1908
Messrs Tennant, Sons & Co. Ltd, Cardiff

20 April 1909
Joseph Bloomer & Co., Brierley Hill
A Boulton & Co., Shrewsbury

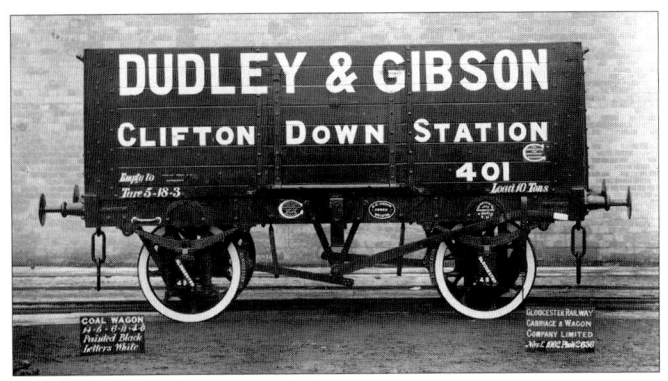

Above & Right: Three wagons for Messrs Dudley & Gibson of Bristol. Wagon No. 401, photographed in November 1902 was painted black with white lettering. The solebar carries an owner's plate which reads 'A. E. Gibson Owner Bristol'. Wagon No. 403 is painted 'chocolate' with white lettering shaded black and with black ironwork. Photographed in July 1909. Finally, wagon No. 101 which was painted as per 403 when photographed in February 1924. The company was trading in 1935 as Dowding, Dudley & Gibson Ltd. *GRC&WCo.*

Below: Two wagons lettered for Critchlow & Sheppard of Cheltenham whose address in 1906 was 3 Imperial Buildings, St. Georges Road. Wagon No. 9 was photographed in September 1903 and was painted 'lead colour' with white lettering and black shading and ironwork. It was photographed together with wagon No. 11. No. 15, together with No. 13, was photographed in June 1904. Painted 'red' with white lettering shaded black they also have end doors fitted. Not trading in 1935. *GRC&WCo.*

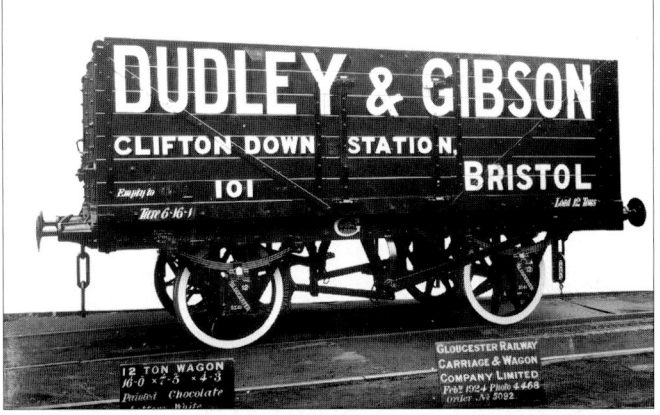

Redler & Co., Birmingham
Graham, Roberts & Co., Newport

12 July 1909
Wm Cory & Son, London
T. L. Leadbeter & Co., Newport
Williams & Co., Cinderford

18 October 1909
J. & W. Bellhouse, Manchester

19 April 1910
Buckland & Co., Chepstow

19 July 1910
Meggitt & Jones Ltd, Cardiff

11 April 1911
Payne & Son, Hereford
Co-operative Wholesale Society Ltd

23 January 1912
A Thomas & Co., Swansea
Christopher Jones, Cardiff
Huntley & Co. Ltd, Lawrence Hill, Bristol

A wagon for Matthew Grist of Merrett's Mills, Woodchester on the Midland Railway's Nailsworth Branch. He opened a ledger account in January 1905 and is listed in a 1906 trade directory as a 'washed wools and mill-puffs manufacturer'. Still trading in 1935. *GRC&WCo.*

Photographed in January 1914 Edward R. is probably the son of Edward J. who opened a ledger account in 1905. Painted 'red', lettered white, black shading and ironwork. *GRC&WCo.*

William Butler had a works at Upper Parting, Gloucester and probably collected coal gas tar in barrels from gasworks in the Forest. There were also several chemical works in the Forest which may have provided trade. *GRC&WCo.*

T. L. Leadbeter's wagon No. 211 was painted 'bright red', lettered white lettering with black shading and ironwork in January 1905. Possibly the same firm as on page 124. *GRC&WCo.*

23 April 1912
Watkins & Leonard, Lawrence Hill, Bristol

11 July 1912
James Waldie & Sons Ltd, Glasgow

15 October 1912
British Red Ash Collieries Ltd, Dock Street, Newport
Granville Smith & Co., Baldwin Street, Bristol

21 January 1913
Accounts outstanding
Bradford & Son, Yeovil
New accounts
Evans & Reid Ltd, Cardiff & London
Bradbury, Son & Co. Ltd, London

22 April 1913
Henry Hosegood & Son, Bristol
Clements & Son, Bristol
J. E. Turner & Co., The Docks, Gloucester
J. L. Garlick & Co., The Docks, Gloucester
G. J. Smith, The Docks, Gloucester
T. Robinson & Co., Gloucester

14 July 1913
C. E. Ford & Co., Bristol
Smith & Cornock, The Docks, Gloucester
J. W. Tombs, The Docks, Gloucester
A. T. Turner & Co., Broad St., Hereford
Wait, James & Co., The Docks, Gloucester
John Weston & Co., Commercial Road, Gloucester

14 October 1913
J. Snow, Whiteladies Rd., Bristol

20 January 1914
William Lewis, Newport
H. Stanley L. Cook trading as Wm H. Essery, Swansea
F. Kemble, Birmingham
Pitt & Morris, Gloucester
Western Counties Agricultural Association Ltd, Plymouth

21 April 1914
Jordan & Co. Ltd, Cheltenham

14 July 1914
Direct Coals Ltd, Yeovil

13 October 1914
Holman Ltd, Cardiff
Geo. Dunlop, Reading

13 July 1915
E. Foster & Co., London
E. Lawrence & Co., Swansea

Left: Photographed in September 1905 was wagon No. 2 for Payne & Son. Painted 'bright red' with white lettering and black shading and ironwork. *GRC&WCo.*

Two views of the screens at Eastern United Colliery reveal comparatively few differences between the upper view taken in the mid 1930s and that below taken during or just after the Second World War. Close scrutiny of the upper photograph reveals wagons for Thomas Silvey, Twining, Lightmoor Colliery, Lowell Baldwin, Princess Royal Colliery, Northern United Colliery and, in the row behind, two wagons for Colthrop's who had paper mills at Thatcham and an Eastern United Colliery wagon.

The view below shows a variety of wagons all in the national requistioned pool, apart from the National Smelting Co. 20-ton steel wagon, which, as it belonged to the Great Western Railway was 'not common user' and the small curved lettering beneath AVON denotes this.

COAL HANDLING

IT is difficult to be precise about the operation of the vast numbers of private owner wagons in the Forest of Dean. The majority of them would have been used in the carriage of coal between the various collieries and the shipping ports of Lydney, Bullo, Sharpness and even as far as Newport. There were also nightly coal trains off the Severn & Wye system to Stoke Gifford Yard near Bristol and off the Forest of Dean Branch from Bullo to Gloucester and Swindon. At these destinations the wagons would be sorted for onward transmission, mainly towards the West Country.

It was the West Country and Ireland which were the biggest takers of Forest coal, much of which traditionally went by sea. With such a long coastline and many small ports and inlets sea-borne trade was a natural for the West Country with small ketches and the Severn Estuary trows sailing from Lydney and Bullo. Some of these vessels took as little as 20 tons of coal and would land it on some remote beach in Somerset or Devon for the use of the local community. The majority of these vessels were owned by the Master and traded out of ports such as Appledore in Devon.

Vessels were also owned by some of the coal factoring businesses such as Sullys, A. J. Smith, Thomas Silvey and Barker & Lovering. They would come to load with regular orders for customers.

Lydney Docks, with its multiple coal tips, could handle a wider variety of vessels than Bullo which in later years only had one tip inside the basin, the rest being on a riverside wharf. Hence Bullo, which shipped a lot of coal for the Stroud valleys, via the Stroudwater and Thames & Severn canals, fell out of use much earlier. Although in the early 1890s it was as busy as Lydney by 1903 it was handling only 8 cargoes a month. This gradually dwindled away but as late as 1922 an occasional shipment was still being made.

Lydney itself had a disadvantage in that it could not handle larger vessels, especially with the increasing use of steamships, and it was also a difficult harbour to work into because of the tidal range and speed on the Severn. Thus, with the opening of the Severn railway bridge in 1879 and the development of the docks at Sharpness the Severn & Wye Railway was able to offer alternative shipping arrangements. A coal tip at Sharpness was first brought into use in January 1880 and six years later a deep water tip was built in the docks themselves.

For a period at Lydney individual colliery or coal

A steamship, possibly belonging to one of the coal factoring firms, loading under the No. 9 tip at Lydney. Vessels such as this could only use this tip, it being the only one situated in the tidal basin. A **CRUMP** wagon is being manhandled towards the empty wagon road having come off the tip and been turned on a turntable.

The tip at Bullo was of a more basic nature to those at Lydney. At one time there was a second tip on the opposite side of the basin and several along a deep water riverside wharf off to the right. At this time in the docks life, c.1920, it was available to shipping only as a tidal basin. Being loaded here is the trow *Finis*, the last vessel to use the dock on a regular basis. One regular cargo was Eastern United coal to Cadbury's works at Frampton-on-Severn.
courtesy Harry Trigg

factoring companies could rent one of the tips for their own use with a couple being left as 'common user' tips. However, complaints were soon raised that it meant some companies had preference over others, especially if their tips were at the lower end of the canal. It was therefore agreed that in certain conditions vessels for traders with tips at the upper basin could load at no extra charge in the lower basin thereby saving a trip up the canal. The practice of hiring out tips did not end until the 1890s. Most of the collieries employed shipping agents to oversee the shipping of the coal and also to secure 'spot' cargoes when a ships' master came looking for a load.

One important aspect of work done on the tips was the mixing of coal to customers requirements. This would be done by tipping one wagonload of 'x' coal with one of 'y'. If the coal came from two different collieries, i.e. Princess Royal and Lightmoor, then the order was often handled through a factor.

An example of the charges made for this service by the railway company comes from 1909:

'The Secretary reported that he has been in further correspondence with the Forest of Dean Coal Owners Association who submitted the memorandum set out

Forest coal was also taken over the Severn Bridge, which opened for traffic in 1879, to the dock at Sharpness where larger vessels could be loaded and also as block trains to Stoke Gifford yarY north of Bristol. This postcard view is the only known photograph showing a coal train on the bridge. The locomotive is a 2021 class 0-6-0 saddle tank and the wagons could be from Princess Royal Colliery.

From another postcard, this shows part of Sharpness Docks with the original Severn & Wye coal tip of 1880 standing above the swing bridge. It remained *in situ* until 1971. A saddle tank can also just be discerned sorting out wagons for the tip. In the foreground the roof of the signal box at Sharpness Station can be seen.

Two views of the deep-water coal tip in Sharpness Docks. It was approached via the viaduct which was originally of timber construction with the actual coal tip enclosed in the timber building. The viaduct was later replaced by a ferro-concrete structure together with a new tip. In the lower illustration a Princess Royal Colliery wagon can be seen posed on the new tip.

hereunder as representing the method of charging at Newport for the service of mixing coal for shipment. This having been confirmed by the Mineral Managers, it was agreed that the same regulations be adopted at Lydney and Sharpness viz:

    Mixing 1 wagon   1d. per ton
    Mixing 2 wagons $^7/_8$d. per ton
    Mixing 3 wagons $^3/_4$d. per ton
    Mixing 4 wagons $^5/_8$d. per ton
    Mixing 5 wagons $^1/_2$d. per ton
    Mixing 6 wagons $^3/_8$d. per ton
    Mixing 7 wagons $^1/_4$d. per ton
    Mixing 8 wagons $^1/_8$d. per ton
    No charge for lots of 9 or more

The charges include the sorting of the empties after shipment.

Examples:-
a. 3 specified trucks to be mixed with 7 specified trucks in a particular order to be charged at $^3/_4$d. per ton on 3 and $^1/_4$d. per ton on 7.
b. 3 specified trucks to be mixed with 9 specified trucks in a particular order to be charged at $^3/_4$d. per ton on 3 and no charge on 9.
c. 9 specified trucks to be mixed with 9 specified trucks in a particular order – no charge.

If however, the trucks to be mixed in a particular order belonging to one firm, or, if belonging to more than one firm, the empty trucks are not required to be sorted out after shipment, no charge is made for mixing lots of more than 5.

Examples:-
a. 3 specified trucks to be mixed with 5 specified trucks in a particular order to be charged at $^3/_4$d. per ton on 3 and $^1/_2$d. per ton on 5.
b. 3 specified trucks to be mixed with 6 specified trucks in a particular order to be charged at $^3/_4$d. per ton on 3 and no charge on 6.
c. 6 specified trucks to be mixed with 6 specified trucks in a particular order – no charge.

No charge is made for arranging groups of trucks for the purpose of keeping coal separate in a vessel, or in any hold of a vessel, provided that the trucks in a group are not required to be arranged in a particular order for such groups.

No charge is made for putting bunker coal in position for shipment at any required point of the load.'

As well as specialised handling at the docks it was necessary that the colliery and the customer liased closely to ensure that the correct number of wagons were in the colliery yard for loading on certain days. This was especially important at collieries such as Lightmoor where a specific type of coal might only be wound and put through the screens on one day a week. If the factors' wagons were not there ready they could not be loaded.

The collieries and the coal factors kept a very close check on the whereabouts of their wagons – not least to ensure that they were not standing empty in a siding and incurring demurrage charges. Within coal factors offices ledgers were kept detailing the movements of every wagon and how much money it had earned each month. Returns of wagon whereabouts were made each day by the Railway Clearing House so that the railway companies could charge their respective traffic dues. These returns were gathered by number takers situated in marshalling yards or at junctions such as Lydney. Also at Lydney on the Severn & Wye line was a weighbridge over which every wagon of coal out of the Forest passed so that the tonnage carried could be accurately charged for. This was probably why the tare weight of the wagon seen on page 89 has been altered. If a repair had been done to the wagon so that its tare weight was lighter then if filled with ten tons of coal the factor did not want to pay for an extra hundredweight of wagon!

It can be seen therefore that the handling of coal, both at the colliery, the docks and, later still, when in the hands of the factor, needed considerable management and organisation. There is still a lot to be discovered and written on the subject, particularly at the coal factor and coal merchant level to understand exactly how those businesses operated.

Wagons could also be tipped using the dockside cranes at Sharpness as witnessed by this view of a Princess Royal wagon being upended over a dumb barge. Presumably once loaded the barges were taken up the Gloucester-Sharpness canal. The cradle for the crane was ordered from Stothert & Pitt of Bath in November 1912 to enable several large orders for Forest coal to be shipped.

The Unknowns, Coal

THERE are several collieries or colliery owners in the Forest who may have had wagons but of which, so far, no record has been found. Collieries which had siding provision are the most likely to have had their own wagons, either lettered for the colliery itself or for the owner. These unknowns have come from a variety of sources, mainly the Gloucester Wagon Co's order books but also from the Severn & Wye letter books which give more details of the non-Forest wagons trading into the area. Just occasionally the railway company minute books give a mention to a wagon or a trader.

Working along the various lines starting on the Great Western's Forest of Dean Branch it is known or it is likely that there should have been wagons for…

Hawkwell Colliery and Hawkwell Tinplate Works

The colliery was bought by Jacob Chivers in 1874 and by 1876 he had deepened the existing shaft to the Coleford High Delf coal. The colliery was worked under the title of the Hawkwell Colliery Co. In 1878 Chivers began the Hawkwell Tinplate Works and in 1881 took into partnership Alfred Charles Bright. In 1880 there are two entries in the books of the Western Wagon Co. for wagons for J. Chivers & Co. and for Jacob Chivers & Son. J. Chivers & Co. took five 10-ton wagons in October 1879 on seven years redemption hire and it is likely that these were destined for Hawkwell. Those for Jacob Chivers & Son probably went to Jacob's previous interests in a tinplate works at Kidwelly which was at this date being managed by his son.

In 1883 Bright took over both concerns following the death of Chivers and in October 1893 A. C. Bright & Co. Ltd was incorporated. One of the shareholders was Edwin Marcus Letcher who was related to Bright by marriage. Both the colliery and the tinplate works had a siding off the Churchway Branch.

Bright may have inherited wagons when he took over from Chivers and certainly in October 1893 he signed a repairing contract with Gloucester for twenty 10-ton wagons for a period of five years. Interestingly, it was on the same day as Letcher had taken out his contract. Were both of these for wagons concerned with Hawkwell?

A. C. Bright & Co. Ltd was not to last long and the company went into liquidation in December 1895 with both the colliery and tinplate works closing down.

E. M. Letcher

Edwin Marcus Letcher may have been connected with Chivers at Hawkwell Colliery or could have been acting as a colliery agent. An advert appeared in the local press in November 1887 for E. Marcus Letcher concerning Hawkwell Colliery. On the 12th February 1879 the GC&WCo. let two 10-ton secondhand wagons on hire to E. M. Letcher Jnr. for a 6 month period.

In January 1885 Letcher purchased 10 wagons from the Swansea Wagon Co. and also signed a repairing agreement on eleven wagons. He was obviously in financial difficulties in February 1889 when he sold the wagons back to the wagon co.

In December 1891 six 8-ton secondhand wagons were let to Letcher on deferred purchase over 7 years by the Gloucester Wagon Co. and a repairing contract was signed for one 7-ton and two 8-ton wagons. October 1893 saw a repairs contract over 5 years for ten 10-ton wagons. However, the 8th July 1896 saw: *'Bad debts written off; E. M. Letcher £160.15.0.'*

Churchway Colliery

Churchway Colliery was worked by Messrs Bennett under the title of the Churchway Company. Coal could have been loaded at the Nelson Colliery siding (see below). A siding was laid in at some point between 1856 and 1872 but it is likely that this was to bring coal in to feed the boilers of the pumping engine as the colliery closed for coal production soon after the opening of the railway. The colliery was then taken over by the Bilson & Crump Meadow Collieries Co. Ltd, later the Lydney & Crump Meadow.

Nelson Colliery

The colliery was served by a broad gauge siding laid in 1856 and an account of 1857 records three wagons a day in and three out. It was owned by Thomas Bennett. Closure is likely to have been before the end of the broad gauge in the Forest in 1872 and by 1881 the colliery was in the hands of the Lydney & Crump Meadow Collieries Co. Ltd.

Meadow Cliff

The Meadow Cliff Colliery Co. was incorporated in August 1915 to work the Roberts Folly gale. In March 1917 a James Stone, coal factor, of Bournemouth became a director and a year later he was joined by Frederick and Charles Baker who were both coal merchants in Southampton. The company was by now in difficulties and in 1922 Godfrey Meek of Lydney was appointed managing director. He had apparently handled all of the collieries previous output in his capacity of coal factor. However, in June 1923 all plant and buildings were seized by H.M. Collector of Taxes and were sold off. The siding was lifted in 1924.

In September 1915 an order was placed with the Gloucester Railway Carriage & Wagon Co. for six secondhand 12-ton wagons let on deferred payment over 7 years at £18 5s. 0d. each and in December 1915 a repairing contract was signed. An inventory taken of the company's assets in 1922 records the six wagons. It is possible that these were lettered up for one of the owning coal merchants or factors rather than for the colliery itself.

Haywood Colliery

Haywood was worked by the Littledean Woodside Coal Company who built a narrow gauge railway to interchange sidings in 1874. Behind the concern was Edwin Crawshay, son of Henry. In March 1886 the Haywood Colliery Co. Ltd was formed but the colliery, despite reaching the famed Coleford High Delf seam of coal, did not prosper and the company was wound up in 1888 with the colliery closing.

Regulator Colliery

Owned by Mr Bennett, the colliery was provided with a siding soon after the opening of the broad gauge line but it was probably removed before the conversion of the line.

Speedwell Newbridge Colliery

Speedwell Newbridge Colliery was situated at Nailbridge and in 1881 Mr Goodrich Langham began development in connection with which the moribund Mitcheldean Road & Forest of Dean Junction Railway's line between Whimsey and Nailbridge was opened as far as sidings at Nailbridge in 1885. With his colliery producing coal he hired five secondhand 8-ton wagons in November for one month from the Gloucester Wagon Co. The next mention is in September 1890 when six secondhand 10-ton wagons were let on hire for one year. By this time the colliery was outputting 1,000 tons a month.

In October 1893 thirty new 10-ton wagons were let on deferred purchase over 7 years to the Speedwell Newbridge Colliery Co. Ltd. However, in January 1896 the Speedwell Company were asking that a bill for £65 at two months might be accepted from them in renewal of part of their bills for £125 12s. 10d. which fell due on the 19th inst. It was resolved that as they had paid the difference in cash it be acceded to. In April 1897 they appear to have changed their purchase to a hire, as an agreement was signed for thirty secondhand 10-ton wagons let on hire monthly at £6 15s. 0d. to the trustees of the Speedwell Newbridge Colliery Co. Ltd. The effects of the colliery were sold off in June 1897. Some of the wagons were returned to the Gloucester Wagon Co. who purchased them for £480. They were promptly resold to the Wimberry Colliery Co. (page 27) for £619 9s. 9d.

Arthur Morgan
A latecomer to the scene was Arthur Morgan. He was managing director for Henry Crawshay & Co. but he also had other business interests which may have had wagons, such as the Cinderford Crushing Co. (see page 163). In connection with coal Morgan announced in March 1917 that he wished to go into the coal factoring business and this he seems to have done as he was supplied with coal from Lightmoor.

Over on the western side of the Forest on the Severn & Wye lines…

Trotter Thomas & Co.
Trotter Thomas & Co. have been mentioned on page 14 in the broad gauge section. In January 1871 they placed an order with the Cheltenham & Swansea Wagon Co. for two broad gauge wagons at £80 each and for three, secondhand, narrow gauge wagons (late Hall) on 7 years deferred purchase at £8 per wagon per annum. The broad gauge wagons were probably for use with Wimberry Colliery whilst the narrow gauge wagons could well have been for use on the recently completed Severn & Wye Mineral Loop which was built to standard gauge and with mixed gauge from Tufts Junction down to Lydney.

Gollop & Ridler
They were known to have had interests in Speech House Hill Colliery (see page 25), in a brickworks at Staple Edge on the Forest of Dean Branch and in Wallsend Colliery on the Forest of Dean Central Railway. They are included here as they were also coal merchants and shippers in Lydney trading as Gollop, Ridler & Co. Although no order can be found, possibly because it was placed pre-April 1866 with Shackleford & Ford of Cheltenham, Gollop & Ridler are recorded in the books of the Cheltenham & Swansea Wagon Co. as 'giving up' five broad gauge wagons in April 1871. They still owned 15 broad gauge wagons at the time of the gauge conversion in May 1872 and it was possibly in anticipation of this that in January 1872 they hired seventy 10-ton wagons for 3 years. This is the only reference to them in the Gloucester Wagon minutes. By 1873 they were also hiring wagons from the Western Wagon Co. as in that year they appear in the books as debtors! August 1873 shows them to have had 10 standard gauge wagons on simple hire and this number was maintained until 1877/78. In August of the latter year the wagons were said to be 'idle' at Cardiff. This could well be because of the fact that James Ridler died in August 1877. The partnership of Gollop & Ridler continued trading until December 1880 at which point it was dissolved. James Gollop is also recorded as owning a Severn trow, the *Eliza*, built in 1864 which probably traded out of Lydney with Forest coal. In October 1881 James Gollop formed Gollop & Co. Ltd with two other members of the family including Francis Gollop of Lydney a coal agent. Included in the agreement were sixty-two wagons on hire from the North Central Wagon Co. under a lease dated 15th June 1879. The company went into voluntary liquidation in September 1884.

Ridler & Weedon (later Weedon & Co.)
Another Lydney partnership, trading in 1870 as coal merchants at Lydney Basin. By 1876 they appear to have become Weedon & Co. and by 1889 are listed as Richard Weedon.

In October 1870 six broad gauge wagons were ordered from the Cheltenham & Swansea Wagon Co. by Ridler & Weedon on 5 year redemption hire at £22 pwpa including repairs. In March 1872 a further ten wagons were purchased on seven years redemption hire at £13 per wagon per annum plus £2 10s. per wagon per annum for repairs. On the 16th August 1872 Messrs Ridler & Weedon applied for their agreements for hire and maintenance of 10 wagons to be cancelled and substituted by others for 3 wagons only – it was 'decided to meet their wishes as far as this company [C&SWCo.] can do'.

Lückes & Nash
Messrs Lückes & Nash had interests in many collieries throughout the Forest including Speech House, Haywood (as part of the Littledean Woodside Coal Co.), Hopewell Engine and Mapleford Engine (as the Western Counties Colliery Co.), Rudge, Pillowell (including the Whitecroft Patent Fuel Works), and also in the Crow's Nest, Staunton and High Meadow Iron Mines. These varied interests were well scattered across the Forest thus their wagons could have appeared anywhere – apart from in front of a camera!

In September 1871 they hired 17 broad gauge wagons from the Cheltenham & Swansea Wagon Co. and then in January 1872 they purchased 20 wagons on 7 year redemption terms followed in March by a further 10 wagons.

On the 14th January 1873 they hired fifteen 10-ton wagons for 3 years from the Gloucester Wagon Co. In September they purchased a total of fifteen10-ton wagons over 7 years. The next reference in the Gloucester minutes is in June 1876 when some secondhand wagons were bought on deferred purchase over 7 years. The order was for 'thirty-five 8-ton wagons (now themselves on hire and purchase.)'.

A repairing contract was signed in February 1877 with the Swansea Wagon Co. (previously the Cheltenham & Swansea Wagon Co.) for the maintenance of 24 wagons.

Messrs Lückes & Nash always seem to have sailed close to the wind in their various interests and in December 1877 a three months bill for £462 10s. 4d. due by Messrs. Lückes & Nash to the Gloucester Wagon Co. was returned dishonoured. In January 1878 writs were issued against them and as they were already involved in other legal proceedings it was expected that they would present a petition for liquidation. This they duly did and Messrs Lückes & Nash disappeared from the Forest's industrial scene.

With the number of concerns in which Lückes & Nash had an interest it is entirely possible that some of the wagons may have been lettered for the relevant works.

Compressed Coal Co.
Another of Lückes & Nash ventures was the Patent Fuel Works at Whitecroft (see page 42) who in the late 1860s formed the Compressed Coal Co. to produce patent fuel using small coal from Pillowell Colliery which was compressed into briquettes at the Whitecroft works. In December 1867 an agreement was signed with the Cheltenham & Swansea Wagon Co. for the hire of seven wagons. In October 1869 ten wagons were hired for one year at £15 per wagon. The works at Whitecroft were for sale in 1877.

A. W. Latham
Although Arthur Latham has been mentioned several times already in connection with collieries that he worked (Darkhill page 44) and his coal factor and merchants business (Phœnix Coal Co., page 83), he is included here again as some wagons cannot be attributed to any of the other concerns. In September 1898 he took six 10-ton wagons from the Western Wagon & Property Co. on seven year redemption hire. How they were lettered up is unknown but they were taken back by the wagon co. *circa* June 1900 which suggests that the bills

were not paid. In February 1899 Latham also took twenty-three 8 and 10-ton wagons from the same supplier, again on seven year redemption hire. A note against the order states that £800 was given for the wagons and then crossed out is 'together with an equitable deposit of the Conveyance of Hopewell Engine Colliery'. Again there were payment difficulties and the wagons were 'given up' on the 3rd July 1901. The note then continues that the wagons were paid out by the Lincoln Wagon Co. on the 24th March 1903. What is unclear from this is whether Latham was still running the wagons after mid-1901 and if he then sold them on to the Lincoln Wagon Co. to raise capital.

Lydney Gas Works
The gas works was started in 1860 and was located close to Lydney Town Station on the Severn & Wye. On the 8th August 1876 a secondhand 8-ton wagon was bought for cash from the Gloucester Wagon Co.

John Powell
On the 22nd August 1913 the coal merchants business of John Henry Powell of Lydney was up for sale including one railway wagon. Nothing else is known.

Williams & Stephens
Williams & Stephens of Lydney had twelve 10-ton wagons supplied in September/October 1876 by the firm of Baxendale & Heald who had a wagon works in Llantrisant. Wagon numbers were 31-42 and they were registered by the GWR. The only reference in trade directories which might fit is one in 1876 for Richard Williams, a coal merchant and ship owner, who also had interests at Dudbridge, Stroud.

Birchen Grove Colliery
The Birchen Grove Colliery Co. Ltd was incorporated in November 1888 to work the Lydbrook Colliery. Sidings for the colliery were just south of Upper Lydbrook Station. It is possible that the company was only working part of the colliery alongside the Forest Steam Coal Co. (page 43). In November 1889 four secondhand 8-ton wagons were let on hire for 1 year by the Gloucester Wagon Co. The company ceased trading in March 1891 when the colliery was sold to the Lydbrook Colliery Co. Ltd (page 39) and in July 1891 the Gloucester Wagon Co. wrote off bad debts for wagon rents and repairs.

Venus Colliery
The Venus Colliery Co. was formed in 1895 by W. G. Moorby and James Linneker of Unstone, Yorkshire, to work the Venus & Jupiter gale which was located to the west of Parkend. A siding off the Coleford Branch was brought into use at the end of October 1895. A ledger account was opened with the Severn & Wye in October 1896. In November 1896 the Gloucester Wagon Co. let fifteen secondhand 10-ton wagons on hire for 11 months. By December 1896 it would appear that the fleet had been reduced as only five 10-ton wagons were hired for 10 months and, indeed, work at the colliery had stopped by May 1897. Again the Wagon Co. were forced to write off a bad debt in July 1897. The colliery company went into liquidation in October 1900.

Forest of Dean Mining Co. Ltd
Wagons for the Forest of Dean Mining Co. Ltd were ordered from the Cheltenham & Swansea Wagon Co. in July 1867 and were presumably for the broad gauge. The company had been formed to work the High Delf Engine gale in the Whitecroft/Parkend area. It is unknown if any work was done.

Messrs Morrells
In the Western Wagon Co's books is one reference to a bad debt in 1873 which was put down to *Morrell execs.*' Unfortunately what the debt was for, or the number of wagons involved is not recorded but it may well have had a Forest connection. In September 1877 the executors of James and Robert Morrell of Oxford still had an interest in Union Colliery in Bixslade. Around 1838 the Morrells had formed the Lydney and Forest of Dean Coal Company. Union was forfeited back to the Crown in 1877 having not been worked for five years. Thus it would appear that the Morrell interest in the Forest did end *circa* 1872/73. This date would also suggest that they may have been running broad gauge wagons.

Flour Mill Colliery Co.
There are entries in the Western Wagon Co's books from August 1875 through to August 1878 relating to wagons supplied to the Flour Mill Colliery Co. In 1875 they had 20 wagons on redemption hire and by August the following year this had increased to 40. There was a Flour Mill Colliery Co. Ltd formed in December 1873 to work the colliery of that name near Bream and also Ellwood Colliery but the company went into liquidation in January 1875. Possibly the Flour Mill Colliery Co. retained an interest in Ellwood Colliery for a period.

and one possibly for the Forest of Dean Central Railway ...

Dean Forest Central Collieries Ltd
In December 1915 four 12-ton wagons were purchased on seven year redemption hire from the Western Wagon & Property Co. These wagons were built at the WW&PCo's works in Cardiff at a cost of £98. The Dean Forest Central Collieries Ltd had offices in Church Square, Blakeney and were working the Wellington Colliery on Moseley Green. This had been purchased on behalf of a syndicate in February 1915. How much work was done is unknown but by 1918 the wagons had been taken back by the wagon company and put into their simple hire stock.

A later unknown ...

Godfrey Meek
Godfrey Meek is listed as a coal factor from Newnham in 1931. Meek had been connected with Meadow Cliff Colliery, becoming managing director in 1922 having already had a mortgage on the property and also having handled all of the output from the colliery in 'his capacity as a coal factor'. Meadow Cliff was closed by 1924 and what happened to Meek between then and 1931 is unknown.

The only evidence that he had wagons comes in *The Nailsworth and Stroud Branch* by Colin Maggs. Oakwood Press, 2000. On page 96 is reproduced some sketches of wagons seen on the branch in the late 1920s-early 30s and there is a wagon for Godfrey F. Meek Colliery Agent:

GODFREY F. MEEK
COLLIERY   AGENT

Meek is still to be found in 1935 trade directories.

One from the 'Industrial User' category:

Berkeley Farmers Association Ltd
They acquired an 8-ton wagon from the Gloucester Carriage and Wagon Co. in 1913 which had previously been let to 'John Mabbett' (possibly H. J. Mabbett of Berkeley, see page 111). Further details are unknown.

...And then there are the wagons for which we have a photograph but no information. In this case a KELLY wagon at Cannop Colliery in the 1930s. But where were they based? A. H. Kelly of Newport is one possibility.

Also at Cannop was the wagon for W. Hall [?] & Co. Ltd. Again, at present they cannot be traced through directories as to where they were based.

One frustrating aspect of seeking out wagons in photographs is when part of a structure or building, or indeed another wagon, gets in the way of an interesting looking vehicle. Here the footbridge at Lydney Junction obscures most of a wagon which appears to be an 'unknown' livery. The top line reads '?ATT???? & ??' – either & Son or & Co. Ltd. Below can be made out E. ??? RD – East somewhere?. Below that again is 'DUD' – possibly Dudbridge in the Stroud area or Dudley?

And finally, an entire right-hand side of a wagon for ??T & SON, *Merchants* of ?? WATER [Bridgwater?].
Photographed in 1908 at Lydney, but who was the owner?

Another source for 'unknown' wagons are the surviving Severn & Wye letter books, now in private hands. These deal mainly with claims against the company and thus carry details of wagons off the road here and there.

22 August 1898 **Knight & Co's** wagon 51 off at Lydney. [Probably John Knight of Gloucester who traded as John Knight & Co. and had a wharf in Gloucester Docks.]

4 March 1899 **Bath Coal Co's** wagon No. 3 off Coleford Jcn. [Established c.1887 and still trading in the 1980s.]

20 March 1899 **R. T. James** wagon No. 1 and **Thomas Burrows** wagon No. 3 off Lydney S&W yard.

29 August 1899 **Briton Ferry Chemical Co's** wagon No. 107.

18 September 1899 **James Poole's** wagon No. 129 off at 14M.P. Loop Line.

16 December 1899 **Goodlands** wagons No's 4 & 8 damaged. [Goodlands were coal merchants from Taunton.]

20 February 1900 **A. Bruce's** Creosote Tank No. 11 off Sharpness.

25 May 1900 **J. R. Nobles** wagon No. 10 off road and partially over embankment at Tufts.

30 May 1900 **J. Grist & Co's** [Dudbridge, Stroud] wagon No. 101 off Lydney Jnc.

1 September 1900 **Kingsbury** wagon No. 99.

3 November 1900 Repairs to wagons of Messrs **E. Thomas & Co.**, Bryn Cottage, Rhyader.

9 July 1901 **E. H. Weeks**, Chepstow, wagon off Lydney Jct.

20 August 1903 **E. H. Weeks** wagon No. 12 off road at Lydney Jct.

21 August 1903 **John Fowler & Co's** wagon No. 75 off road at Lydbrook Jct.

12 February 1904 **F. J. Smith's** wagon No. 65 damaged at Lydney Jct.

14 March 1904 **Wellington's** wagon No. 5 off road at Lydney.

13 February 1905 **E. Finch & Co's** wagon No. 1 off road at Wimberry.

6 May 1905 **G. Gay & Sons** wagon No. 2 off road at Crump Meadow New Sidings.

16 February 1906 Messrs **Happerfields** wagon No. 87 damaged at Lydney Jct.

3 March 1909 **E. Bowks [Bowles?] & Sons** wagon No. 1 off road 3/3 Lydney.

13 March 1911 **Central Coal Co's** wagon No. 114 off at Serridge Jct. [Bath and Bristol, wagon No. 114 was one of a batch (110-119) built in November 1910 by the Midland Wagon Co.]

17 April 1913 **British Wagon Co's** wagon No. 23 off at Hopewell Siding Wimberry Branch. [Probably on a short term hire.]

5 September 1906 **Goodland's** wagon [Taunton] No. 2 defective underframe.

1 October 1906 **J. Toomer & Sons** wagon No. 54 lock buffered and two axles bent at Lydney Jct. [J. Toomer & Son of Swindon, founded 1850. Later wagons supplied by Thomas Hunter Ltd. Painted red.]

26 April 1907 **Gloucester Carriage & Wagon Co's** wagon No. 12234 drawbar hook broken.

15 May 1907 **Philip Earls & Co's** [Cardiff] wagon No. 3402 off Lydney Jct. Yard.

24 August 1907 **Gloucester Carriage & Wagon Co's** wagon No. 30411 damaged.

6 May 1908 **Lames & Sons** wagon No. 12 damaged.

29 November 1917 Repairs **Burnyeat Brown & Co's** wagon No. 654.

11 December 1917 Wagon repairs **Powell Duffryn** Wagon 332 repaired Lydney.

1 March 1919 **Steam Coal Collieries** Wagon No. 810 derailed at Miery Stock Sidings.

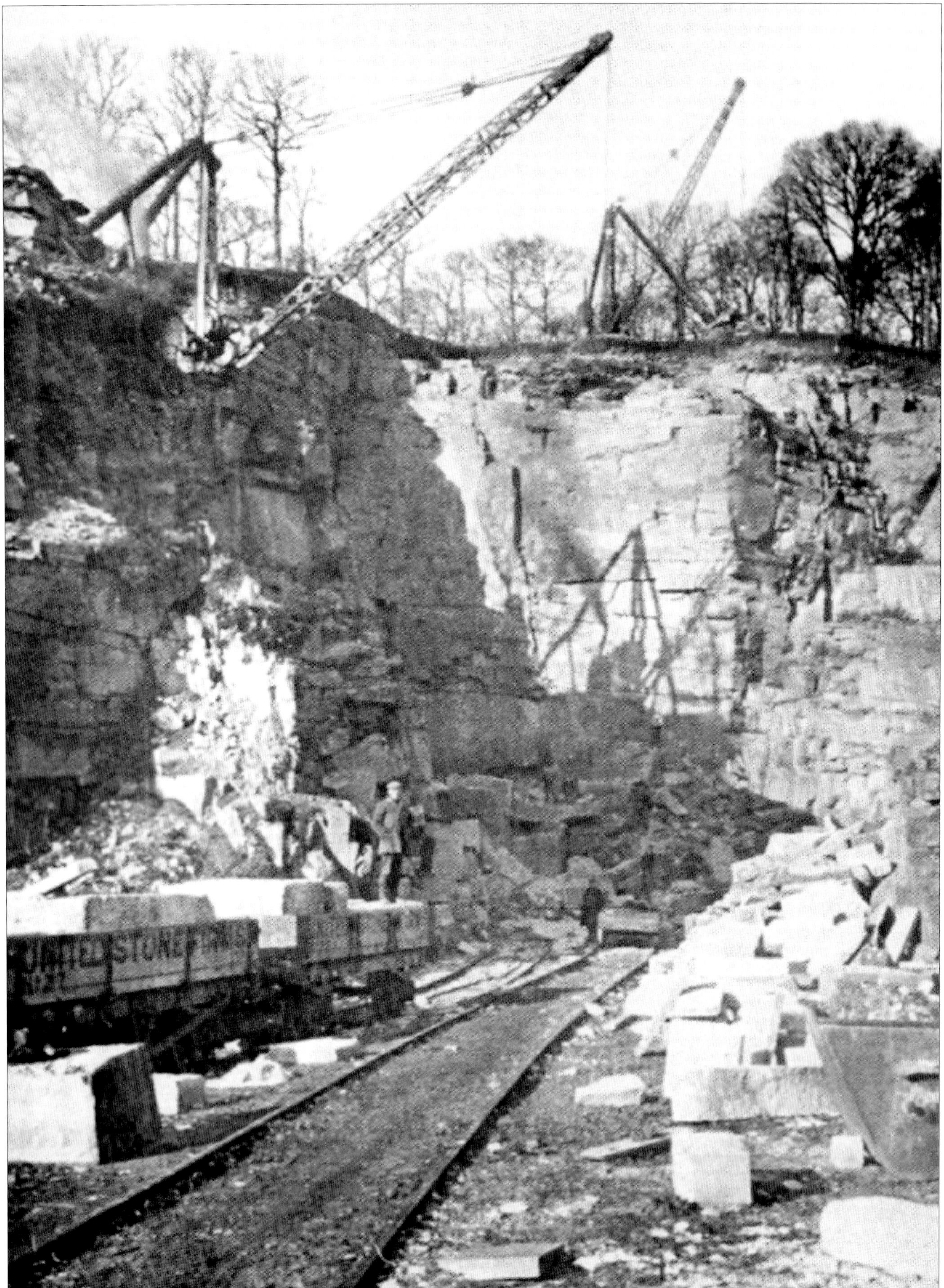
UNITED STONE

STONE

THE history of stone quarrying in the Forest of Dean is a long one. At the end of the nineteenth century there were several small quarry companies, each with their own stone works. Those that were rail connected were virtually all on the western side of the Forest and served by the Severn & Wye Railway.

It was the quarries in valleys such as Bixslade and Wimberry Slade which led to the retention of parts of the tramroad system up to the Second World War and beyond.

Later quarrying developments came in the east of the district and saw some large quarries developed, such as Shakemantle and Drybrook, which were served by the Forest of Dean Branch.

As mentioned, quarrying was in the hands of several small companies such as E. R. Payne, Trotter, Thomas & Co., David & Co., and Porter Bros. By a series of amalgamations in the early part of the twentieth century the majority of the quarries came under one concern. The first amalgamation actually came in 1891 when David & Sant Ltd was created from David & Co., Trotter, Thomas & Co. and Porter Bros. In 1900 David & Sant became part of Forest of Dean Stone Firms which in 1909 also acquired E. R. Payne & Son Ltd and was itself taken over the following year by the United Stone Firms. They also acquired the Forest interests of the Cardiff firm of E. R. Turner & Sons as well as taking over many other quarrying interests throughout the West Country and in West Wales.

In 1913 United Stone Firms went into liquidation but continued trading under the receiver until 1926. The company was then restructured and taken out of receivership as United Stone Firms (1926) Ltd. Like the original firm they were in liquidation in 1932 and continued under the receiver until 1939. It was then acquired by the Forest of Dean Stone Firms Ltd who continue to this day with a stone works at Bixslade.

At Mireystock on the Severn & Wye's Lydbrook Branch was a siding serving a quarry and stone works of Mireystock Quarries Ltd but it is unknown if they had wagons of their own.

Whitecliff near Coleford had a quarry and limekiln operated by the Whitecliff Lime Co. and later the quarry was further developed and is still in use today.

Later a quarry was developed at Shakemantle south of Cinderford and on the site of a previous iron mine (see page 160). This quarry came to be owned by the Basic Lime & Stone Co. Ltd in 1911. In 1916 the leases were transferred to the Porthywaen Lime & Basic Co. Ltd of Oswestry. In 1930 they were taken over by the Steetley Lime & Building Stone Co. who traded at Shakemantle as the Steetly Lime & Basic Slag Co. They continued to work the quarry until 1948. Any of these companies may have worked wagons into Shakemantle.

Another late development was Drybrook Quarry at the extreme end of the Forest of Dean Branch. In 1926 it was operated by Drybrook Quarries Ltd, part of Joseph Ward of Sheffield. Again, they may have used their own wagons.

Shakemantle was one of the later quarries to start up in the Forest around 1911.

> ESTABLISHED 1760
>
> # E. R. PAYNE & SON LIMITED
>
> FOREST OF DEAN STONE MERCHANTS AND QUARRY OWNERS
>
> SAWING, PLANING, AND MOULDING MILLS

E. R. PAYNE & SON

Edwin R. Payne was a long-established business before the arrival of the railways having started in business in 1760. He set up a stone works at Parkend in 1870 and traded as E. R. Payne & Son. In 1905 a limited company was formed to take over the former business. Included in the sale to the new limited company were quarries at Wimberry, Bixhead, Point and Dark Hill and stone works at Parkend and Point Quarry. The company now set up a new stone yard in Point Quarry. Sidings served the Parkend works and Point Quarry and the company also had a crane on Bicslade Wharf. The new company was not a success and was wound up in May 1909, the business being taken over by the Forest of Dean Stone Firm.

THE WAGONS

The record books of the GRC&WCo. show that on the 13th July 1875 Edwin R. Payne acquired six 8-ton wagons for cash and that they were secondhand ex the Bristol Mineral Co. Payne would appear to have also had wagons on hire as in December 1875 a 10-ton wagon was rehired to James Smith of Stroud 'late Edwin R. Payne'.

There is one mention in the S&W letter books and that is of wagon No. 3 off the road at Point Quarry sidings on the 9th March 1899.

Included in the formation of the limited company in 1905 were six 8-ton wagons. These are probably the wagons which were the subject of a repairing contract taken out with the GRC&WCo. on the 14th June 1905 for five 8-ton and one 10-ton wagon for a period of 4 years. When Payne's interests were sold off in 1909 there were five 8-ton wagons listed. From a photograph in the auction catalogue it is just about possible to make out that at least one wagon still carried E. R. Payne & Son. The livery is unknown, from the photograph below it is possible to see that the lettering was shaded and appears to be white which probably rules out a stone coloured wagon. The likelihood is that they were either grey or red with white lettering shaded either black or red.

The auction catalogue photograph which shows an E. R. Payne wagon. It is the two-plank dumb-buffered example nearest the camera and on the original it is just possible to make out **'YNE & SON'**. What the rest of the lettering was is unknown.

Another partial view of a stone wagon, this time one belonging to David & Sant Ltd. It is just possible to discern the **DAV** on the top plank of what is a two or three-plank wagon. Standing next to it is a wagon built by the Midland Carriage & Wagon Co. which may give a clue as to where David & Sant obtained their wagons.
The Quarry and Builders' Merchant

DAVID & SANT

David & Co. had a stone works at Parkend and in 1892 amalgamated with other quarry companies to form David & Sant Ltd. This brought a stone works at Speech House Road and a second works at Parkend into their ownership. The amalgamation probably also brought more railway wagons but no details are known.

THE WAGONS

Little is known of the wagons apart from the partial view of a wagon reproduced above. It would appear that the livery was a stone coloured body with black lettering shaded red.

The prospectus for the formation of Forest of Dean Stone Firms in 1900 states that David & Sant were to bring into the new concern '37 nearly new 10-ton railway wagons'.

In the S&W letter books it is shown that on the 28th June 1898 wagon 105 was off road at Coleford Jnc. On the 23rd February 1899 wagon 135 was off at Parkend and on the 29th May wagons No's 170 and 90 were off at Travellers Rest. All of these were fairly close to

FOREST OF DEAN STONE FIRMS

The Forest of Dean Stone Firms was itself the result of an amalgamation between a couple of other quarrying concerns in 1910.

Again from the prospectus for the formation of the company it would appear that the only wagons coming in from the various concerns were those from Messrs David & Sant. Five more however, would have been acquired with the purchase of the business of Edwin Payne in 1909, though, as Forest of Dean Stone Firms itself was taken over the following year by United Stone Firms, it is possible that these wagons never received a repaint.

An entry in the S&W letter books for the 8th January 1904 records 'Dean Forest Stone Firms' wagon No. 5 and GW wagon No. 46906 damaged at Coleford Jct. on the 2nd of the month. The reference to 'Dean Forest Stone Firms' may be an error for Forest of Dean Stone Firms.

The Gloucester records only show that on the 10th July 1911 bad debts for repairs done to Forest of Dean Stone Firms wagons were written off. This would be after the company had been taken over by United Stone Firms.

No other details of their wagons are known and no photographs have been seen.

Photographed in December 1902 was this two-plank drop-sided wagon for E. Turner & Sons. Painted 'stone colour' with black lettering, shaded red and with black ironwork. Branded *'Empty to Bixslade Siding. Severn & Wye Railway.'* *GRC&WCo.*

E. TURNER & SONS

James Edward and William Henry Turner traded as E. Turner & Sons from Penarth Road, Cardiff. In 1899 they obtained a lease on a quarry at Dark Hill and also set up a stone works at Fetterhill. In 1900 they leased a quarry at Bixslade and set up a second stone works at the lower end of Bixslade, a works which still exists today. In 1910 the Forest of Dean interests of Turners were taken over by the United Stone Firms.

THE WAGONS

December 1902 saw two wagons photographed at Gloucester for Turners. One, No. 25 was a 6-plank coal wagon, whilst No. 26 was a drop-side stone wagon. Both were painted 'stone colour' with black lettering and ironwork and with red shading on the letters.

The only mention in the Severn & Wye letter books is on the 21st August 1908 when wagon No. 6 was derailed at Coleford Jct.

What happened to the wagons when Turners sold their Forest interests is unknown. It is possible that they were maintained to be used in connection with Turner's works in Cardiff.

Wagon No. 25 was listed on the information board as a 'coal wagon'. Presumably used to take coal to their stone works for use in steam crane boilers etc. *GRC&WCo.*

152

Three wagons of United Stone Firms alongside the Cannop Stone Works at Speech House Road. The two on the left are both two-plank wagons, that on the extreme left being a drop-side wagon whilst that numbered 32 has a centre side door. On the right is a dumb-buffered single plank wagon possibly numbered 135. The stone works here was originally established by Trotter, Thomas & Co. and was later operated by David & Sant and Forest of Dean Stone Firms.

UNITED STONE FIRMS

Set up in 1910 United Stone Firms Ltd took over most of the stone firms in the Forest of Dean for the sum of £31,500. However, the new company soon ran into difficulties and from July 1913 continued in business under the receiver with Walter Bryant of Coleford as secretary. In 1926 a new company, United Stone Firms (1926) Ltd was formed with Walter Bryant, William Langford and W. Neville as the first directors. As well as in the Forest of Dean they held quarries at Porthgain, Pembrokeshire; Hallatrow, Somerset; De Lank, Cornwall; Portland, Dorset and in Ireland.

The new company did not fare much better than its predecessor and a receiver was appointed in July 1931. In 1939 the Forest of Dean interests were sold to the Forest of Dean Stone Firms.

THE WAGONS

With such an amalgamation of companies as went into United Stone Firms the wagon fleet must have been from quite a variety of builders. Whilst it is known where some of the Forest of Dean quarry owners' wagons came from, others are unknown. All known details come from the wagon photographs reproduced here.

The Severn & Wye letter books also show that on the 3rd August 1917 United Stone Firms wagons No's 28 & 64 were off at the catch points at Point Sidings and that on the 17th May 1918 their wagon No. 5 and LNWR wagon No. 61420 were off the road at Point Quarry.

Livery, like most of the Forest quarry wagons, was 'stone' colour with black lettering.

Wagons being loaded (or unloaded) at the Cannop works. The stone looks very pale and could be Portland stone being brought into the works for dressing. Wagon No. 13 stands in the foreground. The wagons beyond appear to be railway company wagons. The photograph is taken from an empty coal wagon and shows detail of the metal strip which ran along the upper edge of the top plank.

Above: The end of a United Stone Firms wagon in the siding at the Fetterhill Stone Works which reveals that it was built by the Midland Carriage & Wagon Co. of Birmingham, the builders number may well be 37088.

Left: At Point Quarry Sidings off the Coleford Branch of the Severn & Wye three more United Stone Firms wagons can be seen. The nearest is a single-plank wagon. Then comes wagon No. 33 which is of similar appearance to No. 32 on the previous page. The furthest wagon appears to be numbered 24. Page 148 has another view of the Point Quarry sidings with wagon No. 27 visible.

Seen at Bicslade Wharf in 1939 are a pair of United Stone Firms (1926) Ltd wagons. Both are two-plank drop-side wagons but the further one has raised rounded ends. The nearest wagon is numbered 41 whilst the other is numbered in the 50s.

CLEE HILL GRANITE Co.

The Clee Hill Granite Co. worked quarries near Ludlow, Shropshire. The Severn & Wye letter books reveal that a Clee Hill Granite Co's wagon, No. 431, was damaged at Lydney on the 27th November 1904. It is likely that the wagon was bringing in a load of stone as there are many references in local newspapers of the various councils taking Clee Hill stone for road repairs as it was more durable than the local stone. From the wagon number it is possible that it was a fairly new wagon. One newspaper report of 1901 quoted a price for Clee Hill stone in trucks at Coleford Station but the council deemed it 'out of reason'!

The wagons were painted 'lead colour' with white lettering, shaded red and with black ironwork. At least three batches were supplied by the Gloucester Wagon Co.

154

A lime wagon for the Whitecliff Lime Company photographed at Gloucester in September 1886. It was painted 'stone' colour with black lettering and ironwork. The sloping roof, to keep the contents dry, is fitted with a sliding door on both sides to enable loading.
GRC&WCo.

WHITECLIFF LIME Co.

A private siding agreement was taken out with the Great Western Railway on the 15th October 1885 for a siding to serve a quarry and limekiln off the GWR's Coleford Branch, between Wyesham Junction on the Wye Valley line and Coleford, which had opened for traffic in September 1883. The sidings were ready for use by July 1886. Behind the Whitecliff Lime Co. were Goodrich Langham and Herbert Curwen. In 1904 the company was taken over by the Monmouth Steam Saw Mills Co. Ltd (see page 131) and in 1914 the Whitecliff Lime & Stone Co. was formed. Behind this company were the Monmouth Steam Saw Mills Co. with George Jones, Thomas Gwilliam and Ernest Boulton. By August 1930 the owners were Thomas Swan & Co. Ltd who operated until soon after the Second World War when the quarry was bought by Fred Watkins who traded as Fred Watkins (Whitecliff Quarries) Ltd. In the mid-1960s the quarry passed to Man-Abell (Whitecliff Quarry) Ltd.

After 1917 the quarry traffic was worked via the Severn & Wye's Coleford Branch and this continued until 1967.

THE WAGONS

In September 1886 three secondhand 10-ton wagons were let on seven years deferred purchase by the Gloucester Wagon Co. with the Lime Co. to keep the wagons in repair. In May 1887 a further three 10-ton wagons were let over 7 years deferred purchase.

Presumably between 1904 and 1914 wagons lettered for the Monmouth Steam Saw Mills were used which is possibly borne out by a Gloucester order dated 6th April 1914 when three secondhand 8-ton wagons were let on hire for 10 months to the Whitecliff Lime & Stone Co. which were described as 'late Monmouth Steam Saw Mills'. In September 1915 three 8-ton wagons were sold to the Whitecliff Lime Co. on seven years deferred payment.

From the Severn & Wye letter books it can be seen that on the 30th April 1907 Whitcliff Lime Co's wagon No. 1 was off the road at Coleford Jct.

One of the smaller quarries in the Forest served by a railway siding belonged to John Cooper who applied for one off the Forest of Dean Branch in June 1854 in connection with his 'Forest Stone Trade'. The siding, situated between the tunnels at Soudley, was removed by 1892. It is unknown whether Cooper had any wagons of his own.

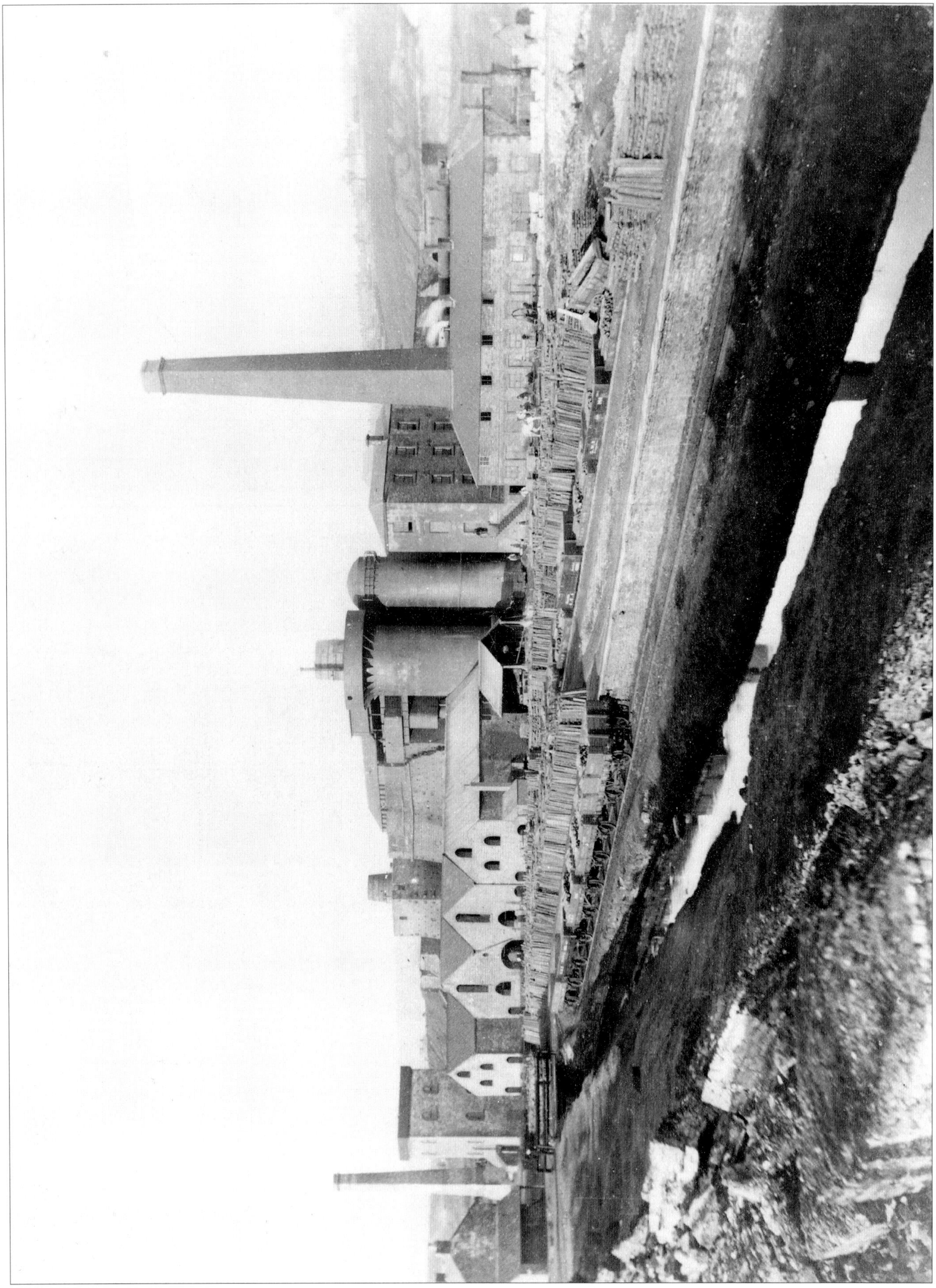

METALLIFEROUS

THE Forest of Dean coalfield lies on top of iron ore deposits which formed in the crease limestone. From early times iron was mined around the edge of the area leaving telltale surface workings known as 'scowles'. Later, deep mining was introduced, especially around the Cinderford and Milkwall/Bream areas. Even several South Wales ironmasters took the rich ores from the Forest to smelt in their blast furnaces.

The availability of iron ore, together with a plentiful supply of timber for making charcoal, led to the early establishment of an iron-smelting industry with many charcoal blast furnaces throughout the Forest. Later development of coke-fired blast furnaces led to the building of several such furnaces in the Forest – at Cinderford, Parkend and Soudley.

With the production of iron came many other connected industries, especially tinplate production but also wire works, forges and foundries, the latter supplying castings for use in the collieries and mines. Tinplate works were established at Lydbrook, Lydney, Parkend and Cinderford.

However, the heyday of Forest of Dean iron mining and working ended in the 1890s. The importation of cheaper foreign ores led to a decline in the demand for Forest ore. The last major iron mine working was at Shakemantle, south of Cinderford, which closed in 1899 but small quantities continued to be won until the end of the Second World War in the Milkwall and Sling area. A further spin-off of iron ore extraction is the finding of areas of iron oxides (ochre and red) known as 'colour'. This led to the setting up of several colour works in the area to produce pigments for use in paints. There were works at Milkwall (The British Colour & Mining Co.), Coleford (William Henry Fryer) and Lydney (William Jones, later Wellington, Jones & Co.).

The last blast furnace, at Cinderford, closed down in 1894. Tinplate continued to be made at Lydney until 1957.

One of the six 10-ton wagons bought by the Milkwall Ironstone Co. Although described as a 'coal wagon' it is likely that it was used for the transportation of iron ore – especially as it is branded *'Empty to Milkwall, GWR & Mid. Severn & Wye Joint Rly.'*. GRC&WCo.

EASTER IRON MINE

The story of this concern near Milkwall is rather complex with several owners through its working life all of whom had wagons but many also had other interests in the Forest. The mine was first galed in April 1846 and in June 1852 was leased to Osman Barrett, James Michaelmas Barrett and J. G. Borlase who traded as Barrett Brothers (see page 163). This partnership was wound up in August 1874. Until the Severn & Wye opened their Coleford Branch railway in July 1875 all traffic would have been taken down the Milkwall Tramroad for transshipment at Parkend.

Easter Hematite Iron Ore Co. Ltd
Incorporated in March 1874 to take over the Easter Iron Mine, Milkwall, from Messrs Barrett Brothers. The chairman of the company was Capt. Heyworth. In February 1880 the Gloucester Wagon Co. let ten secondhand 8-ton wagons on hire for an unspecified period. In March 1883 there is a record of a further hiring of ten secondhand wagons comprising six 7-ton, two 8-ton and two 10-ton wagons for a one year period. Whether these replaced the original hiring or were extra is unknown. Work appears to have ceased at the mine by December 1883 and the company was wound up in January 1884 but may well have continued trading.

Milkwall Ironstone Co.
The Milkwall Ironstone Co. was formed circa 1910 to work the Easter Iron Mine.

In November 1911 they bought six 10-ton wagons on 7 years deferred payment from the Gloucester Wagon Co. These three-plank wagons were painted 'chocolate' brown with white lettering and black shading and ironwork.

However, the company was not to last long and in July 1916 sold out to the Easter Iron Ore Mines Ltd which went into voluntary liquidation in 1924. The buildings at Milkwall alongside the Sling Branch then passed to the British Colour & Mining Co. Ltd.

Memorandum.

FROM
R. WATKINS & SONS,
West Dean and Newland
Iron and Colour Mines,
BREAM, LYDNEY.

— Also Proprietors of Coal, Limestone, and Gravel. —

Telegrams: "WATKINS, WHITECROFT."

July 21st 1897

A Baylies Esq
Arlind

RICHARD WATKINS

Richard Watkins leased New Dun Pit Iron Mine near Sling from Henry Crawshay from *circa* 1877. A siding, served by a tramway from the mine was provided by the Severn & Wye in 1880 at the end of a branch from Milkwall Station.

In April 1902 Crawshay's interests were assigned to Messrs Watkins who also acquired Sling Pit the following year. By 1921 the works were in the hands of Fred Watkins who began to develop an engineering works where secondhand machinery was reconditioned. The works still operate on the site today.

THE WAGONS

Twelve 10-ton wagons were acquired from the Western Wagon Co. in March 1880 over five years redemption purchase and seven 10-ton wagons were added in November 1885 over seven years.

In 1902 the railway Joint Committee were trying to recover siding dues and seized two of Richard Watkins wagons, No's 16 and 19 until the debt was paid.

No details of Richard Watkins livery can be traced. The wagons would later have been lettered for Fred Watkins but livery details are unknown apart from what can be deduced from the photograph reproduced below.

Below: A variety of wagons belonging to Fred Watkins stand on the siding at the end of the Sling Branch with the loading chute and buildings of the New Dun Pit Iron Mine behind. The clearest wagon is the seven-plank, side and end door No. 35 in front of the chute. The smaller lettering reads '**IRON ORE AND COLOUR MINES**' whilst bottom right reads 'Coleford'. The four plank to its left, which also appears to have an end door, is lettered '**MINE OWNER AND COAL FACTOR**'. Unfortunately its number is obscured.

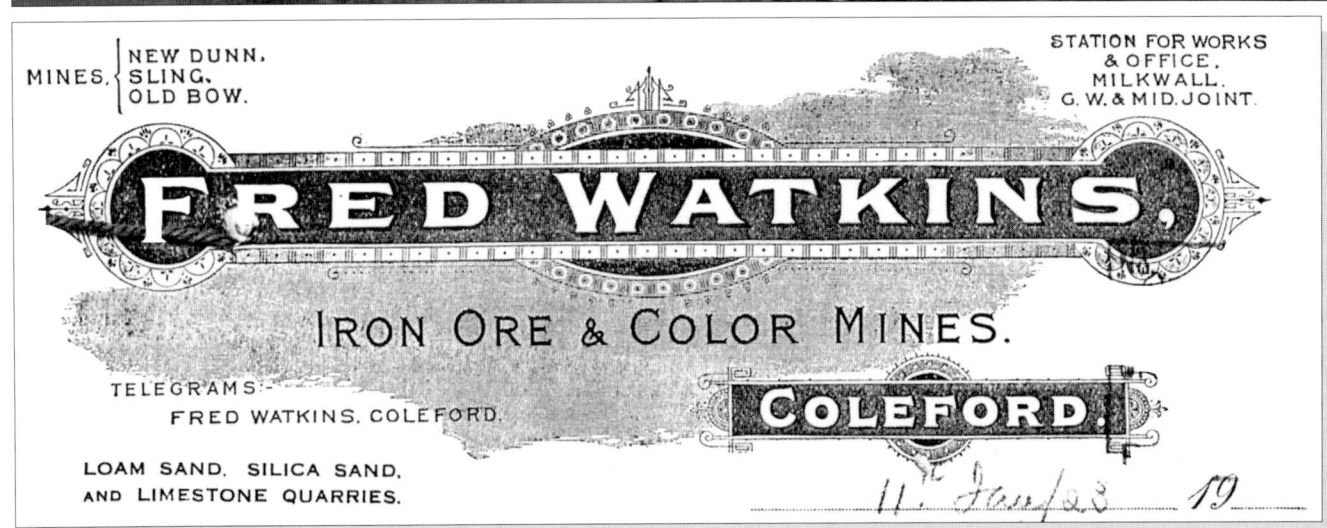

MINES: NEW DUNN. SLING. OLD BOW.

STATION FOR WORKS & OFFICE.
MILKWALL.
G.W. & MID. JOINT.

FRED WATKINS,
IRON ORE & COLOR MINES.
COLEFORD.

TELEGRAMS:
FRED WATKINS, COLEFORD.

LOAM SAND, SILICA SAND,
AND LIMESTONE QUARRIES.

Taken from a very faded original this is the only photograph known to show the 'covered way' at Parkend where the Severn & Wye Railway passed underneath the access to the furnace tops at the Parkend Ironworks. The arch of the covered way can be seen in the centre of the view. The broad gauge branch serving the ironworks by which ore and coke would have been delivered ran above the house on the left. Turntables were provided in the coke yard to facilitate the movement of wagons from one siding to another. The Parkend Tinplate Works were off to the left.
courtesy Tony Wright

FOREST OF DEAN IRON Co.

The Forest of Dean Iron Co. was formed in 1824 by Moses Teague, William Montague and Benjamin Whitehouse who took a lease on blast furnaces at Parkend. In 1826 Montague was joined by John James and in 1847 James became the sole lessee. In 1854 he bought the works outright and took Charles Greenham on as manager and, later, partner. Following a depression in trade, the works were sold in 1875 to Edwin Crawshay and then were taken over by Henry Crawshay & Son. At the end of 1877 the works closed and were not to reopen, demolition starting in 1890.

THE WAGONS
With the arrival of the broad gauge at Parkend in 1869 the Forest of Dean Iron Co. may well have had some broad gauge wagons. With the gauge conversion in 1872 comes the first record in Gloucester Wagon Co. records which shows that ten 8-ton wagons were purchased in March 1872 on seven year redemption hire. In September 1873 twenty 8-ton wagons were ordered on the same terms. The minute books of the Western Wagon Co. gives the Forest of Dean Iron Co. as debtors in 1873. Later in the year there is a record that they had 33 wagons on simple hire. The following year, 1874, this number had reduced to 27 and in 1876 it was down to 10 but 40 wagons were being purchased on redemption hire. The problems of the works is reflected in the minutes of the Wagon Co. when in August 1877 it is shown that 17 wagons were idle, of which 11 were at Lydney. The Iron Company still had 10 wagons on simple hire and 40 on redemption hire. After August 1878 there is no futher mention of the Forest of Dean Iron Co.

PARKEND TINPLATE Co.

The tinplate works at Parkend were built by James and Greenham between 1851 and 1853. They then sold them to Samuel Ries who leased them to Nathaniel Daniels who traded as the Parkend Plate Co. In 1856 the works were bought by the Allaways of Lydney Tinplate Works. They were for sale in 1872 and in 1875 were bought by Edwin Crawshay. In 1879 they were leased to Charles Morris of Llanelly, trading as the Parkend Tinplate Co. The works closed in September 1881.

THE WAGONS
The only reference to wagons for the tinplate works comes in the minutes of the Western Wagon Co. On the 24th August 1880 the Parkend Tinplate Co. ordered eight 10-ton wagons on five year redemption hire. These were seized back in May 1882 and resold to the Dean Forest Coal Co.

The site of the tinplate works siding at Parkend. The works themselves were on the right of this view looking south towards Parkend Station.

Above: The Shakemantle Iron Mine of Henry Crawshay & Co. A tramroad connection to Cinderford Ironworks came in at high level on the ledge behind the buildings. The Forest of Dean Branch lies hidden in the valley, the siding runs in front of the large engine house.

Left: A cruel enlargement off another view of the Shakemantle site reveals three wagons lettered up for Crawshay. Simply lettered **HENRY CRAWSHAY & Co.** with a running number on the left and **CINDERFORD** on the right.

HENRY CRAWSHAY & Co.

As well as owning the various collieries already mentioned (Lightmoor, Eastern United and Northern United) Henry Crawshay had many more interests throughout the Forest including iron mines and ironworks. His interest at Parkend has already been noted in this section. However, it was with the Cinderford Ironworks that Henry's father, William, a noted ironmaster from Merthyr Tydfil in South Wales, became involved in the Forest. William became a partner with several others in the Cinderford Iron Co. in 1832.

With the opening of the Forest of Dean Branch as a broad gauge railway in 1854 a siding was built into the ironworks together with a connection to Lightmoor Colliery. Also in that year William Crawshay transferred 50% of his interest to his son Henry. In 1862 Henry was able to issue a notice stating that he would carry on the works alone, trading as the Cinderford Ironworks. Henry died in 1879 but the works continued under the name of Henry Crawshay & Co. until Henry Crawshay & Co. Ltd was formed in 1889. They closed in 1894.

To supply the ironworks iron ore mines were developed in the Cinderford area with most of the ore being brought to the surface at Shakemantle. The iron mine finally closed in 1898. A siding was provided with connections at either end from the opening of the FoD Branch but as Crawshays built their own tramroad connection between the iron mine and the ironworks it was probably used mainly for incoming traffic or ore sold to other ironworks.

THE WAGONS

Little is known of wagons supplied to Henry Crawshay & Co. Ten 10-ton wagons were supplied from the Western Wagon Co. in January 1880 and were booked to Henry Crawshay & Sons. These were followed in September 1881 by twenty 8-ton wagons.

As the photograph reproduced here is the only known view of wagons so lettered it is impossible to determine the livery. Numbers appear to be in the 200s, possibly 237, 247 and 252. They are likely to have been used in connection with other of Crawshays non-colliery interests but could well have been run into Lightmoor Colliery if they were short of wagons there.

Looking south-east off the top of Bradley Hill Tunnel *circa* 1875/6 with the Forest of Dean Branch curving round towards Haie Hill Tunnel. In the centre of the view can be seen the Soudley Ironworks with their works locomotive standing in the sidings. The coke wagons in the sidings certainly belong to the Great Western Iron Company, the rest are not identifiable.

GREAT WESTERN IRON Co.

The Great Western Iron Co. worked the blast furnaces at Soudley for a relatively short period between 1875 and 1877. Iron making on this site had been started in 1836. By 1863 the furnaces were being worked by Messrs Goold Brothers who have already been mentioned several times in this volume. They certainly had wagons and these could, and probably were, used in conjunction with the Soudley works. However, none of them can be directly put down to the works here and no images of them have been seen. The Goold period of ownership was during the time that the Forest of Dean Branch was broad gauge. The works closed for a period during 1867 and Goolds managed to sell them off in 1873.

There were then several changes of ownership until in May 1875 they were bought by Messrs Morrison and Beauclerk who formed the Great Western Iron Co. Ltd. After a promising start, during which time a brand new furnace was built, the works succumbed to foreign competition in 1877 and the furnace was blown out – the new one had never seen any use. The works were demolished during 1899.

THE WAGONS

Originally broad gauge wagons for Messrs Goold Brothers would have worked to the ironworks as mentioned on page 14. Whether any converted or standard gauge wagons for the Goolds worked to Soudley is uncertain.

A series of three photographs of the works, one of which is reproduced at the head of the page, are the only evidence found of wagons for Soudley Ironworks during the ownership of the Great Western Iron Co. Even these only give distant views from which it is only possible to make out the main lettering.

Suppliers for any of the wagons have not been found.

An enlargement off the above view where the wording **GREAT WESTERN** can be made out along the top planks.

From another view taken on the same occasion is this enlargement of some coal wagons. Again **GREAT WESTERN** can be discerned with a wagon number in the centre. The second line appears to read **IRON Co**. After that, frustratingly, the lettering cannot be defined.

The tinplate works at Lydney.

RICHARD THOMAS

In 1871 Richard Thomas took a lease on a tinplate works at Lydbrook which had been idle for several years. In 1875 he took over the lease on the works at Lydney. Both had sidings off the Severn & Wye Railway. In 1884 Richard Thomas & Co. Ltd was formed to operate the two works. The works at Lydbrook closed in 1925. Lydney worked through until the Second World War when the buildings were requisitioned by the Admiralty. After the war the works re-opened under Richard Thomas & Baldwin, finally closing in 1957.

THE WAGONS

Details of wagon purchases by Richard Thomas are thin on the ground. In March 1894 he took twenty 10-ton wagons from the Western Wagon Co. which had been built by B. P. Blockley. They were to be paid for over three years but there are no records of payments after September. Whether this was because the wagons were paid for at this point or if Thomas defaulted is unknown.

The Severn & Wye letter books show that R. Thomas & Co's wagon No. 206 was off the line on the 22nd August 1898 at Lydney, and wagon No. 12 was off at Lydney Engine Shed Box on the 1st August 1899.

On the 19th February 1904 wagon No. 39 was off the road at Parkhill Siding on the Oakwood Branch. On the 1st November wagon No. 57 was damaged at Lydney Jct. It should be added that some of these wagons might have been being used in connection with Thomas's Lydbrook Colliery.

Taken at Lydney this fine group of workers sadly obscure part of a Richard Thomas wagon lettered up for his tinplate business. The five-plank side and end door wagon is obviously of some age. It is lettered **RICHARD THOMAS** & *Company Limited*. **LYDNEY IRON & TIN WORKS**. There is also something in the centre of the side door which might be a number 11 or some form of identification mark. Livery is unknown.

The Lydbrook works were in the bottom of the valley, connected to the Severn & Wye by a 1 in 25 incline which can be seen running behind the chimney.

The Unknowns, Metalliferous

The Forest of Dean Iron & Steel Co. Ltd
Nothing is known of this concern but they appear in the Gloucester order book when on the 13th March 1877 they placed an order for sixty new 8-ton wagons on deferred purchase over seven years. It could be an error in the Gloucester minutes for the Forest of Dean Iron Co.

Dean Forest Hematite Iron Ore Co.
The Dean Forest Hematite Iron Ore Co. (Jarrett Bros) ordered from the Western Wagon Co. six 10-ton wagons in March 1880 on seven years deferred purchase and five 8-ton wagons over five years in October 1885. Wagons may well have been used in conjunction with iron mines on the Lydney Park estate and loading may well have taken place at Tufts Junction where a loading bank existed on the Oakwood Branch.

The Forest Hematite Co.
Again, nothing at present is known of this company. In April 1891 five 8-ton wagons were ordered from the Western Wagon Co. The company cannot have had a long life as no payments for the wagons were made after January 1894 and it is assumed that the wagons returned to the wagon company.

Staunton Iron Co.
Yet another company of whom nothing is known which might have Forest connections. On the 5th November 1869 twenty-two colliery trams were ordered from the Cheltenham & Swansea Wagon Co. but it was minuted that this was not to be accepted unless better terms could be agreed. Later in the month an order for 12 low-sided wagons on 7 years redemption hire was taken on.

Osman Barrett
On the 30th March 1870 an order was placed with the Cheltenham & Swansea Railway Carriage & Wagon Co. by Osman Barrett of Mitcheldean for 15 broad gauge wagons on seven years redemption hire including repairs at £20 per wagon per annum. Barrett had many interests throughout the Forest including a share in Foxes Bridge Colliery as well as Easter Iron Mine and Fair Play Iron Mine. The wagons referred to may have been lettered for one of these concerns or for Barrett Brothers.

There are also two entries in the Gloucester Wagon Co. books. One, dated the 9th July 1878 is for repairs to one wagon for cash. The other of the 14th July 1880 writes off a bad debt for wagon repair, probably that repaired in 1878.

Osman Barrett snr. died in 1890.

W. H. Fryer
In March 1876 10 wagons were ordered by W. H. Fryer on seven year redemption hire at £11 15s. 0d. pwpa from the Cheltenham & Swansea Wagon Co. Fryer had interests in iron mines in the Milkwall/Sling areas and in 1875 had been seeking the provision of siding accommodation by the Severn & Wye. It is likely that the wagons were used in conjunction with these. Details of lettering and livery unknown.

Jacob Chivers
Already mentioned under coal unknowns at Hawkwell Colliery he may also have had wagons in connection with his Hawkwell Tinplate Works.

A. C. Bright
Also had wagons in connection with Hawkwell Tinplate Works but no further details are known. It is interesting to speculate that tinplate was often boxed and dispatched in covered goods wagons i.e. box vans. Did Chivers or Bright, or indeed Richard Thomas, ever have any privately owned box vans running in the Forest.

Whimsey
Whimsey was the northern limit of the Forest of Dean Branch and here interchange sidings were provided with several tramroad lines. A major traffic from this point was iron ore brought down from the Wigpool and Westbury Brook mines.

Westbury Brook Iron Mine
Westbury Brook Iron Mine was owned by Sir Josiah John Guest of the Dowlais Iron Co. It is likely therefore, that wagons lettered up for Dowlais were used for the transportation of the iron ore. The mine closed in 1893.

A Dowlais ironworks wagon photographed at Gloucester in October 1899. Painted black with white lettering. Were such wagons seen in the Forest in connection with the iron ore trade? GRC&WCo.

Wigpool Iron Mine
Wigpool was, at the time of the arrival of the broad gauge, in the hands of Messrs Allaway who had interests in the ironworks at Cinderford and in the tinplate works at Lydbrook and Lydney. They certainly had broad gauge wagons as mentioned on page 13. In December 1871 they formed the Lydney & Wigpool Iron Ore Co. Ltd. Ore production at Wigpool ceased in 1883. An auction in 1887 makes no mention of railway wagons but one of the mortgagees of the property, Samuel Fox of the Stocksbridge Ironworks, Sheffield, may have acquired some of them as there were internal user wagons at the works which were always referred to as 'the Lydneys'.

Ebbw Vale
Another South Wales concern with an iron mining interest in the Forest was the Ebbw Vale Co. They had iron mines in the Oakwood Valley close to Bream. Where the ore was loaded is uncertain but it could well have been at the Marsh Sidings at Parkend where the Oakwood Tramroad terminated on a transshipment wharf. Ore may well have been taken to Lydney for shipping to Newport.

Cinderford Crushing Co.
The Cinderford Crushing Co. was formed by Arthur Morgan, E. W. Morgan, G. F. Morgan, F. G. Washbourn and William Crawshay. It was started in 1894 with the closure of Cinderford Ironworks to dispose of the accumulation of slag and cinders. This material was mainly used as railway ballast and for road construction. The company later took similar material from the Soudley Ironworks site and also from several collieries. Arthur Morgan was also removing material from sites in South Wales. It can only be assumed that the company may have had wagons but it is possible that the material was removed using railway company wagons. This was probably the case at Cinderford where the Great Western took regular trains of ballast off the siding to the old Cinderford Ironworks.

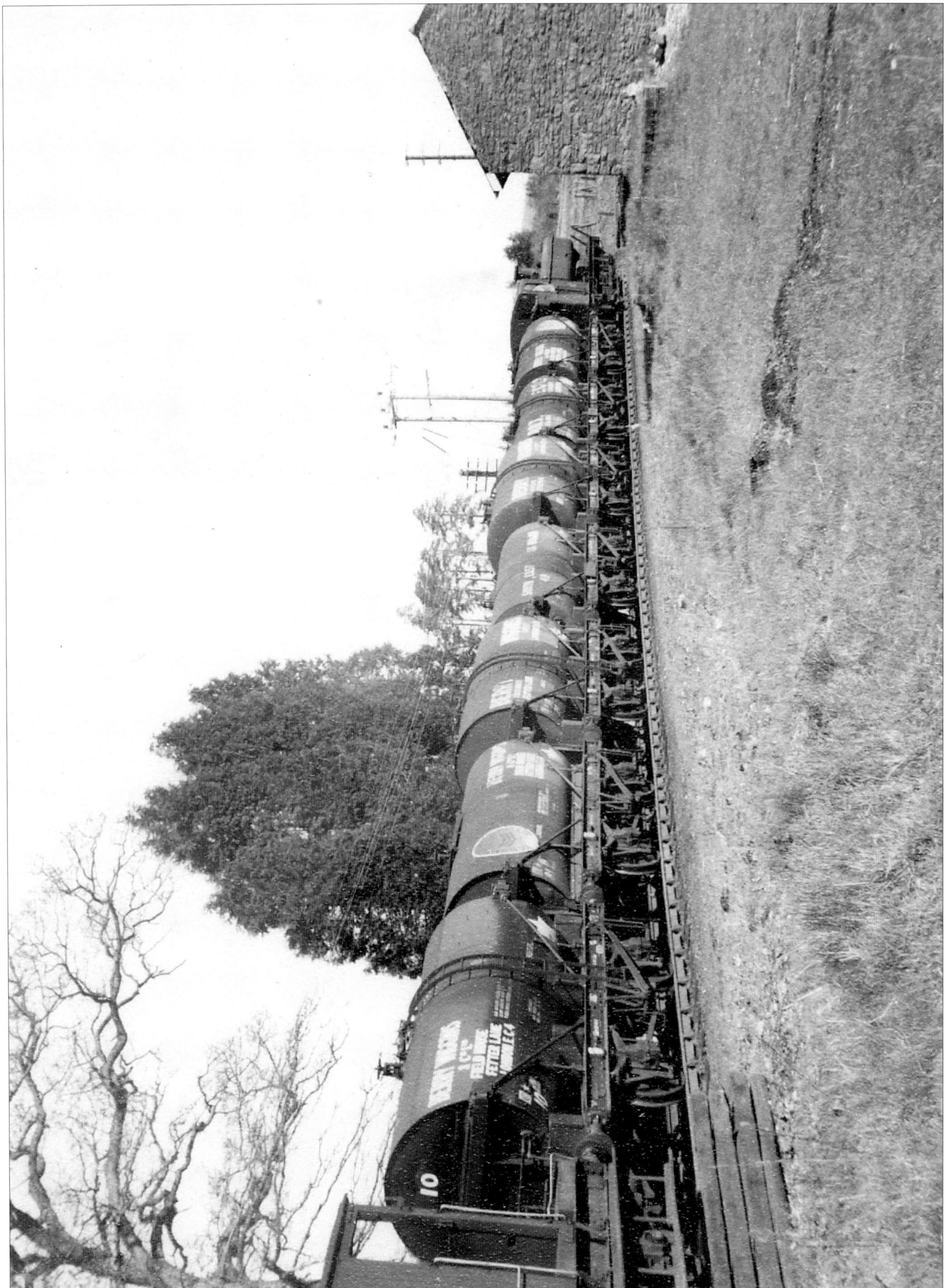

An early view of the Whimsey depot, probably c.1950 with a variety of Berry Wiggins' tankers stood on the siding, all displaying variations in livery. *Chapman, Cinderford*

BERRY WIGGINS

Berry Wiggins produced bitumen from a plant at Sharnel Street on the Isle of Grain, Kent. They had a head office in Stratford, East London. The company was trading in 1924 and possibly earlier. It was not until 1949 however, that they set up a depot at Whimsey. Initially it would appear that they just used the siding behind the goods shed but eventually they took over the entire site of the Cinderford Goods Station including the goods shed itself.

The bitumen was brought to Whimsey in lagged tank wagons. These could be heated to warm the bitumen and allow it to flow, either into storage tanks or directly into road tankers for distribution around west Gloucestershire and Herefordshire.

Traffic for Berry Wiggins was virtually the last to use the Forest of Dean Branch and with the removal of the depot to Lydney in 1967 the branch was closed. Up until this date Berry Wiggins tank wagons were a daily sight with about six or seven wagons being brought in and the empties returned – the last private owner traffic in the Forest.

THE WAGONS

The company had a large fleet of tank wagons for both Class A (highly inflammable) and Class B liquids and also for bitumen. The photographs show the variety of different outlines of the tanks suggesting that they were obtained over a long period and from a variety of different builders. Charles Roberts of Wakefield and the Cambrian Wagon Co. are known to have provided wagons to the fleet. Later it would seem that many of the tank wagons were hired from the British Railway Traffic and Electric Co.Ltd (B.R.T. & E. Co. Ltd).

The wagons were painted black with white lettering. The circular plate on the sides was a pale yellow with red sergeant's stripes. There has been a suggestion that Berry Wiggins' wagons were painted dark green. This could be a possibility for earlier wagons or for those involved in Class A traffic. Certainly from memory (always dangerous!) and from colour photographs and film the wagons in the 1960s were black.

A close-up of wagons being discharged into a road tanker. Wagon No's 49 and 61 are identifiable. *Chapman, Cinderford*

In this builder's official photograph the yellow circular plate with its red stripes is prominent. The smaller lettering at the top reads 'Liquaphalt' which was Berry Wiggins' trade name for its bitumen whilst under the stripes reads 'British Made' and lower still 'Stratford E. 15'. The white star denotes that the wagon was suitable for running as 'fast traffic' – up to a maximum of 35 mph.   *HMRS*

A view from above gives good detail of the tank fillers and vents. Notice also the different sizes of tanks and styles of lettering. Neither of these wagons, No's 28 and 82, carry the sergeant's stripes roundel. The **BERRY WIGGINS** spread across the length of the tank as on No. 28 appears to be the earlier form of lettering.

Ben Ashworth

Tank No. 131 at Whimsey gives detail of the address lettering and also the small 'For repairs' lettering which appears under the & Co. Ltd.   *Alec Pope*

166

Above & right: Two tank wagons belonging to B.R.T.&E.Co. Ltd whose offices were at 13 Grosvenor Crescent, London. They had a large fleet of wagons and these were on hire to Berry Wiggins. The livery was black with white lettering. *both Alec Pope*

Wagons belonging to the South Eastern Gas Board also worked into the depot at Whimsey. These had a red oxide painted barrel with white lettering and black solebar and running gear. No's 49 and 35 are seen here. *Left: Alec Pope, right: Ben Ashworth*

SHARPNESS CHEMICAL Co.

Very little can be found on the Sharpness Chemical Co., a company history file does exist in the Public Record Office but has still to be consulted. However, it appears that the company was formed in 1903 and that they were tar distillers located next to the gas works in Sharpness Docks. Both wagons were built by R. Y. Pickering of Glasgow; No. 24 was painted on the 14th October 1903 and was registered by the Midland Railway, No. 33 was painted on the 2nd November. No. 24 as well as the registration plate and the diamond-shaped builder's plate, carries an owner's plate which reads Sharpness Chemical Co. Sharpness Docks Glos.

MISCELLANEOUS

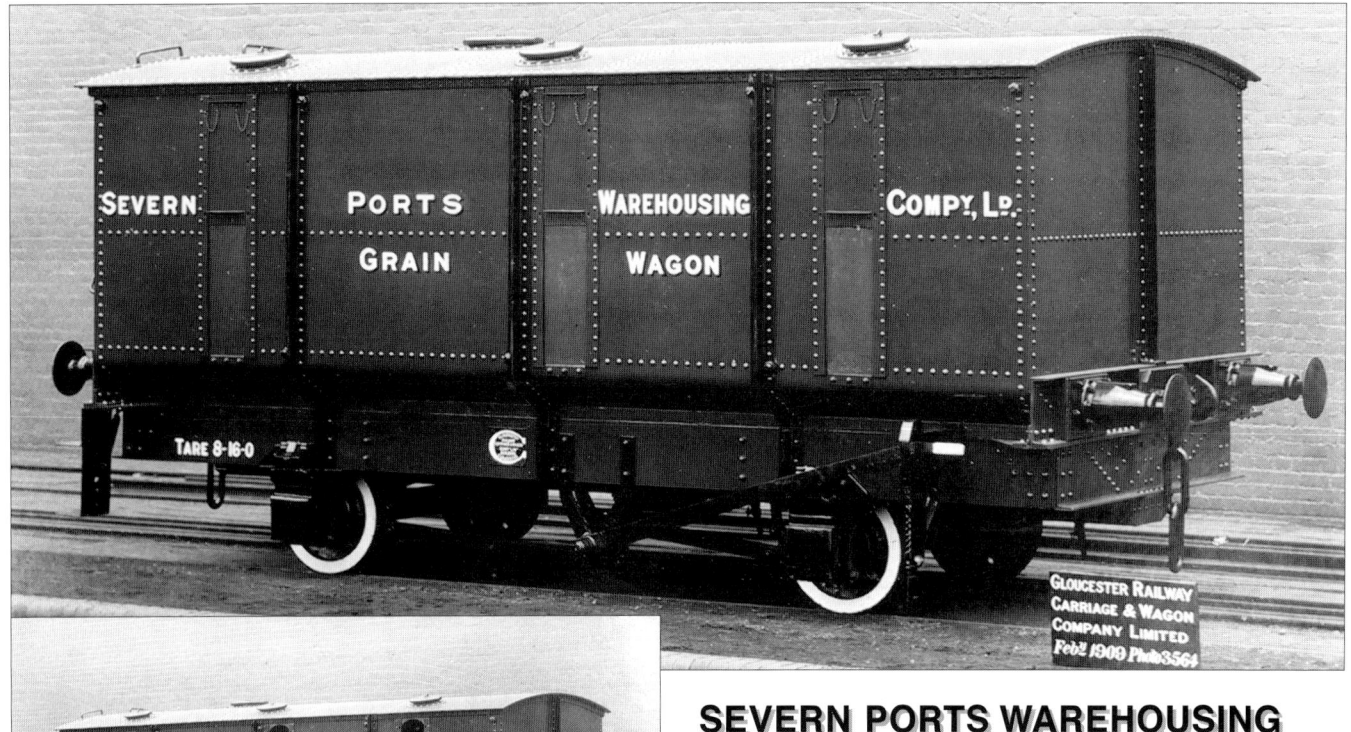

SEVERN PORTS WAREHOUSING

Remaining in Sharpness Docks we have this grain wagon built by Gloucester and photographed in February 1909. It was presumably an 'internal user' wagon only as it carries no railway company registration plates but this could be because it was photographed prior to registration. A postcard view of the docks does show the wagon in use on the quayside but more details would be welcome. *GRC&WCo.*

SPILLERS

Finally, the only known view of a privately owned covered goods wagon in the Forest. The Great Western Railway originally introduced their 'Iron Mink' wagons in 1884 (an example stands to the left of the Spillers wagon). So successful were they that private builders copied the design. Messrs Spillers were flour millers with mills in Cardiff and between 1906 and 1907 they acquired 300 such vehicles from Messrs Harrison & Camm of Rotherham. After a court case over freight rates Spillers sold their wagons to the Great Western in 1911. Thus it is possible to date the view above to circa 1910/1911 and it is likely that flour was being delivered for use in a local bakery.

A Great Western 0-6-0 saddle tank pulls a wagon out of the works at Bullo. Sadly it is not a Forest of Dean wagon.   *collection Pete Ball*

LOCAL WAGON BUILDERS

CHELTENHAM

At Cheltenham from an early period were the wagon works belonging to William Shackleford. He was trading as early as 1852 and at some point went into partnership with a Mr Ford, trading as Shackleford, Ford & Co. In 1866 a limited company was formed to take over the business but soon it was discovered that the two principals in the business had been 'misappropriating' money. They were removed from the scene and it was decided to rename the company the Cheltenham & Swansea Wagon Co. Ltd, presumably to get away from any reference to the disgraced Shackleford and Ford. The company were certainly supplying wagons, both broad and narrow (standard) gauge, to the Forest of Dean and were probably the nearest wagon company to the Forest at this time.

The business does not seem to have thrived, there were bank loans to be paid off and wagons were being put out to finance with other companies including the Bristol Wagon Co. and the Scottish Wagon Co. Some contracts were even being made straight over to the banks so that they were guaranteed their money. In 1870 the works at Cheltenham were sold off and all wagon building was then concentrated at Swansea. To reflect this the company name was changed once again, this time to the Swansea Wagon Co. Ltd. In 1886 the company became part of the Gloucester Carriage & Wagon Co. and in 1894 the Swansea works were closed down.

BULLO PILL

Joseph Boucher had been doing work for the Cheltenham & Swansea Wagon Co. in September 1866 as cheques were being made out to him but it is believed that the building of wagons at Bullo only started when Boucher transferred his business from London around 1873. A siding agreement for a connection to the works was taken out in July of that year. Trade directories describe Boucher's business in 1874 as being a railway carriage and wagon builder and a brass and ironfounder who would undertake wagon repairs on the Great Western mainline between Reading and Chepstow.

On the 18th March 1875 the Bullo Pill & Forest of Dean Wagon Co. Ltd was incorporated with a capital of £50,000 in 2,500 £20 shares to 'acquire the iron foundry, steam engine, forges, hydraulic clipping and other machinery, tanks, saw mills, shops, offices, buildings, stock in trade, plant, railway trucks let on hire, nine dwelling houses, land tenements, hereditaments and premises with the appurtenances and other property called the Bullo Pill Waggon works situate at Bullo Pill lately carried on by Joseph Boucher'. However the property was not transferred to this company and in June 1880 it was stated that the company never carried on business and so was dissolved.

Boucher may have been trading throughout this period as the Newnham & Bullo Wagon Works Co. until in January 1884 he filed for bankruptcy with debts of £11,500. In June 1888 the works were put up for auction under an action from the Sheriff of Gloucester but it is unclear as to whether they were sold as in 1889 the works were being run by William Boucher, possibly a son of Joseph and trading as the Forest of Dean Wagon Co. and then in February 1890 it was converted into a limited company.

Incorporated on the 21st February 1890 the Forest of Dean Wagon Co. Ltd had a capital of £5,000 in 1,000 £5 shares. The subscribers included Stephen Wallace Hadingham. The assets that the company was to acquire included 74 railway wagons (let on hire) and 10 railway trucks 'recently bought of Sir Hussey Vivian'. It also acquired the debts of the company, said to be £1,895 4s. 7d. and, not surprisingly perhaps, the company was wound up on the 31st March 1892 with William Boucher and Phipps Williams to take over all liabilities and assets for the paid up capital, viz: £3,290. Boucher and Williams formed a partnership to trade as Messrs Boucher, Williams & Co.

In April 1893 the Standard Wagon Co. Ltd was incorporated to take over the works at Bullo. This time the capital was put at £10,000 and the subscribers included William Boucher who was also to be manager. In January 1894 an agreement was signed with Stephen Haddingham, a bank manager from Newnham, for the purchase of 125 wagons on seven-year redemption hire from the British Wagon Co. for the sum of £1,500.

However, once again, financial liabilities became too great and in May 1895 the company went into liquidation and was taken over as a going concern [!] by a company with exactly the same name as its predecessor. The subscribers were also the same but the capital to be raised was down to £5,000. The new company was closely connected with the Railway Wagon & Engineering Co. Ltd of Swansea who also had William Boucher as their engineer. This latter company had been incorporated in December 1894.

The new Standard Wagon Co. was as unsuccessful as the first and in February 1899 was wound up. Yet again, a new company was formed and again was given an almost identical title, this time the Standard Wagon & Carriage Co. Ltd. The capital was a massive £50,000 of which £28,600 was to purchase the Bullo works. Again no investors could be found and the wagon side of the business was sold to the Albion Carriage Co. Ltd who had works at Grange Court, which lay between Newnham and Gloucester on the mainline, and which also had Boucher as managing director. Once more it failed and was wound up in September 1902.

William Boucher and Charles Boucher then traded for a while as the National Wagon Company doing wagon repairs and also producing buffers and in 1903 took out a patent for an 'improved buffer'. In October a new company, the National Trading Co. Ltd was formed to acquire the works and the rights to the buffer. The subscribers were Hubert Gopsill Brown of Gloucester, merchant; Wm Harris jnr of Newnham, wagon builder; Felix Russell of Newnham, wagon builder; Charles William Stafford Boucher of Newnham, wagon builder; William Robert Trigg of Severn View, Newnham, an insurance agent; David Northway of Westbury, wagon builder; and Thomas King of Newnham, also a wagon builder. The manager once again was William Boucher but as with all the other companies the new one was in trouble by 1906 and was dissolved in May 1907.

Possibly no more work was done at the works after this date and the siding agreement was terminated in May 1916.

Of interest is the interaction between various wagon builders. The records of the Western Wagon Co. show that they were both selling wagons to, and buying wagons from Boucher! Presumably Boucher was buying wagons to hire out but it is possible that he was buying wagons in order to complete wagon orders. The same applied the other way with the Western Wagon Co. buying in wagons when the price was right.

There is a minute in the Western Wagon Co's books for the supply of 141 8- and 10-ton wagons to the Standard Wagon Co. in October 1896 and then in 1899 the taking of some of them back into stock following the demise of the Standard Wagon Co.

In December 1901 the Western Wagon Co. sold 122 wagons to the Albion Carriage Co. of which Western Wagon had acquired fifty from the Lincoln Wagon Co. Whilst being paid for the wagons of the Albion Carriage Co. had to carry Western Wagon Co. owner's plates (and some possibly Lincoln Wagon Co. plates as well). All very confusing for the historian and modeller!

There is also a reference in 1888 to a person named Mountjoy, a Newnham wagon builder who had a works at Bullo Pill but nothing further is known. The 'works' may well have been just a repairing hut in Bullo Yard.

Two views taken inside Gloucester Wagon Co. showing the construction of private owner coal wagons. In the upper view the underframes are being assembled whilst in the lower view finishing touches are being made to a rake of RCH 1923 standard seven-plank wagons. *Neil Parkhouse collection*

GLOUCESTER

The history of the Gloucester Wagon Co. is well documented elsewhere (Mike Christensen, The Gloucester Wagon Co. Ltd, *British Railway Journal*, No's 6, Winter 1985, & 7, Spring 1986) so only a short history is needed here.

The Gloucester Wagon Company Ltd was formed in February 1860 and leased land in Gloucester on which to build their works. The company grew quickly and were to produce many wagons for Forest of Dean companies as witnessed by this volume. They also supplied smaller wagon builders, such as Boucher at Newnham, with wagon parts, especially castings or forged metalwork – drawbar hooks, side knees, axleguards, brakeracks, brakework, wheels, etc. being some of the material.

The company continued to trade right through the period covered by private wagon ownership and as well as supplying wagons for purchase also had many out on simple hire – between June 1874 and June 1875 for example over 6,900 wagons were out on hire and over 5,200 had been sold on redemption hire. The ending of private wagon usage at the end of the Second World War must have come as quite a blow to the company. Presumably any wagons that it still had on hire were requisitioned and added into the general pool.

The records of the company, now held at the Gloucestershire Records Office, and especially the photographic albums, have proved invaluable in compiling this work and I thank the staff for their tireless efforts in wheeling the volumes in and out of the store.

APPENDIX ONE
CRAWSHAY ORDERS

The Crawshay Minute Books, now held in the Gloucestershire Records Office, contain details of orders placed for the period April 1908 to August 1917. They give virtually the only insight into the working of one of the Forest's collieries and, as such, are invaluable. The orders are reproduced below to give some idea of the monthly trade for one of the larger housecoal collieries in the Forest of Dean – Lightmoor – and for one of the new deep gale collieries – Eastern United.

Note: FOR = Free on rail. FOB = Free on board.

15 APRIL 1908
The Manager reported he had made the following contracts since the last meeting:-
1,000 tons of small coal for **Dean Forest Coal Co.**, Cinderford, at 6/9 per ton F.O.R. in buyers trucks at colliery less 6d. per ton rebate and 2^1/$_2$% discount for delivery to **Messrs Richard Thomas & Co.**, Lydney at the rate of 50 tons per week.
1,200 tons of small coal to **Messrs Sully & Co.** at 6/9 per ton in buyers trucks at colliery less 6d. per ton rebate and 2^1/$_2$% discount for delivery to **Messrs Princess Royal Colliery Co.** at the rate of 50 tons per week.
1,300 tons of small coal to **Dean Forest Coal Co.** at 6/9 per ton in buyers trucks at colliery less 6d. per ton rebate and 2^1/$_2$% discount for delivery to **Messrs Princess Royal Colliery Co.** at the rate of 50 tons per week.

21 MAY 1908
It was reported that the following contracts had been made since the last meeting:-
Graham Bros. & Co. 3,200-4,000 tons of small coal at 7/- per ton less 6d. per ton rebate and 2^1/$_2$% discount for delivery to Swindon between now and 31 March 1909.
John Hollow & Sons 1,000 tons of coal for delivery between now and 31 March 1909 as follows: 500 tons of large coal at 15/- per ton FOR Lydney and 500 tons of nut coal at 14/- per ton FOR Lydney from now till 30 September 1908 with 1/- per ton advance from that date to 31 March 1909.
Great Western Railway Co. 5,000 tons of best Forest coal at 13/- per ton net in buyers trucks at Lightmoor Colliery delivered between now and 30 April 1909.

18 JUNE 1908
It was reported that the following contracts had been made since the last meeting:-
May 22 1,000 tons of best Forest coal at 14/6 per ton from now until 30 September next and 15/6 from 1 October to 31 March 1909 for **Mr Cornelius Hyde**, Ballinacurra.
May 23 5-700 tons of best Forest coal at 14/6 per ton from now until 30 September next and 15/6 from 1 October to 31 March 1909 for Mr **Timothy Fenton**, Ballycotton.
25 May 1,500 tons of best Forest coal to be taken in odd sailor cargoes between now and 30 September next at 14/6 per ton FOR Lydney. The whole of these contracts were on account of **Messrs Suttons Ltd**

16 JULY 1908
It was reported that the following contracts had been made since the last meeting:-
600 tons of small coal at 8/- per ton net delivered Chepstow for the **Chepstow Gas Co.** The delivery is required between now and 30 June 1909.
120-150 tons of rough small coal at 6/3 per ton in buyers wagons at colliery less 5% for cash against invoice for delivery during July, August and September next to **Mrs. A. L. Kilmister**.

27 AUGUST 1908
It was reported that the following contracts had been made since the last meeting:-
Mrs. A. L. Kilmister 2,500-3,000 tons of large coal for foreign shipment at 13/- per ton at pit less 5% for cash. Delivery from 1 November 1908 to 30 April 1909.
Also a further 2,500-3,000 tons on offer to the same person for foreign shipment at the same price.
Sully & Co. 750-1,000 tons of rough small coal at 6/9 per ton at pit less 6d. per ton rebate and 2^1/$_2$% discount for delivery over the next twelve months for Exmouth.
Dean Forest Coal Co. 500-750 tons of rough small coal at 7/- per ton at pit less 6d. per ton rebate and 2^1/$_2$% discount for delivery between now and 31 July 1909 for **Ralph, Preece, Davis & Co.**, Hereford.
Sully & Co. 720 tons of rough small coal at 6/- per ton at pit less 6d. per ton rebate and 2^1/$_2$% discount for delivery over six months ending 28 February 1909 for Paignton.

17 SEPTEMBER 1908
It was reported that the following contracts had been made since the last meeting:-
A. L. Kilmister 1,500-2,000 tons of large coal at 13/- per ton in wagons at pit less 5% for cash. Delivery in about eight equal monthly quantities from 21 October 1908 to 21 March 1909 for foreign shipment only.
A. Hathaway 50 tons of cobbles at 17/6 per ton net cash delivered Usk station in about equal monthly quantities from 1 October 1908 to 31 April 1909.
Sully & Co. Ltd 250 tons of rough small coal at 5/- per ton at pit less 6d. per ton rebate and 2^1/$_2$% discount, for immediate delivery to the **Princess Royal Colliery Co.**
Dean Forest Coal Co. 250 tons of rough small coal at 5/- per ton at pit less 6d. per ton rebate and 2^1/$_2$% discount, for immediate delivery to the **Princess Royal Colliery Co.**

The question of giving **Mrs. A. L. Kilmister** the sole agency for our Starkey coal at Mill Street station Newport was discussed and considered very advisable to do so until further notice.

A letter was read from the **Dean Forest Coal Co.** asking for a special rebate on small coal to be sent to W. Tapscot of Charfield. It was decided no special rebate could be made on same at present.

15 OCTOBER 1908
Received from **Messrs Sully** re small coal and the Secretary reported that he had this morning practically completed arrangements with **Messrs Sully & Co.** and the **Dean Forest Coal Co.** for 2,000-2,500 tons of small coal to each party for the **Princess Royal Colliery Co.** at 3/11 per ton FOR at colliery in buyers wagons less 2^1/$_2$%, no other rebate, for delivery between now and 31 March 1909.

It was reported that the following contracts had been made since the last meeting:-
Bird & Son Ltd 150 tons of rough small coal at 8/- per ton delivered East Moors, Cardiff, less 2^1/$_2$% in about equal monthly quantities from 1 October 1908 to 30 April 1909.
Mrs. A. L. Kilmister 120-150 tons of rough small coal in about equal monthly quantities 1 October to 31 December 1908 at 5/- per ton in buyers wagons at pit less 6d rebate and 5% for cash against invoice for delivery to Cadoxton.
James Smith ^{2}/$_3$ in summer of what we supply in winter, current prices.
New Bowson Coal Co. Small coal for Gloucester Electricity Works 4/6 per ton less 2^1/$_2$% in buyers wagons at colliery.

19 NOVEMBER 1908
It was reported that the following contracts had been made since the last meeting:-
Dean Forest Coal Co. 2,000-2,500 tons of small coal for Princess Royal Colliery Co. Ltd at 3/11 per ton less 2^1/$_2$% in buyers wagons at colliery in equal monthly deliveries to 31 March 1909.
Sully & Co. 2,000-2,500 tons of small coal for Princess Royal Colliery Co. Ltd at 3/11 per ton less 2^1/$_2$% in buyers wagons at colliery in equal monthly deliveries to 31 March 1909.
New Bowson Coal Co. small coal for the Newent Waterworks at 5/- per ton, less 6d. rebate, 2^1/$_2$% discount, in buyers trucks at colliery for six months ending 30 April 1909. Quantity 1-3 trucks per week is required.
E. Jarrett 200 tons of rough small coal for Dudbridge at 5/- per ton less 6d rebate, 2^1/$_2$% discount, in buyers trucks at colliery, delivered in about equal monthly quantities between now and 31 March 1909.

18 FEBRUARY 1909
Following contracts made since last meeting:
Sully & Co. Ltd 6,100 tons rough small for Princess Royal Colliery Co. at 3/11 per ton in buyers wagons at colliery less 2^1/$_2$% from 22 January 1909 to 31 March 1910.
Sully & Co. Ltd 300 tons rough small for Teignbridge at 4/9 per ton in buyers trucks at colliery less 6d. rebate and 2^1/$_2$% over 12 months ending 31 December 1909.

Sully & Co. Ltd 250 tons rough small for Fremington at 4/9 per ton in buyers trucks at colliery less 6d. rebate and 2½% from now to 31 March 1909.
A. L. Kilmister 100/200 tons rough small to Cadoxton at 4/6 per ton in buyers trucks at colliery less 5% from now to 31 March.

18 MARCH 1909
Contracts made since last meeting:
Dean Forest Coal Co. 5,000 tons rough small coal for Princess Royal Colliery Co. in about equal monthly quantities over the twelve months ending 31 March 1910 at 3/11 per ton less 2½% in buyers trucks at colliery.
Dean Forest Coal Co. 2,000 tons rough small coal for Princess Royal Colliery Co. in about equal monthly quantities during January, February and March 1909 at 3/11 per ton less 2½% in buyers trucks at colliery.
New Bowson Coal Co. 2,000 tons rough small in about equal monthly quantities over the twelve months ending 31 March 1910 at 5/- per ton in buyers trucks at colliery less 6d. rebate and 2½%
New Bowson Coal Co. 210 tons rough small in about equal monthly quantities over the twelve months ending 31 March 1910 at 5/- per ton in buyers trucks at colliery less 6d. rebate and 2½%

22 APRIL 1909
Following contracts made since last meeting:
Edgar Jarrett 200 tons rough small at 5/- per ton less 6d. rebate and 2½% in buyers wagons at colliery in equal monthly quantities during April, May and June 1909.
Gloucester Union 100 tons rough small at 7/4 per ton net delivered Gloucester Station as required between now and 30 September 1909.

13 MAY 1909
Contracts made:
Sully & Co. about 60 tons per week of rough small coal at 4/6 per ton in buyers wagons at pit less 2½% from 1 April to 30 September 1909 for delivery to Gloucester Electricity Works.
New Bowson Coal Co. about 4 trucks of rough small coal per week at 4/6 per ton in buyers wagons at pit less 2½% from 1 May to 31 October 1909 for Newent Water Works and Gloucester Baths.

14 MAY 1909
Contracts made:
The Ross Gas Co. Ltd 500 tons of nuts at 14/6 per ton delivered Ross station in about equal monthly quantities between 12 May 1909 and 12 May 1910 less the usual 2½%.
The Chepstow Gas Co. Ltd 700 tons of rough small coal at 7/6 per ton delivered Chepstow in about equal monthly quantities until 31 May 1910. Terms net cash.

25 AUGUST 1909
Contracts:
Dean Forest Coal Co. 1,000 tons of rough small in about equal monthly quantities from 1 September 1909 to 31 August 1910 at 5/6 per ton in buyers trucks at colliery less 6d. per ton rebate and 2½%.
Dean Forest Coal Co. 2,000 tons of rough small in about equal monthly quantities from 1 August 1909 to 31 July 1910 at 5/6 per ton in buyers trucks at colliery less 6d. per ton rebate and 2½%.
Great Western Railway Co. 4,000 tons of best Forest coal for delivery between now and the end of June 1910 at 12/6 per ton net in buyers wagons at colliery.

18 NOVEMBER 1909
Contracts:
Edgar Jarrett 500 tons of small coal for Dudbridge. Delivery between now and 30 June 1910 at 5/3 per ton in buyers wagons at Lightmoor Colliery less 6d. rebate and 2½%.
Dean Forest Coal Co. 100 tons of small coal for delivery to Messrs Chadborne Sons & Taylor over the next six months at 5/6 per ton in buyers wagons at Lightmoor Colliery less 6d. and 2½%.

16 DECEMBER 1909
Contracts:
Dean Forest Coal Co. 180 tons small coal for W. Tapscott at 5/3 per ton in buyers wagons at colliery less 6d rebate and 2½% for delivery between now and 20 May 1910.
Edgar Jarrett 52 truckloads of small coal for Woolaston at 5/3 per ton in buyers wagons at colliery less 6d. rebate and 2½%. Delivery between 22 November 1909 and 22 November 1910.
Mrs. A. L. Kilmister 1,500/2,000 tons of small coal for foreign shipment at 4/6 per ton in sellers wagons at colliery less 5% discount cash as usual delivery between 1 January and 30 June 1910.

Gee & Co. Gloucester 12-18 truckloads small coal at 7/6 per ton net cash delivered Gloucester GWR at the rate of 1, 2 or 3 trucks per month as required.

21 JANUARY 1910
Contracts:
A. L. Kilmister 1,500 tons Forest large for foreign shipment at 13/- per ton in sellers wagons at colliery less 5% for cash. Delivery in equal quantities during January, February and March 1910.
A. L. Kilmister 240/360 tons rough small coal for Cadoxton at 5/- per ton in buyers wagons at colliery less 5% for cash. Delivery 40 to 60 tons per month from 1 January to 30 June 1910.
A. L. Kilmister 800/1,000 tons rough small for foreign shipment at 4/6 per ton coal and wagon at colliery less 5% for cash. Delivery during February and March 1910.
A. L. Kilmister 2,000 tons rough small for foreign shipment at 4/6 per ton coal and wagon at colliery less 5% for cash. Delivery in equal monthly quantities from 1 January to 31 July 1910.

17 FEBRUARY 1910
H. Lancaster & Co. 6 to 12 trucks small coal at 9/6 per ton net delivered Newent station between 22 January and 22 July 1910 as required.

17 MARCH 1910
Contracts:
Great Western Railway Co. 1,500 tons large coal including the nuts at 12/- per ton net in buyers trucks at colliery delivery as required over next six months.
Dean Forest Coal Co. 3,750 tons rough small coal at 4/4 per ton net in buyers trucks at colliery less 1d. per ton difference in rate on all sent to Lydney basin. Delivery to the Princess Royal Colliery Co. in equal monthly quantities over the next twelve months.
Sully & Co. Ltd 3,750 tons rough small coal at 4/4 per ton net in buyers trucks at colliery less 1d. per ton difference in rate on all sent to Lydney basin. Delivery to the Princess Royal Colliery Co. in equal monthly quantities over the next twelve months.

21 APRIL 1910
Contracts:
Edgar Jarrett 750 tons rough small coal 6/6 per ton in buyers wagons at colliery less 9d. per ton rebate net cash delivered in about equal monthly quantities between 26 March and 26 September 1910 to the Hereford Corporation.

26 MAY 1910
One contract for 100 tons small coal at 6/- per ton, no rebate or discount for delivery to the order of **Messrs George Jones & Co**., Chepstow over the next two months.

25 AUGUST 1910
Secretary reported he had secured a contract for 3000 tons of large coal for the **Great Western Railway** at 12/- net in their trucks at colliery delivered as required between July 1910 and 30 June 1911.

15 SEPTEMBER 1910
Contracts:
George Jones & Co. 100 tons small coal 6/- per ton net in buyers trucks at Lightmoor Colliery for delivery to Chepstow in about equal quantities over the next two months.
Dean Forest Coal Co. 2,100 tons of small coal at 5/- per ton net in buyers wagons at Lightmoor Colliery. Delivery at the rate of 300 tons per month from 1 September 1910 to 31 March 1911 to W. J. Mills of Bristol.
E. Jones & Son 250 tons small steam coal at 6/3 per ton net in R. Thomas & Co's wagons at Eastern United Colliery, delivering 30 tons per week for the next two months.

20 OCTOBER 1910
Contracts:
Dean Forest Coal Co. 200 tons Eastern United block coal 10/- per ton net in buyers wagons at colliery. Delivery in about equal monthly quantities over the next twelve months to Ralph, Preece & Co. of Hereford.
Edgar Jarrett 500 tons rough small coal at 5/6 per ton net in buyers trucks at colliery. Delivery to Grist & Co., Dudbridge at the rate of about 70 tons per month.
E. Jones & Son 2,500 tons Eastern United rough small High Delf steam coal at 6/1 per ton net in R. Thomas & Co's wagons at colliery. Delivery at the rate of 50 tons per week to commence on completion of contract for 250 tons made 9 September 1910.
Stonehouse Brick & Tile Co. 1,000 tons rough small High Delf steam

coal at 6/9 per ton less 2¹/₂% at colliery, half in buyers and half in sellers wagons, delivered in about equal monthly quantities over the next six months.
George Jones & Co. 200 tons rough small coal at 6/- per ton net in buyers wagons at colliery 6d. per ton extra if in sellers wagons. Delivery to Chepstow in about equal quantities over the next four months.

18 NOVEMBER 1910
Contracts:
Dean Forest Coal Co. 3 trucks rough small coal per week over the next eight months, 1 November 1910 to 30 June 1911 5/6 per ton in buyers trucks at colliery less a rebate of 9d. per ton only, no discount, to Messrs Poole Bros. of Bristol.
Edgar Jarrett 52 ten ton truckloads rough small coal for Woolaston at 5/6 per ton in buyers wagons at colliery less 9d. per ton rebate only, no discount. Delivery at the rate of one truckload per week over the next twelve months 1 December 1910 to 30 November 1911.
Dean Forest Coal Co. 1000 tons rough small coal 5/6 per ton in buyers wagons at colliery less 9d. per ton rebate only, no discount. Delivery in about equal monthly quantities over next twelve months 1 November 1910 to 31 October 1911 to Messrs Ralph, Preece, Davies & Co., Hereford.

15 DECEMBER 1910
Contracts:
George Jones & Co. 200 tons rough small coal at 5/- per ton in buyers trucks at colliery, 6d. per ton extra if in sellers trucks, net cash. Delivery to Chepstow in about monthly instalments over four months.

15 FEBRUARY 1911
Contracts:
Jones & Son 650 tons of Eastern United small coal at 6/1 per ton net no rebate in Thomas's wagons at colliery. Delivery at the rate of 50 tons per week until the end of December 1911, to commence on completion of present contract dated 20 September 1910.
Great Western Railway Co. 1000/1500 tons Forest large housecoal hard at 12/- per ton net delivered Bilson Junction in buyers wagons. Delivery as required.

16 MARCH 1911
Contracts:
Great Western Railway Co. 1000 tons large housecoal, hard, at 12/- per ton net in buyers wagons at Bilson Junction, delivery as required.
George Jones & Co. 200 tons rough small coal at 5/- per ton in buyers wagons at colliery. Delivery to Chepstow in about equal quantities over the next four months
The Radstock Coal Co. 1000 tons rough small coal at 5/6 per ton in buyers wagons at colliery less 9d. per ton rebate. Delivery in about equal monthly quantities between now and 31 August 1911.

21 APRIL 1911
Contracts:
Stonehouse Brick & Tile Co. 1000 rough small High Delf steam coal at 6/9 per ton less 2¹/₂% for cash in the month following delivery as usual. Half the quantity to be sent in sellers and half in buyers wagons. Delivery in about equal monthly quantities over the next six months following completion of present contract.
Dean Forest Coal Co. 2000/2500 tons rough small coal at 5/6 per ton in buyers trucks at colliery less 9d. per ton rebate. Delivery in about equal monthly quantities over the next twelve months to Mr W. J. Mills of Bristol.
Dean Forest Coal Co. 2000 tons rough small coal at 5/6 per ton in buyers wagons at colliery less a rebate of 9d. per ton. Delivery in about equal monthly quantities over the next twelve months or as much as colliery can conveniently supply to Whimsey Station for Messrs Powell, Gwinnell & Co.
H. Lancaster & Co. 160 tons Lightmoor rough small coal at 10/- per ton delivered Newent in about equal monthly quantities between now and the end of April 1912.

18 MAY 1911
Contract:
Ross Gas Co. Ltd 200 tons Eastern United small steam coal at 8/8 per ton delivered to Ross station over the next ten weeks.

15 JUNE 1911
Contracts:
Sully & Co. Ltd 3900 tons rough small coal 4/9 per ton in buyers wagons at colliery less 1d. per ton difference in rate on all coal sent to Lydney Basin, all other points strictly net. Delivery in about equal monthly quantities over the next twelve months to order of Princess Royal Colliery Co.
Dean Forest Coal Co. 3900 tons rough small coal 4/9 per ton in buyers wagons at colliery less 1d. per ton difference in rate on all coal sent to Lydney Basin, all other points strictly net. Delivery in about equal monthly quantities over the next twelve months to order of Princess Royal Colliery Co.
George Jones & Co. 100 tons Eastern United small steam coal at 6/3 per ton net in buyers wagons at colliery, 6d. per ton extra if in sellers wagons. Delivery to Chepstow in about equal weekly quantities over the next two months.
East Dean Rural District Council 300 tons Eastern United small steam coal at 9/- per ton net delivered Greenbottom Pumping Station between 1 July and 31 December 1911.

20 JULY 1911
Contracts:
Renwick, Wilton & Co. Ltd 350/450 tons Lightmoor rough small coal at 6/9 per ton FOR Lydney. Delivery in about equal monthly quantities over the next twelve months.
Chepstow Gas Co. 1000 tons Eastern United small coal at 7/9 per ton in buyers trucks, 6d. per ton extra if in sellers trucks. Delivery as required between 21 June 1911 and 21 June 1912.
Co-operative Wholesale Society, Bristol, 1000 tons block or through High Delf coal at buyers option, block at 10/- per ton, through at 7/6 per ton net in buyers wagons at Eastern United Colliery, 6d. per ton extra if in sellers wagons. Delivery in about equal monthly quantities between 1 July 1911 and 30 June 1912 to the Bristol Co-operative Society, Lawrence Hill.
Great Western Railway Co. 5000 tons Forest large house coal 12/- per ton in buyers trucks at Bilson Junction. Delivery as required over next twelve months.
Henry Pritchard & Co. Ltd 60 tons through & through steam coal at 11/6 per ton delivered Redcliffe Wharf, Bristol between now and end of year.
Co-operative Wholesale Society, Bristol 1000 tons rough small High Delf steam coal at 5/10 per ton in buyers wagons at Eastern United Colliery, 6d. extra if in sellers wagons. Delivery at the rate of about one truck per day to Co-operative Wholesale Society, Avonmouth Mill, Avonmouth.

30 AUGUST 1911
Contracts:
A. Morgan 500 tons Eastern United small steam coal 6/3 per ton in sellers wagons at colliery, delivered as required in monthly quantities between now and 31 March 1912.
Stonehouse Brick & Tile Co. 1000 tons rough small Eastern United steam coal 6/9 per ton at colliery, half quantity to be sent in buyers and half in sellers wagons. Delivery in about equal monthly quantities between now and 31 March 1912 to commence on completion of present contract.
George Jones & Co. 100 tons small High Delf steam coal 6/3 per ton in buyers wagons at colliery. Delivery in about equal weekly quantities over the next two months.
Gloucestershire County Council Up to 30 tons High Delf block coal. Delivery as required to certain Forest districts.
E. Jarrett 500 tons Lightmoor rough small coal at 6/- per ton in buyers wagons less 9d. per ton rebate. Delivery to Lydney Docks as required for shipment during the next two or three months.
Ross Gas Company 500/1000 tons through & through High Delf coal at 10/- per ton d/d Ross. Delivery not less than ten tons per week but more if required.
W. Sisson & Co. Ltd 12 trucks through & through steam coal at 9/9 per ton d/d Gloucester as required.

21 SEPTEMBER 1911
Contracts:
Princess Royal Colliery Co. Ltd 1000 tons Eastern United small steam coal at 6/6 per ton net in sellers wagons at colliery to be sent to Lydney Basin in about equal weekly quantities over the next ten weeks.
Gee & Co. Ltd 7-14 truckloads Eastern United small steam coal at 9/- per ton delivered direct Gloucester Docks GWR at the rate of one or two trucks per month between now and 31 March 1912.
New Bowson Coal Co. 300/500 tons Eastern United small steam coal at 6/3 per ton in buyers wagons at colliery. Delivery in about equal monthly quantities to Cheltenham net cash.
J. Stephens, Son & Co. Ltd 1000 tons Eastern United small steam coal at 8/3 per ton net delivered direct Gloucester GWR in buyers wagons in about equal monthly quantities from 6 September 1911 to 30 June 1912.

Suttons Ltd 500 tons best Forest coal at 14/- per ton net FOR Lydney. Delivery as required between 1 October 1911 and 30 April 1912 for Martin & Blackwood.
E. Jarrett 650/1000 tons at buyers option Lightmoor bank small coal at 5/3 per ton net in buyers wagons at colliery. Delivery to the Bristol district excluding Lawrence Hill in about equal monthly quantities between 1 September 1911 and 30 April 1912.
Dean Forest Coal Co. 1000 tons Lightmoor small coal for delivery to Whimsey for Powell, Gwinnell & Co. at the rate of 75-150 tons per week at 6/- per ton in buyers wagons at colliery less 9d. rebate.
Dean Forest Coal Co. 52 truckloads Lightmoor small coal for delivery to Caldicot at the rate of two trucks per week between 8 September 1911 and 29 February 1912 at 6/- per ton in buyers trucks at colliery less 9d. rebate.
E. Jarrett 1200 tons Lightmoor small coal for delivery to Lydney Basin over the next six months in about equal monthly quantities at 5/3 per ton net in buyers wagons at colliery.

19 OCTOBER 1911
C & G Ayres 60-70 tons small steam coal at 8/3 per ton net in buyers wagons at colliery 9d. per ton extra if in sellers trucks. Delivery in about equal monthly quantities between 20 September 1911 and 31 March 1912.
Renwick, Wilton & Co. Ltd 250/300 tons Lightmoor rough small coal 7/- per ton FOR Lydney. Delivery at the rate of about equal shipments of 60-80 tons between 1 November 1911 and 31 October 1912.
W. Sisson & Co. Ltd 12 trucks through & through High Delf steam coal at 11/- per ton delivered Gloucester GWR Town station as required to follow on after completion of present contract.
Gloucester Union 140 tons Lightmoor rough small coal at 9/- per ton delivered Gloucester GWR over next six months.
George Jones & Co. 100 tons Lightmoor rough small coal at 6/6 per ton net in buyers trucks at colliery. Delivery at the rate of about two trucks per week until the whole quantity is taken.
Suttons Ltd 10,000 tons best Forest coal at 14/3 per ton for any portion of the quantity taken per steamer FOR Lydney, 6d. per ton extra for that taken per sailing vessel net. Delivery is required for shipment between now and 30 April 1912 in about equal monthly quantities.

16 NOVEMBER 1911
Contract:
Central Coal Co. 150 tons Lightmoor rough small coal 6/6 per ton net in buyers wagons at colliery. Delivery about 50 tons per month until end of January 1912.

14 DECEMBER 1911
Contracts:
Dean Forest Coal Co. 250 tons Eastern United High Delf block coal at 12/- per ton net in buyers wagons at colliery. Delivery in about equal monthly quantities between date and 31 March 1912 to W. J. Mills of Bristol.
Dean Forest Coal Co. 100 tons Eastern United High Delf block coal at 11/9 per ton net in buyers wagons at colliery. Delivery in about equal monthly quantities between date and 30 April 1912 to W. Tapscott, Charfield.
George Jones & Co. 100 tons Lightmoor rough small coal at 6/6 per ton in buyers wagons at colliery. Delivery at rate of about two trucks per week.
Great Western Railway Co. 2,000 tons Forest large housecoal at 13/- per ton in buyers wagons at Bilson Junction. Delivery as required.
Dean Forest Coal Co. 1,500 tons Lightmoor bank small coal at 7/- per ton net in buyers wagons at colliery less 9d. per ton rebate. Delivery in about equal monthly quantities between date and 30 April 1912 to W. J. Mills, Bristol.
Dean Forest Coal Co. 1,000 tons Lightmoor rough small coal at 7/- per ton net in buyers wagons at colliery less 9d. per ton rebate. Delivery to Whimsey for Lansley & Cullis at the rate of 75-150 tons per week.

18 JANUARY 1912
Contracts:
East Dean Rural District Council about 300 tons Eastern United High Delf steam coal at 9/9 per ton, delivered direct Greenbottom Pumping Station at the rate of about 50 tons per month between 1 January and 30 June 1912.
George Jones & Co. 200 tons Lightmoor rough small coal at 6/- per ton net in buyers trucks at colliery. Delivery at rate of about two trucks per week.
Central Coal Co. 900 tons Lightmoor rough small coal at 6/- per ton in buyers trucks at colliery. Delivery in equal quantities of 150 tons per month over next six months.

16 MAY 1912
Contracts:
I. W. Baldwin & Co. 100 tons Eastern United block coal 11/6 per ton in buyers wagons at pit and any quantity up to 100 tons of through & through steam coal at 9/6 per ton net in buyers wagons at pit for delivery in the month of May to Messrs F. Biss [?] & Co.
I. W. Baldwin & Co. 1,000/1,200 tons Eastern United small steam coal 7/6 per ton net in buyers wagons at colliery. Delivery at the rate of 25 tons per week from 6 May 1912 to 6 May 1913 to Cirencester.
I. W. Baldwin & Co. Two cargoes of about 40 tons each of Eastern United small steam coal at 7/6 per ton net in buyers wagons at colliery. Delivery during the month of May 1912 to Critchley Bros., Brinchcombe.
W. Sisson & Co. Ltd Ten trucks of through & through steam coal 12/6 per ton net delivered Gloucester Town Station as required.

20 JUNE 1912
Contracts:
Dean Forest Coal Co. 300 tons Eastern United block coal 11/6 per ton net in buyers trucks at colliery. Delivery in equal monthly quantities from 21 May 1912 to 21 May 1913 to Mr W. Tapscott.
I. W. Baldwin & Co. 1,000 tons of Eastern United block coal 10/6 per ton net in buyers trucks at colliery. Delivery in about equal monthly quantities over next twelve months to W. Perch & Co.
H. Pritchard & Co. Ltd 60 tons Eastern United through coal 13/- per ton net. Delivered Redcliffe Wharf, Bristol at the rate of one or two trucks per month as required.
Central Coal Co. 900/1,200 tons Eastern United or Lightmoor small coal, buyers option, 7/6 per ton net in buyers trucks at colliery. Delivery in about equal monthly quantities during June, July and August 1912.
Dean Forest Coal Co. 250 tons Eastern United block coal 11/3 per ton in buyers trucks at colliery. Delivery in about equal monthly quantities over the next 12 months for Messrs Webb, Hall & Webb, Ross.
Dean Forest Coal Co. 250 tons Lightmoor rough small coal at 7/6 per ton in buyers wagons at colliery less 3d. per ton rebate. Delivery in about equal monthly quantities over the next twelve months to W. L. Buchanan, Gloucester.
Ross Gas Co. Ltd 1,500/2,000 tons Eastern United through coal at 11/6 per ton delivered Ross Station in about equal monthly quantities over the next twelve months.
L. Twining & Co. 300/400 tons Eastern United through coal at 10/- per ton in buyers trucks at colliery. Delivery about 5 trucks per month over next twelve months to Swindon.
A. E. Flower 100 tons Eastern United block coal 17/- per ton d/d Ledbury or 13/6 in buyers trucks at colliery as required over the next six months.
Thomas W. Ward Ltd 150 tons Eastern United small coal at 7/- per ton in buyers wagons at pit. Delivery over next 10-14 days.
Church of England Temperance Society 120 tons Eastern United block coal at 15/6 per ton delivered direct to Abbotswood House, Cinderford, as 5 or 6 ton lots as required over next twelve months.
Thomas W. Ward Ltd 400 tons Eastern United small coal at 7/- per ton in buyers trucks at colliery. Delivery at the rate of 40 tons per week.
East Dean Rural District Council. Half Council's requirements of High Delf small steam coal at 10/9 per ton delivered direct Greenbottom as required during July, September and November 1912.
Read & Sons 40-50 tons bank cobbles at 13/6 per ton in buyers trucks at colliery less 6d. per ton rebate. Delivery to the Dursley Union between date and 30 September 1912.
S. Jefferies & Sons 350 tons Eastern United small coal at 7/3 per ton in buyers trucks at pit. Delivery in about equal monthly quantities over next eight months.
Thomas W. Ward Ltd 500 tons Eastern United small coal at 7/- per ton in buyers wagons at colliery. Delivery in about equal quantities over the next two months.

18 JULY 1912
Contracts:
J. Stephens, Son & Co. Ltd 1,000 tons Eastern United small coal at 9/3 per ton in buyers wagons. Delivered Gloucester GWR in equal monthly quantities after completion of existing contract.
T. W. Ward Ltd 200 tons Eastern United small coal at 7/- per ton in buyers wagons at pit. Delivery in about equal monthly quantities after completion of contracts dated June 1, 7 & 14th and before 30 September 1912.
T. W. Ward Ltd 2,000 tons Eastern United small coal at 7/3 per ton in buyers wagons at pit delivered in about equal monthly quantities between 1 September 1912 and 1 September 1913.
C. & G. Ayres 80/100 tons Eastern United small coal 7/6 per ton in buyers wagons at pit, 1/- per ton extra if in sellers wagons. Delivery over twelve months from 1 July 1912.

Dean Forest Coal Co. 1,000 tons Lightmoor small at 6/6 per ton in buyers wagons at pit less 3d. per ton rebate. Delivery in about equal monthly quantities over next twelve months to Poole Bros.
Chepstow Gas Co. 1,000 tons Eastern United small at 9/6 per ton in buyers wagons. Delivered Chepstow in about equal monthly quantities between date and 30 June 1913.
Dean Forest Coal Co. 500 tons Eastern United block at 11/6 per ton in buyers trucks at pit. Delivery in equal monthly quantities 1 July 1912 to 30 June 1913 for W. Tapscott.
Great Western Railway Co. 2,000 tons Forest large housecoal at 13/- per ton deliveries to 30 September 1912 and 14/- per ton subsequent supplies. Delivery as required.
Lydney & Crump Meadow Collieries Co. Ltd 200-260 truckloads Eastern United small at 7/3 per ton in buyers wagons at pit. Delivery at the rate of 15 - 20 truckloads per week over next three months.
I. W. Baldwin & Co. about 50 tons monthly Eastern United small coal at 7/3 per ton in buyers trucks at pit. Delivery from 1 July 1912 to 31 March 1913 to the Newent Water Works.
I. W. Baldwin & Co. 2,500 tons with option of increasing to 4000 tons Lightmoor small coal at 6/- per ton in buyers wagons at pit. Delivery in about equal monthly quantities over the next twelve months.
I. W. Baldwin & Co. 3,000/4,000 tons Eastern United block coal at 10/11 per ton in buyers wagons at pit. Delivery in equal monthly quantities over next twelve months after completion of the present contract.
Dean Forest Coal Co. 1,250 tons Lightmoor small coal at 6/- per ton in buyers wagons at colliery. Delivery in about equal monthly quantities over the next six months to F. Silvey & Co., Bristol.
Gloucester Farmers Ltd 250 tons Eastern United small at 10/3 per ton carriage paid to Gloucester GWR in equal monthly quantities over the next twelve months.
Dean Forest Coal Co. Eastern United through coal at 9/3 per ton in buyers wagons at colliery. Delivery in about equal monthly quantities over the next twelve months for R. P. Davies & Co.
Dean Forest Coal Co. 1,500 tons Eastern United small at 7/3 per ton in buyers wagons at colliery. Delivery in about equal monthly quantities over the next twelve months for R. P. Davies & Co.
Dean Forest Coal Co. 4,000 tons Lightmoor small 6/3 per ton in buyers wagon at colliery less 3d. per ton rebate. Delivery in about equal monthly quantities over next twelve months after completion of present contract to Princess Royal Colliery Co. Ltd
Sully & Co. 4,000 tons Lightmoor small 6/3 per ton in buyers wagon at colliery less 3d. per ton rebate. Delivery in about equal monthly quantities over next twelve months after completion of present contract to Princess Royal Colliery Co. Ltd
A. H. Nott 100 tons Eastern United small at 7/6 per ton in buyers wagons at colliery. Delivery in about equal monthly quantities over the next twelve months.
J. C. Hill & Co. Ltd 750 tons Eastern United block coal at 14/- per ton delivered Oakfield Works, Cwmbran, in about equal monthly quantities from 1 August 1912 to 31 July 1913.

19 SEPTEMBER 1912
Contracts:
Berkeley Gas Co. 100 tons Eastern United small coal 10/6 per ton. Delivered Berkeley in about equal monthly quantities over twelve months from 24 July 1912.
Suttons Ltd 17,500 tons best Forest coal 15/- per ton FOR Lydney 1 September - 30 September 1912 and 16/- per ton FOR Lydney from 1 October 1912 to 31 March 1913. Delivery at rate of 2500 tons per month from 1 September 1912 to 31 March 1913.
J. B. Williams & Co. 7 truckloads Eastern United small coal at 10/2 per ton delivered direct Llanthony, Gloucester at the rate of one truck per month from September 1912 to 31 March 1913.
E. Jarrett 64 truckloads Lightmoor small coal at 6/3 per ton in buyers wagons at colliery delivered in about equal monthly quantities over next twelve months.
Berkeley Gas Co. 230 tons Eastern United small at 10/6 per ton and 50 tons Eastern United through coal at 12/- per ton. Both delivered to Berkeley in about equal monthly quantities over twelve months commencing 24 July 1912.
Direct Coal Supply Co. 1,000/1,500 tons Eastern United through coal at 9/3 per ton in buyers wagons at pit. Delivery in about equal monthly quantities over next nine months and 500 tons Eastern United block coal at 11/6 per ton in sellers wagons at pit. Delivery in about equal monthly quantities over next twelve months.

17 OCTOBER 1912
Contracts:
J. W. Kilmister About 1,000 tons Lightmoor small coal at 5/11 per ton in sellers wagons at colliery. Delivery as required for shipment in 200-300 ton lots between date and 31 December 1912.
Dean Forest Coal Co. 400 tons Eastern United block coal at 11/6 per ton net in buyers trucks at colliery. Delivery in about equal monthly quantities between 17 September 1912 and 30 June 1913.
Stonehouse Brick & Tile Co. Ltd 1,000 tons Eastern United small coal at 7/3 per ton less 2½% in buyers wagons at colliery. Delivery in about equal monthly quantities over the next twelve months.
Great Western Railway Co. 5,000 tons Forest coal at 14/- per ton in buyers wagons at Bilson Junction. Delivery at the rate of 300 tons per week.
New Bowson Coal Co. 500-700 tons Eastern United small coal at 7/9 per ton in buyers trucks at colliery. Delivery in about equal monthly quantities over next twelve months.
Henry Pritchard & Co. Ltd 100 tons Eastern United through coal at 14/- per ton net delivered Bristol at the rate of one or two trucks per month as required.

21 NOVEMBER 1912
Contracts:
Dean Forest Coal Co. 500 tons Lightmoor rough small coal. Delivery to Ralph, Preece, Davies & Co. in about equal monthly quantities over next twelve months at 6/6 per ton in buyers trucks at colliery less 3d. per ton factors rebate.
C. & G. Ayres 26 truckloads of Lightmoor small coal at 6/3 per ton in buyers wagons at pit. Delivery at rate of one truck per week over the six months commencing 1 November 1912.
Sully & Co. Ltd 500 tons Lightmoor rough small coal at 6/6 per ton in buyers trucks at pit less 3d. per ton rebate. Delivery in about equal monthly instalments between 1 December 1912 and 31 March 1913.
Edgar Jarrett 10,000 tons Lightmoor rough small coal at 6/2 per ton in buyers wagons at pit for foreign shipment at Sharpness over the next twelve months.
Dean Forest Coal Co. 2,500 tons Eastern United small coal at 7/6 per ton in buyers trucks at pit for delivery to the Lydney Coal Co. in equal monthly quantities over next twelve months.
Edgar Jarrett 3,000 tons Eastern United small coal at 7/6 per ton in buyers trucks at pit for shipment at Sharpness in 100-200 ton lots over the next twelve months.
W. Sissons & Co. Ltd 12 truckloads Eastern United through coal at 12/6 per ton delivered GWR Gloucester as required.
I. W. Baldwin & Co. 3,000 tons Eastern United through coal at 8/9 per ton in buyers trucks at pit and 4,000 tons Eastern United small coal at 7/- per ton in buyers trucks at pit, both for delivery in equal monthly quantities over the next twelve months.

12 DECEMBER 1912
Contracts:
Dean Forest Coal Co. 2,500 tons Eastern United small coal at 7/6 per ton in buyers wagons at colliery. Delivery in equal monthly quantities over next twelve months to the Lydney Coal Co.
East Dean Rural District Council. All Eastern United small coal required by them during February, April and June 1913 at 11/9 per ton delivered Greenbottom Pumping Station.
C. & G. Ayres 20 truckloads Lightmoor small coal at 7/- per ton in buyers wagons at pit for delivery at rate of one truck per week from date.
Central Coal Co. 150 tons Eastern United small coal at 8/- per ton in buyers wagons at colliery. Delivery in about equal monthly quantities between date and 31 March 1913.

20 FEBRUARY 1913
Contracts:
Dean Forest Coal Co. 400 tons Eastern United small coal at 8/9 per ton in buyers wagons at colliery. Delivery in about equal monthly quantities between date and 30 April 1913.
Great Western Railway Co. 5,000 tons Forest large housecoal at 14/- per ton delivered Bilson Junction in buyers trucks as required.

13 MARCH 1913
Contract:
Basic Lime & Stone Co. Ltd 180 tons Eastern United block coal at 15/- per ton carriage paid to Shakemantle Siding. Delivery in about equal monthly quantities over next six months.

17 APRIL 1913
Contract:
I. W. Baldwin & Co. 300 tons Eastern United small coal 11/- per ton net in buyers wagons at colliery. Delivery to Newent Water Works in equal monthly quantities 1 April to 30 September 1913.

19 JUNE 1913
Contracts:
J. Stephens Sons & Co. Ltd 300 tons small steam coal 13/3 per ton net in buyers wagons delivered Gloucester GWR in equal monthly quantities during June, July and August 1913.
Great Western Railway Co. 5,000 tons Forest large housecoal 14/- per ton net in buyers wagons at colliery and 15/- per ton for all supplied subsequent to 1 September 1913.
George Jones & Co. 100 tons small steam coal at 11/- per ton net in buyers wagons at pit. Delivery as required over next three or four months.
Gloucestershire County Council requirements of coal to various schools over next twelve months as under:

      Rubbles delivered St. Whites at 19/6 per ton net
      Forest   "   Soudley   " 20/- per ton net
      "   "   Lydbrook " 21/6 per ton net

Suttons Ltd Various cargoes ranging from 90 to 200 tons each best Forest coal for shipment before 31 August 1913 at 16/- per ton net FOR Lydney.

24 JULY 1913
Contracts:
City of Cork Steam Packet Co. 1,000 tons best Forest coal at 16/6 per ton FOR Newport until 31 August 1913 and 1/- per ton advance from 1 September 1913. Delivery in equal monthly quantities from date to 31 March 1914.
I. W. Baldwin & Co. 1,000 tons Eastern United block coal at 13/3 per ton in buyers trucks at pit. Delivery in equal monthly quantities from 1 July 1913 to 30 June 1914 for W. Perch & Co.
I. W. Baldwin & Co. 1,500 tons Eastern United block coal at 13/- per ton in buyers trucks at pit for delivery to Messrs A. J. Smith Ltd after completion of present contract and before 31 December 1913.
Central Coal Co. 100/200 tons Lightmoor small coal at 10/- per ton in buyers trucks at pit. Delivery in about equal monthly quantities between 1 October and 31 December 1913.
John Williams & Co. Ltd 150/200 tons Eastern United small coal at 10/9 per ton in buyers wagons at pit. Delivery in about equal monthly quantities between date and 30 June 1914.

28 AUGUST 1913
Contracts:
Berkeley Gas Co. 300 tons High Delf block coal at 15/9 per ton delivered Berkeley between 26 July 1913 and 26 July 1914.
Ross Gas Co. Ltd 1,000 tons High Delf through coal at 13/6 per ton delivered Ross in about equal monthly quantities between date and 31 August 1914.
Henry Pritchard & Co. Ltd 100 tons High Delf through coal at 14/6 per ton delivered Redcliffe Wharf, Bristol as required.
Suttons Ltd 600 tons best Forest coal at 16/- per ton FOR Lydney from date to 31 August 1914 with 1/- per ton advance on all taken between that date and 31 March 1914. Delivery as required for Mr C. Hyde.
I. W. Baldwin & Co. 1,000 tons each High Delf through and small coal at 10/3 and 8/6 per ton respectively in buyers wagons at colliery. Delivery to commence at expiration of existing contract for Messrs A. J. Smith Ltd
Dean Forest Coal Co. 200 tons High Delf small coal at 9/9 per ton net cash in buyers trucks at colliery for delivery in about equal monthly quantities over next twelve months to Messrs Ralph, Preece, Davies & Co.
Dean Forest Coal Co. 2000 tons Lightmoor small coal at 7/9 per ton in buyers wagons at pit less 3d. per ton rebate for delivery in equal monthly quantities over next twelve months for Messrs R. P. Davies & Co.
Dean Forest Coal Co. 2500 tons Lightmoor small coal at 7/6 per ton less 3d. rebate in buyers wagons at pit. Delivery in equal monthly quantities over next twelve months for Princess Royal Colliery Co. Ltd
Sully & Co. 2500 tons Lightmoor small coal at 7/6 per ton less 3d. rebate in buyers wagons at pit. Delivery in equal monthly quantities over next twelve months for Princess Royal Colliery Co. Ltd
T. W. Ward Ltd 2600 tons High Delf small coal at 7/9 per ton in buyers wagons at colliery. Delivery in about equal monthly quantities between date and 30 April 1914 for Bath Electricity Works.

18 SEPTEMBER 1913
Contracts:
Sully & Co. 500 tons High Delf small coal 9/- per ton net in buyers wagons at colliery. Delivery to the Exeter Brick & Tile Co. in about equal monthly quantities from 19 August to 30 November 1913.
Sully & Co. Ltd 500 tons Lightmoor small coal at 8/- per ton in buyers wagons at pit less 3d. per ton rebate for delivery to the Exeter Brickworks in about equal monthly quantities from 1 December 1913 to 31 August 1914.
Victor Grey & Co. All High Delf nuts that can be spared at 11/- per ton net at colliery. Delivery over six months commencing 1 September 1913.
W. Sisson & Co. Ltd 200 tons High Delf through coal at 13/6 per ton net at Gloucester GWR as required.
Bain Sons & Co. 500 tons best Forest coal at 17/6 per ton less 3d. per ton rebate FOR Lydney. Delivery as required between date and 31 March 1914.

16 OCTOBER 1913
Contracts:
Edgar Jarrett 120 truckloads Lightmoor small coal 7/3 per ton in buyers wagons at pit. Delivery in about equal monthly quantities from 15 September 1913 to 15 September 1914
J. Stephens, Son & Co. Ltd 500 tons of Eastern United small at 11/6 per ton delivered Gloucester GWR in buyers wagons over next six months.
Dean Forest Coal Co. 3,000 tons of Eastern United small at 8/- per ton in buyers wagons at colliery. Delivery in about equal monthly quantities.
Edgar Jarrett 3,400 tons Lightmoor small at 7/6 per ton in buyers trucks at colliery. Delivery in about equal monthly quantites from 1 September 1913 to 30 June 1914 to Swindon Electricity Works.
Church of England Temperance Society 100 tons Eastern United block at 16/6 per ton delivered Abbotswood House as required.
C. & G. Ayres 50 tons Eastern United small at 8/- per ton in buyers wagons at colliery. Delivery to Reading over the next six months.

20 NOVEMBER 1913
Contracts:
Lucas & Co. 12 truckloads Lightmoor small coal 11/1 per ton delivered Bristol, Midland Rly., at rate of one ton per week until 31 December.
Princess Royal Colliery 5,000 tons Eastern United small coal at 8/9 per ton F.O.R. at Lydney or Sharpness. Delivery in about equal monthly quantities over next twelve months.
H. Lancaster & Co. 50 tons Eastern United small coal at 12/9 per ton delivered Newent as required after completion of present contract.
John Griffiths 240 tons Eastern United through coal at 10/- per ton in buyers wagons at colliery. Delivery in equal monthly quantities over next seven months.
Dean Forest Coal Co. 1,000 tons Eastern United through coal 9/3 per ton in buyers trucks at colliery. Delivery in equal monthly quantities over next twelve months to R. P. Davies & Co. Hereford.
E. Jarrett & Co. 2,000 tons Lightmoor small coal 6/3 per ton in buyers wagons at colliery. Delivery about 50 tons per week to the Great Western Railway.
Dean Forest Coal Co. 500 tons Eastern United small coal at 7/9 per ton in buyers wagons at colliery. Delivery to R. P. Davies & Co. in about equal monthly quantities over next twelve months.
George Jones & Co. 100 tons Eastern United small coal at 8/9 per ton in buyers trucks at colliery. Delivery as required to Messrs Finch & Co. over next three months.
Dean Forest Coal Co. 2,000/3,000 tons Lightmoor small coal at 6/6 per ton less 3d. per ton rebate in buyers trucks at pit. Delivery twelve trucks per week from 1 November to 31 December 1913 and twenty-four trucks per week afterwards to Crindau.
Dean Forest Coal Co. 2,860/3,120 tons Eastern United small coal 7/- per ton in buyers trucks at colliery. Delivery 110/120 tons per week over next six months to Mr Hunt of Bridgwater.
Dean Forest Coal Co. 1,000 tons Eastern United small coal at 7/3 per ton in buyers wagons at colliery in equal monthly quantities over the next six months to Poole Bros. of Bristol.
Thomas W. Ward 2,000 tons Eastern United small coal at 7/3 per ton in buyers trucks at colliery. Delivery in equal monthly quantities over next twelve months to Bristol.

18 DECEMBER 1913
Contracts:
I. W. Baldwin & Co. 1,000 tons Eastern United High Delf block coal at 12/6 per ton in buyers trucks at colliery for delivery to A. J. Smith Ltd in about equal monthly quantities over the nine months following the completion of present contract.
I. W. Baldwin & Co. 2,000 tons Eastern United High Delf through coal at 9/- per ton in buyers trucks at colliery. Delivery as above.
I. W. Baldwin & Co. 6,000 tons Eastern United High Delf small coal at 7/- per ton in buyers trucks at colliery. Delivery as above.
I. W. Baldwin & Co. 2,000/3,000 tons Lightmoor small coal at 6/6 per ton less 6d. rebate in buyers trucks at pit. Delivery to A. J. Smith Ltd in about equal monthly quantities over nine months ending 11 August 1914.
Great Western Railway Co. 3,000 tons best Forest coal at 14/- per ton

delivered direct Bilson Junction as required.

C. & G. Ayres 100 truckloads Lightmoor small coal at 6/3 per ton in buyers trucks at pit for delivery to Loudwater at the rate of one truck per week during January 1914 and two trucks per week subsequently until 31 December 1914.

Dean Forest Coal Co. 3,000 tons Eastern United High Delf small coal at 7/6 per ton in buyers trucks at colliery. Delivery 100 tons per week to Llandore from date until 30 June 1914.

Victor Grey & Co. 500 tons Lightmoor small coal at 6/3 per ton in buyers trucks at colliery delivered to Llandore in equal weekly quantities between 1 January and 30 June 1914.

Victor Grey & Co. 1,200 tons Eastern United High Delf small coal at 7/6 per ton in buyers wagons at colliery. Delivery to Briton Ferry at rate of 100 tons per week or as near to that quantity as sellers can conveniently supply.

22 JANUARY 1914
Contracts:

Edgar Jarrett 120 tons Lightmoor small 6/6 per ton in buyers trucks at colliery for delivery at the rate of one truck per month to Hereford.

C. W. Williams 200 tons Eastern United small coal at 11/3 per ton delivered Withington Station. Delivery in about equal monthly quantities over next six months.

Sully & Co. 6/700 tons Lightmoor small coal at 6/6 per ton in buyers trucks at colliery. Delivery to the Ilfracombe Electric Light Works in about equal monthly quantities over the next thirteen months.

Monmouth Steam Saw Mills Co. Ltd 130 tons Lightmoor bank coal at 16/- per ton in buyers wagons at colliery. Delivery in about equal monthly quantities between now and 30 June next.

George Jones & Co. 200 tons Eastern United small steam coal 8/- per ton in buyers wagons at colliery. Delivery to Chepstow as required between 1 January and 31 March 1914.

Lucas & Co. 12 truckloads Lightmoor small coal at 10/2 per ton carriage paid to Bristol. Delivery one truck per week between date and 31 March 1914.

19 MARCH 1914
Contracts:

Great Western Railway Co. 8,000 tons best Forest coal at 13/3 per ton delivered Bilson Junction in buyers wagons as required.

16 APRIL 1914
Contracts:

Victor Grey & Co. All Eastern United small coal we can spare up to 2,000 tons over six months from 1 April 1914 for delivery to Briton Ferry at 7/6 per ton net in buyers trucks at colliery.

Lucas & Co. 26 truckloads Lightmoor small coal at 10/2 per ton net delivered Bristol M.R. at the rate of one truck per week until 30 September 1914.

Central Coal Co. 300 tons Lightmoor small coal at 6/6 per ton in buyers trucks at colliery. Delivery in about equal monthly quantities over next three months.

Dean Forest Coal Co. 1,200 tons Lightmoor bank small coal at 6/6 per ton in buyers trucks at colliery for delivery to Mr W. J. Mills of Bristol in about equal monthly quantities from 1 April to 31 December.

21 MAY 1914
Contracts:

Dean Forest Coal Co. 3,000 tons Lightmoor small coal at 6/6 per ton less 3d. rebate in buyers trucks at colliery for delivery to Crindau after completion of the existing contract. [Crindau north of Newport, gasworks] Delivery at the rate of 12 to 24 truckloads per week.

Central Coal Co. 350-500 tons at buyers option Lightmoor small coal at 6/6 per ton net in buyers trucks at colliery for delivery in about equal monthly quantities over twelve months commencing 29 April 1914.

Ross Gas Co. 100 tons Eastern United block coal at 15/2 per ton net delivered Ross at the rate of 25 tons per week.

18 JUNE 1914
Contracts:

Suttons Ltd 500 tons best Forest coal at 16/- per ton FOB Lydney for delivery to Mr Fenton as required between date and 30 September 1914.

I. W. Baldwin & Co. 3,120 tons Lightmoor small coal 6/9 per ton less 6d. rebate in buyers trucks at colliery. Delivery at rate of 60 tons per week over twelve months commencing 1 June 1914.

23 JULY 1914
Contracts:

Dean Forest Coal Co. 350 tons High Delf block coal at 12/3 per ton net in buyers trucks at colliery for delivery over next twelve months to Mr Hunt of Bridgwater.

Suttons Ltd 5 cargoes of 150-200 tons each best Forest coal at 16/- per ton net FOR as required from 1 July to 30 September 1914 for Mr C. Hyde, also a further 6 cargoes comprising about 1100 tons best Forest coal on same terms and over a similar period for various others of Sutton's customers.

Sully & Co. Ltd 500 - 1,000 tons High Delf small coal at 7/9 per ton net in buyers trucks at colliery. Delivery to Taunton mills from 1 July to 30 September 1914.

Dean Forest Coal Co. 3,000 tons Lightmoor bank small coal at 6/6 per ton less 3d. rebate in buyers trucks at colliery. Delivery to Mr W. J. Mills of Bristol from 1 July 1914 to 31 March 1915.

City of Cork Steam Packet Co. Ltd 2,500 tons best Forest coal at 16/6 per ton less 6d. rebate F.O.B. Newport for all taken up to 30 September 1914 with 1/- per ton rise on any quantity taken between 1 October 1914 and expiry of contract viz: 30 April 1915.

Gloucestershire Education Committee. House coal as required to council schools over next twelve months as follows:
    Double View best coal at 19/6 d/d
    St. Whites rubbles at 19/6 d/d
    Soudley best coal at 20/- d/d

T. W. Ward Ltd 500 - 700 tons Lightmoor small coal at 7/9 per ton F.O.B. Lydney for delivery between date and 31 December 1914.

Referring to the contract for 2,500 tons of best Forest coal with the **City of Cork Steam Packet Co. Ltd** the Secretary explained this order was obtained by Capt. Creagh and as he had to make two or three special journeys to Cork to see the buyers it was decided to pay him 25s. towards his out-of-pocket expenses.

27 AUGUST 1914
Contracts:

Great Western Railway Co. 3,000 tons best Forest coal at 13/3 per ton delivered Bilson Junction in buyers trucks as required.

Ross Gas Co. 500 tons High Delf block coal at 14/9 per ton d/d Ross at the rate of 25 tons weekly from 1 August 1914.

Suttons Ltd 6-700 tons Forest coal for Mr M. J. Fleming and 600 tons for Martin & Blackwood at 16/- per ton FOR Lydney. Delivery as required before 30 September 1914.

City of Cork Steam Packet Co. Ltd 2,000 tons best forest coal at 16/6 per ton FOR Newport from date until 30 September 1914 with 1/- per ton rise on any quantity taken between 1 October 1914 and 31 March 1915. Delivery in equal monthly quantities between date and 31 March 1915.

Sully & Co. Ltd 1,000 tons Lightmoor small coal at 6/6 per ton less 6d. rebate in buyers trucks at colliery. Delivery in about equal monthly quantities over twelve months from 22 July 1914 for Messrs Bradford & Sons.

Sully & Co. Ltd 450-500 tons High Delf small coal at 7/9 per ton in buyers trucks at colliery. Delivery to Exeter Brick Works in about equal monthly quantities over next twelve months.

H. E. Stonyer 24 truckloads High Delf small coal at 11/6 per ton d/d Withington at rate of 2 trucks per month.

Dean Forest Coal Co. 500 tons coal at present prices until 30 September 1914 with 1/- per ton rise from 1 October 1914 to 31 March 1915 for Messrs Varwell, Guest & Co.

17 SEPTEMBER 1914
Contracts:

Dean Forest Coal Co. 30 tons of best Forest coal at 16/6 per ton in buyers trucks at colliery. Delivery to Mr C. W. Jones towards the end of November for charitable purposes.

Henry Pritchard & Co. Ltd 70 tons High Delf through coal at 13/6 per ton delivered Redcliffe Wharf, Bristol as required.

John Griffiths 200-250 tons high Delf through coal at 10/- per ton in buyers trucks at colliery delivered to Severn Tunnel Junction as required between date and 31 August 1915.

15 OCTOBER 1914
Contracts:

John Stephens, Son & Co. Ltd 1,000 tons of High Delf small coal at 9/6 per ton d/d Gloucester in buyers wagons in about equal monthly quantities over next twelve months.

Dean Forest Coal Co. 50 tons High Delf block coal at 12/3 per ton in buyers trucks at colliery. Delivery to Mr Hunt of Bridgwater in about equal monthly quantities over next six months.

Western Navigation Coal Co. 60 tons per week of broken up Lightmoor small coal until 31 March 1915 at 6/6 per ton less 3d. rebate in buyers trucks at colliery.

Berkeley Gas Co. 300 tons High Delf block coal at 14/9 per ton d/d Ross in about equal monthly quantities after completion of present contract until 30 June 1915.

Lucas & Co. 26 truckloads Lightmoor small coal at 10/2 per ton d/d

Bristol at rate of one truck per week until 31 March 1915.

19 NOVEMBER 1914
Contracts:
Dean Forest Coal Co. 200 tons High Delf small coal at 7/3 per ton in buyers wagons at colliery. Delivery to Gloucester Wagon Co. as required.
J. C. Hill & Co. Ltd 300-400 Eastern United block coal at 15/6 per ton delivered Cwmbran at rate of one truck per week from date until 31 July 1915.
H. Lancaster & Co. 100 tons High Delf small coal at 10/3 per ton delivered Newent as required.
E. Jarrett 2,500 tons Lightmoor small coal at 6/3 per ton net in buyers wagons at colliery. Delivery 50 tons per week to the Great Western Railway Company.
Victor Grey & Co. 40-50 tons High Delf small coal from 1 November to 31 December 1914 at 7/3 per ton, coal and wagon at colliery. Delivery to Gorseinon.
I. W. Baldwin & Co. 400 tons High Delf small coal at 6/6 per ton net in buyers trucks at colliery. Delivery at the rate of 100 tons per week for A. J. Smith Ltd
Geo. Jones & Co. 200 tons High Delf small coal at 7/3 per ton in buyers trucks at colliery. Delivery over next three months to Finch & Co. Chepstow.
Dean Forest Coal Co. 1,630 tons High Delf small coal at 7/- per ton in buyers wagons at colliery. Delivery over next six months to Pontymister.

17 DECEMBER 1914
Contracts:
C. & G. Ayres 72 truckloads Lightmoor small coal at 5/6 per ton in buyers trucks at colliery. Delivery six trucks per month over the year 1915 for Loudwater.
Budd & Co. 2,000 tons Lightmoor small coal at 4/6 per ton, coal and wagon at colliery. Delivery 250 tons per week to Newport docks for foreign shipment.
T. W. Ward & Co. Ltd 800 tons High Delf small coal at 7/3 per ton in buyers trucks at pit. Delivery in about equal monthly quantities over the year 1915.
Dean Forest Coal Co. 1,000 tons High Delf small coal at 7/3 per ton in buyers trucks at colliery. Delivery to Newport, Rogerstone or Pontymister after the completion of existing contract for that district.

21 JANUARY 1915
Contracts:
Western Navigation Coal Co. 5-600 tons Lightmoor small coal at 5/6 per ton, coal and wagon at colliery, for shipment over January next.
Victor Grey & Co. 1,000 tons High Delf small coal at 7/6 per ton in buyers wagons at colliery for delivery to Briton Ferry in about equal monthly quantities between date of completion of existing contract and 30 June 1915.
A. J. Smith Ltd 5-600 tons bank coal at 16/- per ton less 6d. rebate in buyers trucks at pit for delivery during December.
Edgar Jarrett 120 trucks Lightmoor small coal at 6/6 per ton in buyers trucks at pit. Delivery to Hereford in about equal monthly quantities over ensuing 12 months.
I. W. Baldwin & Co. 52 truckloads High Delf nuts at 10/9 per ton in buyers trucks at pit for delivery at the rate of one truck per week to A. J. Smith Ltd
I. W. Baldwin & Co. 5,000 tons High Delf small coal at 7/6 per ton in buyers trucks at pit for delivery in about equal monthly quantities over 12 months following completion of present contract.
Dean Forest Coal Co. 104 truckloads Lightmoor small coal at 6/6 per ton less 3d. rebate in buyers trucks at pit. Delivery two trucks per week to Woolaston over the year 1915.
Dean Forest Coal Co. 1,000 tons Lightmoor small coal at 6/6 per ton in buyers trucks at pit. Delivery to Mr W. J. Mills of Bristol in about equal monthly quantities from 1 January 1915.
Dean Forest Coal Co. 250 tons High Delf small coal at 7/6 per ton in buyers trucks at colliery. Delivery at sellers convenience to Gloucester Wagon Co.
Dean Forest Coal Co. 6 truckloads of bank coal per day from end of December to 31 March 1915 for Varwell, Guest & Co.
Budd & Co. 2,000 tons Lightmoor small coal at 7/- per ton, coal and wagon at colliery. Delivery about 250 tons per week after completion of present contract.
Central Coal Co. 150 tons Lightmoor small coal at 6/6 per ton, coal and wagon at pit. Delivery in about equal monthly quantities over six months from 1 January 1915 to Bristol.
Central Coal Co. 60-70 tons Forest or cobble coal at buyers option at Forest 16/6 and cobble 15/6 per ton in buyers trucks at pit. Delivery to Williton in about equal monthly quantities over 3 months from 1 January 1915.
Renwick, Wilton & Co. 50 tons Lightmoor small coal at 6/6 per ton less 3d. rebate in buyers trucks at pit. Delivery to Torre or Paignton over the next fortnight as required and a further 50 tons for similar delivery at 1/- per ton extra.
Western Navigation Coal Co. 1,500 tons Lightmoor small coal at 7/3 per ton, coal and wagon at colliery. Delivery at rate of 500 tons per month over 3 months from 1 January 1915.
J. Meates & Son 150-200 tons Lightmoor small coal at 7/3 per ton in buyers trucks at pit. Delivery two trucks per week between 12 January and 31 March 1915 for Newent.
W. Sisson & Co. Ltd 100 tons High Delf through coal at 13/6 per ton delivered Gloucester GWR as required.
Edgar Jarrett 5000 tons Lightmoor small coal at 7/3 per ton in buyers trucks at pit. Delivery about 100 tons per week over the ensuing 12 months for the Great Western Railway Co.
Renwick, Wilton & Co. Ltd 100 tons Lightmoor nuts at 17/- per ton less 6d. rebate in buyers trucks at pit. Delivery over 3 weeks.

18 FEBRUARY 1915
Contracts:
Central Coal Co. 350 tons Lightmoor small coal 7/6 per ton in buyers trucks at colliery. Delivery in about equal monthly quantities between date and 30 April 1915.
T. W. Ward Ltd 5 cargoes of 100-110 tons each Lightmoor small coal at 12/- per ton F.O.R. Lydney. Delivery one cargo every week or ten days until completion of contract.
The question of making a further contract with the Great Western Railway was considered and it was decided that it was not advisable to make a further contract with them at less that 20/- per ton. It being considered that if we met them by quoting below present list price we should in future get no consideration whatever for doing so.

18 MARCH 1915
Contracts:
I. W. Baldwin & Co. 400 tons High Delf small coal at 10/6 per ton in buyers trucks at pit. Delivery 3 trucks per week to Gloucester Wagon Co.
Western Navigation Coal Co. 500 tons Lightmoor small coal 13/- per ton at pit. Delivery 250 tons in March and 250 tons in April.

22 APRIL 1915
Contracts:
Edgar Jarrett 600 tons Lightmoor small coal at 14/- per ton in buyers trucks at pit. Delivery 150 tons per month to Messrs Guest, Keen & Nettlefolds Ltd
Dean Forest Coal Co. 120 tons Lightmoor small coal 12/6 per ton in buyers trucks at pit less 3d. rebate for delivery to Gloucester Corporation in about equal monthly quantities over next six months.
H. Blandford & Sons 30 tons Lightmoor rubbles at 23/9 per ton delivered Dursley between date and 30 June 1915 as required.
Chepstow Gas Co. 100 tons Lightmoor small coal at 14/10 per ton delivered Chepstow over next three months.
Western Navigation Coal Co. 600 tons Forest coal at 21/6 per ton, coal and wagon at pit. Delivery for foreign shipment during April.
Central Coal Co. 200 tons Lightmoor small coal at 14/- per ton in buyers trucks at colliery. Delivery about one truck per day during April 1915.
Western Navigation Coal Co. 5,400 tons Lightmoor Forest coal at 21/6 per ton, coal and wagon at pit. Delivery from 1 May to 30 September 1915 and 2500 tons Lightmoor small coal at 13/9 per ton, coal and wagon at pit, for delivery over the same period.

20 MAY 1915
Contracts:
Great Western Railway Co. 2,000 tons Forest large coal at 19/- per ton delivered Bilson Junction as required in buyers trucks.
W. Sisson & Co. Ltd 55 tons High Delf through coal at 20/6 delivered Gloucester GWR as required.
Western Navigation Coal Co. 100 tons Forest large coal at 20/- per ton, coal and wagon at colliery, to be dispatched on 18 May for prompt shipment.
Jones & Sons 70 tons Lightmoor small coal at 14/- per ton less 3d. rebate, in buyers trucks at colliery for shipment at Bullo in 4-6 weeks time.

24 JUNE 1915
Contracts:
New Bowson Coal Co. 100 tons High Delf block coal at 18/9 per ton in buyers trucks at pit. 100 tons High Delf through coal at 17/- per ton in buyers trucks at pit. 100 tons High Delf nuts at 17/6 per ton in buyers trucks at pit. 100 tons High Delf small at 15/9 per ton in

buyers trucks at pit. Delivery at sellers convenience commencing 1 June 1915.
Dean Forest Coal Co. 500 tons Lightmoor small coal at 14/- per ton in buyers trucks at colliery less 3d. per ton rebate. Delivery 14 trucks per week to the South Wales Glass co. after completion of present contract.
Suttons Ltd 7,500 tons Lightmoor Forest large housecoal at 21/9 per ton F.O.R. Lydney or Sharpness. delivery in about equal monthly quantities between date and 31 August 1915.
Sully & Co. Ltd 175 tons Lightmoor small coal at 14/- per ton in buyers trucks at pit less 3d. rebate. Delivery in about equal monthly quantities for shipment to Bridgwater between now and 31 May 1916.
Sully & Co. Ltd 300 tons Lightmoor Forest coal at 20/6 per ton in buyers trucks at pit less 9d. per ton rebate. Delivery to the Somerset Trading Co. in about equal monthly quantities between date and 28 September 1915.
A. J. Smith Ltd 500 tons Lightmoor Forest coal at 20/6 per ton from date to 31 August 1915 and 21/6 per ton from then to end of year. Delivery at the rate of two trucks per week commencing immediately.
Western Navigation Coal Co. 1,500 tons Lightmoor nut coal at 18/6 per ton, coal and wagon at pit. Delivery in about equal monthly quantities between 1 July and 30 September 1915 for foreign shipment.
Dean Forest Coal Co. 300 tons Lightmoor large coal, block 21/- per ton, single screened 21/- per ton, rubbles 20/9 per ton, Forest 20/6 per ton, in buyers trucks at pit less 9d. per ton rebate. Delivery in about equal monthly quantities between date and 30 September 1915 to Somerset Trading Co.
Dean Forest Coal Co. 3 cargoes of 100-140 tons each Lightmoor large coal, block, Forest, single-screened or rubbles at current prices. Delivery one cargo per month during June, July & August 1915 to the Combwick Farmers Association.
Church of England Temperance Society 50 tons High Delf block coal at 22/- per ton delivered at Abbotswood House or Lodge as required over next twelve months after completion of existing contract.
Western Navigation Coal Co. 350 tons Lightmoor bank small coal at 14/6 per ton, coal and wagon at pit, less 3d. per ton rebate. Delivery in about equal monthly quantities from 1 June to 30 September 1915.

27 JULY 1915
Contracts:
Central Coal Co. 32 truckloads Lightmoor bank small coal at 15/- per ton in buyers trucks at colliery. Delivery 4 trucks per week from 1 August 1915.
Ross Gas Co. 750 tons High Delf block coal at 22/9 per ton delivered Ross in about equal monthly quantities over next twelve months after completion of existing contract.

26 AUGUST 1915
Contract:
Lydney & Crump Meadow Collieries Co. Ltd 800 tons Lightmoor small coal at 15/- per ton in buyers trucks at colliery less 3d. per ton rebate. Delivery at the rate of 200 tons per week over four weeks.

16 SEPTEMBER 1915
Contracts:
Lydney & Crump Meadow Collieries Co. Ltd 800 tons Lightmoor small coal at 13/- per ton less 6d. rebate in buyers trucks at pit. Delivery if possible to be completed between 31 August and 15 September 1915.
Dean Forest Coal Co. 500 tons High Delf small coal at 14/9 per ton in buyers trucks at colliery. Delivery at rate of 4 or 5 trucks per week or more if convenient to both parties.

21 OCTOBER 1915
Contracts:
John Stephens, Son & Co. Ltd 900 tons High Delf small coal at 15/6 per ton delivered Gloucester in buyers trucks at the rate of 150 tons per month.
City of Cork Steam Packet Co. Ltd 3,000 tons Forest large coal at 22/6 per ton F.O.R. Newport less 6d. per ton rebate. Delivery in about equal monthly quantities between date and 30 April 1916.
Berkeley Gas Co. 300 tons eastern United block coal at 20/9 per ton d/d Berkeley in about equal monthly quantities.
W. H. James 50-60 tons per month High Delf steam coal from 1 October 1915 to 31 March 1916 at 17/8 per d/d Newent Waterworks.
Great Western Railway Co. 10,000 tons Forest large coal at 18/6 per ton d/d Bilson Junction as required.
Sully & Co. Ltd 375 tons Lightmoor small coal at 11/6 per ton in buyers trucks at pit. Delivery in about equal monthly quantities between 1 January and 30 June 1916 for Ilfracombe.
Lucas & Co. 39 truckloads bank small coal at 16/5 per ton d/d Bristol during October 1915 with 1/- per ton reduction on subsequent deliveries to 30 June 1916. Delivery at rate of one truckload per week.
W. Sisson & Co. Ltd 100 tons High Delf through coal at 18/6 per ton d/d Gloucester as required over next six months.
T. W. Ward Ltd 250 tons High Delf small coal at 13/- per ton in buyers trucks at pit delivery at rate of about twenty tons per week.

18 NOVEMBER 1915
Contracts:
T. W. Ward Ltd 300 tons bank small at 11/6 per ton in buyers wagons at pit less 3d. rebate. Delivery one truck per week to Bayliss & Son.
Renwick, Wilton & Co. 250 tons Lightmoor small coal at 12/9, coal and wagon at pit less 3d. per ton rebate. Delivery one truck per week to Plymouth.

16 DECEMBER 1915
Contracts:
A. J. Smith Ltd 2,500 tons Lightmoor small coal at 11/6 per ton in buyers trucks at pit less 3d. per ton rebate. Delivery in equal monthly quantities over seven months from 1 December 1915.
Budd & Co. Ltd 3,000 tons Lightmoor small coal at 11/6 per ton in sellers wagons at colliery. Delivery in about equal monthly quantities over the next four months for foreign shipment.
Edgar Jarrett 2,500 tons Lightmoor small coal at 11/6 per ton in buyers trucks at pit less 3d. per ton rebate. Delivery about 50 tons per week to the Great Western Railway Co.
Edgar Jarrett 60 tons Lightmoor small coal at 11/6 per ton in buyers trucks at pit less 3d. rebate. Delivery about 10 tons per month to Hereford.

20 JANUARY 1916
Contracts:
Lydney & Crump Meadow Collieries Co. Ltd 500 tons Lightmoor small coal at 11/6 per ton less 3d. rebate at pit. Delivery up to 100 tons per week.
Renwick, Wilton & Co. 500 tons Lightmoor small coal at 11/6 per ton less 3d. rebate at pit. Delivery about 50 tons per week.
W. H. James 26 trucks High Delf small coal at 15/1 per ton delivered at Gloucester in buyers trucks at the rate of one truck per week from 1 January to 30 June 1916.
Budd & Co. Ltd 500 tons Forest coal at 22/- per ton in buyers trucks at pit for foreign shipment in equal weekly quantities over January 1916. Also a further 500 tons on same terms for February delivery.

17 FEBRUARY 1916
Contract:
Berkeley Gas Co. 300 tons High Delf block coal at 20/9 per ton delivered Berkeley at the rate of 10-12 tons per week after completion of existing contract.

27 APRIL 1916
Contracts:
Budd & Co. 400 tons Lightmoor Forest coal for foreign shipment at 23/6 per ton in buyers wagons at colliery for delivery in about equal weekly quantities after completion of existing contract.

18 MAY 1916
Contracts:
Western Navigation Coal Co. 300 tons Lightmoor small coal for foreign shipment at 18/- per ton, coal and wagon at pit, less 1^1/4%.
James & Emanuel 600 tons Forest coal for foreign shipment at 25/- per ton in buyers trucks at pit. Delivery at the rate of 100 tons per week.
Budd & Co. 500 tons Forest coal at 25/- per ton in buyers trucks at pit for foreign shipment. Delivery about 100 tons per week.
J. W. Kilmister spot lots of 200-300 tons Forest coal at 25/9 per ton in our own wagons at pit for foreign shipment subject to seven days notice.

15 JUNE 1916
Contract:
Budd & Co. Ltd 500 tons Forest coal for foreign shipment at 25/- per ton in buyers trucks at pit. Delivery at rate of about 100 tons per week.

27 JULY 1916
Contracts:
Great Western Railway Co. 10,000 tons Forest housecoal at 21/- per ton in buyers wagons at Bilson Junction. Delivery at the rate of 300 tons per week commencing on completion of existing contract.
Ross Gas Co. Ltd 750 tons Lightmoor or Eastern United block coal at 23/8^3/4 for Lightmoor block or 20/2^3/4 for Eastern United block subject to any advance authorised by Government, delivered to Ross station in equal monthly quantities over twelve months from completion of

present contract.

31 AUGUST 1916
Contract:
Lydney & Crump Meadow Collieries Co. Ltd 4,000 tons Lightmoor small coal at 14/- per ton in buyers wagons at pit less 3d. per ton rebate. Delivery at the rate of about 100 tons per week for foreign shipment.

14 DECEMBER 1916
Contract:
Dean Forest Coal Co. 500 tons Eastern United High Delf small coal at 15/11 per ton in buyers wagons at pit for delivery to Gloucester Wagon Co. at the rate of 20 tons per week after completion of present contract.

18 JANUARY 1917
Contracts:
Dean Forest Coal Co. 5,000 tons rough small coal at 13/6 per ton in buyers wagons at colliery less usual rebate of 3d. per ton. This price to stand good until 30 June next then subject to any advance allowed by the Government. Delivery to be made if possible at the rate of two trucks daily.
Victor Grey & Co. 300 tons small coal at 13/- per ton in buyers wagons at colliery less usual rebate of 3d. per ton. Delivery at the rate of about 25 tons per week between now and the end of April next.
Thomas W. Ward Ltd 500 tons small coal at 13/- per ton in buyers wagons at colliery, usual hire if in sellers wagons, usual rebate 3d. per ton. Delivery at the rate of 50 tons per week.
Having received an order for 100 tons of Eastern United block coal for the **South Eastern & Chatham Railway Co.** from Messrs W. D. Barnet & Co. Ltd, Exchange Chambers, St. Mary's Ave., London, EC. Mr A. J. Morgan stated that he had seen these people and arranged with them to try the coal at 34/- per ton carriage paid to Cuxton station SECR, this figure being made up as follows:

Coal at colliery	20/- per ton
Truck hire to Cuxton station, or any other on SECR	1/10^{1}/$_{2}$
Railway rate	9/10
Commissions to Messrs Barnet	2/3^{1}/$_{2}$
Total	34/-

It was decided to execute the order. Also to encourage further orders for this coal if satisfactory from the railway co. in future when our output increased.

15 MARCH 1917
Contract:
Central Coal Co. 2,700 tons Lightmoor small coal at 13/- per ton in buyers wagons at colliery. Delivery to be completed if possible on or before 30 June next.

17 MAY 1917
Contracts:
Ross Gas Co. 250 tons of Lightmoor or Eastern United block coal, Lightmoor block at 26/2^{3}/$_{4}$ per ton and Eastern United block at 22/8^{3}/$_{4}$ per ton in buyers wagons at pit. Delivery to be made in equal monthly quantities.
Great Western Railway Co. 4,100 tons of best large housecoal at 22/6 per ton at Lightmoor Colliery of Bilson Junction in buyers wagons at colliery. Delivery at the rate of 300 tons per week between 5 May 1917 and 5 August 1917.

26 JULY 1917
Contracts:
Alfred J. Smith Ltd 3,900 tons Lightmoor small coal at 13/6 per ton in buyers wagons at pit, usual hire and hours, equal deliveries over 12 months from 6 July 1917 or 75 tons per week.
Edgar Jarrett 2,600 tons of Lightmoor small coal for the Great Western Railway at 16/3 per ton from 1 July 1917 to 31 July 1917, 14/3 1 August to 13 September 1917, 13/9 14 September to 31 October 1917 and 12/9 1 November to 30 June 1918 in buyers wagons at colliery, usual hire and hours. Deliveries at the rate of 50 tons per week from the 7 July 1917.
New Bowson Coal Co. 5,000 tons of Lightmoor small coal at 13/3 per ton in buyers wagons at colliery, usual hire and hours. Deliveries in equal quantities over 12 months ending 30 June 1918.
Dean Forest Coal Co. 20,000 tons of Lightmoor small coal at 13/1^{1}/$_{2}$ per ton in buyers wagons at colliery, usual hire and hours. Equal delivery over 12 months ending 30 June 1918.
A. J. Morgan 500 tons of Lightmoor block and single screened coal at 24/- and 23/6 per ton in buyers wagons at colliery net, usual hire and hours, for delivery to the Ealing Borough Surveyor over 3 months from 14 July 1917.
Great Western Railway 4,100 tons of best large housecoal as previously supplied at 22/6 per ton in buyers wagons at colliery, usual hire and hours for delivery at the rate of 400 tons per week on completion of the existing contract.
All the above contracts are subject to the conditions desired by the Controller of Mines under net cash terms.
As regards the 500 tons for **Mr A. J. Morgan** for the Borough Surveyor of Ealing it was decided that so long as he was being charged full list price with no factors rebate it was quite in order to supply him 500 or 1,000 tons if it was at all convenient to do so notwithstanding the minute passed 15 February last.

30 AUGUST 1917
Contracts:
Chepstow Gas Co. 600 tons Lightmoor small coal to end of October 1917 at 15/10^{3}/$_{4}$ per ton and 1 November to 30 June 1918 at 15/4^{3}/$_{4}$ per ton delivered net in equal monthly quantities.
Ross Gas Co. 500 tons Eastern United block coal at 22/8^{3}/$_{4}$ per ton delivered Ross station at the rate of 20-30 tons per week. If unable to supply Eastern United block Lightmoor block coal to be sent at 26/2^{3}/$_{4}$ net.
Both contracts subject to the usual War Clause and the wishes of the Coal Controller.

17 JANUARY 1918
Great Western Railway Co. had asked for a further contract for 4,000 tons of coal.

21 FEBRUARY 1918
Contracts showing the sale of 789 tons per calendar month Forest of Dean large coal to the **Great Western Railway** at 25/- per ton net in their trucks at colliery for a period whilst the existing conditions remain in force was presented and approved.

20 JUNE 1918
Contract:
Dean Forest Coal Co. 10,000 tons Lightmoor small coal for delivery between 1 July 1918 and 30 June 1919 in equal monthly quantities at 15/7^{1}/$_{2}$ per ton at pit, wagon hire extra. Terms strictly net. Contract subject to any action taken by Controller etc., also to any increase in price which may be allowed during period of delivery.

25 JULY 1918
Contracts:
Dean Forest Coal Co. 5,000 tons Lightmoor small coal for delivery between 1 July 1918 and 30 July 1919 at varying prices in buyers wagons at colliery, usual hire extra if in sellers wagons. Cash, monthly less rebate of 3d. per ton.
Dean Forest Coal Co. 3,000 tons Lightmoor bank small coal for delivery between 1 July 1918 and 30 June 1919 in buyers wagons at colliery.
Arthur J. Morgan 5000 tons Lightmoor small coal for delivery between 1 July 1918 to 30 June 1919 in buyers wagons at colliery.

17 JULY 1919
Contracts:
Dean Forest Coal Co. 15,000 tons Lightmoor small coal 19/7^{1}/$_{2}$ per ton net in buyers trucks at colliery in equal monthly quantities over 12 months from 1 July 1919.
Dean Forest Coal Co. 3,000 tons Lightmoor bank small in equal monthly quantities from 1 July 1919 to 30 June 1920. Price:

1 July - 31 July 1919	23/6 per ton
1 August - 14 September 1919	21/6
15 September - 31 October 1919	21/-
1 November 1919 - 30 June 1920	20/-

in buyers wagons at colliery less a rebate of 3d. per ton.
Arthur Morgan 5,000 tons Lightmoor small coal in equal monthly quantities from 1 July 1919 to 30 July 1920. Price:

1 July - 31 July 1919	23/- per ton
1 August - 14 September 1919	21/-
15 September - 31 October 1919	20/6
1 November 1919 - 30 June 1920	19/6

in buyers wagons at colliery less a rebate of 3d. per ton.
Great Western Railway Co. 50-100 tons per week of Lightmoor small coal over 12 months from 1 July 1919. Price:

1 July - 31 July 1919	23/- per ton
1 August - 14 September 1919	21/-
15 September - 31 October 1919	20/6
1 November 1919 - 30 June 1920	19/6

in buyers wagons at colliery.

INDEX

COMPANIES & PARTNERSHIPS

A. Goold & Co.	13, 30-31
Aldridge, R. E.	111
Alfred J. Smith Ltd	70, 94-95, 96, 139
Allaways, Messrs	13, 159, 163
Austin Motor Co.	69
Ayres, C. & G.	121
Bailey, J. E.	72
Baker & Kernick	70, 105
Baldwin, I. W.	60, 70, 82
Baldwin, Lowell, & Co.	65, 68, 70, 81, 99-100, 138
Barker & Lovering	70, 104, 139
Barrett Brothers	157
Basic Lime & Stone Co. Ltd	149
Bath Coal Co.	147
Bedwas	51, 125
Bennett, Messrs	144
Berkeley Farmers Association Ltd	111, 146
Benjamin & Co.	132
Berry Wiggins	7, 165-167
Bilson & Crump Meadow Colliery Co. Ltd	30
Binks, J. C. & Co.	44
Birchen Grove Colliery Co.	146
Blandford, H. & Sons	112
Boucher, Williams & Co.	
Bowkes [Bowles], E. & Sons	147
Brain, T.	13, 15
Bright, A. C. & Co. Ltd	144
Bristol Mineral Co.	150
British Colour & Mining Co.	157
British Railway Traffic & Electric Co. Ltd	165
British Red Ash Collieries Ltd	17, 39, 43
Briton Ferry Chemical Co.	147
Bruce, A.	147
Bryant, Geo. & Co.	36
Bryer Ash, G.	134, 135
Buchanan, W. L.	135
Budd & Co.	125
Burnyeat Brown & Co.	147
Burrows, Thomas	147
Butler, William	135, 137
Cannop Coal Co. Ltd	56
Central Coal Co.	147
Chamberlain, E. A.	127
Cheltenham, Borough of	130
Chivers, Jacob & Son	144
Cinderford Crushing Co.	145, 163
Clee Hill Granite Co.	154
Clutton	101
Coal Agencies Ltd	95
Cole, Edward J.	135, 137
Coleford Red Ash Colliery Co. Ltd	41
Colthrop	138
Compressed Coal Co.	13, 145
Crane, Alexander	115
Critchlow & Sheppard	135, 136
David & Co.	149, 151
David & Sant Ltd	19, 151
Davis, G	119
Dean Forest Central Collieries Ltd	146
Dean Forest Coal Co.	65, 69-70, 71-75, 76
Dean Forest Hematite Iron Ore Co.	163
Dean Forest Navigation Coal & Fuel Co.	42
Dickinson, Prosser & Cox	113
Dowlais Iron Co.	163
Drybrook Quarries Ltd	149
Duck, William	119
Dudley & Gibson	135, 136
Dunkerton Coal Factors	97, 101
Earl, Philip & Co.	147
Easter Hematite Iron Ore Co. Ltd	157
Easter Iron Ore Mines Ltd	157
Ebbw Vale Co.	163
Edgar Jarrett & Co.	33, 60, 77-78
Finch, E. & Co.	147
Flour Mill Colliery Co.	146
Forester & Co.	13
Forest Hematite Co.	163
Forest of Dean Iron & Steel Co. Ltd	163
Forest of Dean Iron Co.	13, 14, 159
Forest of Dean Mining Co. Ltd	146
Forest of Dean Stone Firms	149, 150, 151
Forest of Dean Stone Firms Ltd	149
Forest Red Ash Co.	43
Forest Steam Coal Co.	43, 146
Fowler, John & Co.	147
Fred Watkins (Whitecliff Quarries) Ltd	155
Gay, G. & Sons	147
Gethin, W. C.	133
Goodland	147
Glossop, F. B.	89, 107
Gloucester Corporation	126, 130
Gloucester Gaslight Company	129
Gloucester Wagon Co.	7, 13
Gollop & Co.	44, 145
Gollop & Ridler	13, 145
Gollop, Ridler & Co.	145
Goodlands	117
Goold Bros	13, 14, 31, 161
Graham Roberts & Co.	125
Great Western (Forest of Dean) Coal Consumers Co. Ltd	25
Great Western (Forest of Dean) Collieries Co. Ltd	25
Great Western Iron Co.	161
Greenham & James	13, 14
Grist & Co.	147
Grist, Matthew	135, 136
Gwinnell, H. A.	134, 135
Hall, W.	147
Happerfields, Messrs	147
Hartnell & Son	117
Hawkwell Colliery Co.	144
Henry Crawshay & Co. Ltd	7, 13, 14, 16, 25, 32, 33, 34-38, 65-67, 69-70, 71, 79, 84, 104, 126, 128, 145, 159, 160
Hillier's Bacon Curing Co. Ltd	127
Hirwaun Aberdare Steam Coal Co.	13, 31
Hockaday & Co.	20
Hollins, John	123
Holmes Bros	41
Holpin, F. J.	111
James & Emanuel	94, 125
James, R. T.	147
James, William H.	110
Jarrett Bros	163
Jefferies, Samuel	128
Jones, E. & Sons	65
Joseph Ward	149
Kelly, A. H.	147
Kingsbury	147
Knight, E.	147
Lames & Sons	147
Lansley	133
Leadbeter	32, 124
Leadbeter, T. L. & Co.	136, 137
Lincoln Wagon Co.	7
Littledean Woodside Coal Co.	144, 145
Llewellyn, Samuel	123
Lückes & Nash	14, 25, 145
Lydbrook Colliery Co.	146
Lydney & Forest of Dean Coal Co.	146
Lydney Coal Co.	108
Lydney & Crump Meadow Collieries Co. Ltd	30, 60-63, 67, 79, 119, 144
Lydney & Wigpool Iron Ore Co.	163
Mabbett, H. J.	111, 146
Man-Abell (Whitecliff Quarry) Ltd	155
Mansfield Bros	109
Meek, Godfrey, colliery agent	146
Mierystock Quarries Ltd	149
Milkwall Ironstone Co.	163
Monmouth Steam Saw Mills Co. Ltd	131, 155
Moody, A. E.	111
Moreland, S. J.	128
Morgan Bros	122
Morgan, E. P. & R. L.	76
Morgan, George & Sons	43
Morrells, Messrs	146
Morris, Wm	124
Morrison & Beauclerk	161
Mortimore	120
Mullis, F. G.	132, 133
National Smelting Co.	138
New Bowson Coal Co.	36, 69, 76, 79-81
Newport Coal & Coke Co.	94
New Trafalgar Colliery Co. Ltd	28
Noble, J. R.	147
Old Radnor Co.	135
Palmer & Sawdye	132
Park Colliery Co. Ltd	48
Parkend & New Fancy Collieries Co.	18-20
Parkend & New Fancy Collieries Co. Ltd	18-20
Parkend Coal Co. Ltd	13, 14, 18-19, 85
Parkend Deep Navigation Collieries Co. Ltd	18-24, 33
Parkend Plate Co.	159
Parkend Tinplate Co.	72, 159
Park Iron Mines & Collieries Ltd	48, 77
Park Iron Ore & Coal Co. Ltd	48-49
Pates & Co.	113
Payne, E. R.	149
Payne, E. R. & Son Ltd	149, 150, 151
Payne & Son	136, 137
Pearce	95
Pepler, H. & Sons	119
Phœnix Coal Co.	44, 83-84, 146
Playne, Wm	126
Poole, James	147
Porter Bros	149
Porthywaen Lime & Basic Co. Ltd	149
Pounsbery	133
Powell Duffryn	147
Powell, Gwinnell & Co. Ltd	114
Powell, Osman Trevor	105
Princess Royal Colliery Co. Ltd	52-53, 70, 95, 138
Purified Flock & Bedding Co. Ltd	126
Radstock Coal Co.	117
Ralls & Son	121
Read & Son	89, 92-93
Read & Westmoreland	92-93
Renwick, Wilton & Co.	60, 66, 70, 102-103
Richard Thomas & Baldwin	162
Richard Thomas & Co.	39, 65, 162
Ricketts	60
Ridler & Weedon	13, 14, 25, 145
Royal Forester Colliery Co. Ltd	25
Sawyer, W. & Co.	114
Severn Ports Warehousing	169
Sharpness Chemical Co.	168
Silvey, F. H. & Co.	98
Silvey, Thomas & Co.	96-97, 98, 138, 139
Small, George & Son	32, 116
Smith, F. J.	147
Smith, James	15, 37, 41, 79, 88-91, 107, 150
Somerset Trading Co.	117, 121
South Eastern Gas Board	167
South Herefordshire Agricultural Co-op	130
South Wales Coal Co.	133, 134
Speech House Hill Colliery Co. Ltd	25
Speech House Hill Collieries Co. Ltd	25
Speech House Main Collieries Co. Ltd	25
Speedwell Newbridge Colliery Co. Ltd	144
Spencer Abbott	121
Staunton Iron Co.	163
Steam Coal Collieries	147
Steetley Lime & Basic Slag Co.	149
Steetley Lime & Building Stone Co.	149
Stephens, John, Son & Co. Ltd	129
Stonehouse Brick & Tile Co. Ltd	128
Stone, S. & Co.	119
Stroud Gas Light & Coke Co.	127
Sully & Co.	33, 34, 70, 76, 85-87, 139
Summer & Co.	95
Swan, Thomas & Co.	155
Terrett Taylor & Sons	110
Thomas, E. & Co.	147
Toomer Bros	13
Toomer, J. & Sons	147
Toomer, R & Co.	19, 25
Trafalgar Colliery Co. Ltd	28
Trotter, Thomas & Co.	9, 13, 14, 27, 145, 149
Turner, E. R. & Sons	149, 152
Twining, Lewellin	118, 138
United Stone Firms Ltd	149, 151, 152, 153
United Stone Firms (1926) Ltd	149, 153
Usher, Albert	121
Venus Colliery Co.	146
Victor Grey & Co.	124
Wallsend Limited	44
Wanklyn & Grindell	91
Ward, E. T.	43, 115
Webb Bros	134
Webb, Hall & Webb, Ltd	123
Weedon & Co.	145
Weedon Bros	33
Weeks, E. H.	147
Wellington	147
Wellington, Jones & Co.	157
Western Counties Colliery Co.	145
Western Wagon Co.	7
West Glos. Power Co.	51
Whitecliff Lime Co.	149, 155
Whitecliff Lime & Stone Co.	131, 155
Whittaker, Keighley	25
Whitwill, Cole & Co.	118
Whitwill, Mark & Son	118
Williams & Stephens	146
William Thomas & Co. Ltd	33, 117
Wimberry Colliery Co. Ltd	27, 145
Wm Cory	60, 70
Yates, John	123

DOCKS

Bullo	7, 9, 139, 140
coal tips	11, 13, 139, 140-143
Lydney	7, 9, 11, 22, 70, 87, 95, 96, 115, 139
Newport	7
Sharpness	7, 70, 139, 141-143

INDUSTRY

Coal Factors	69-70
Coal Merchants	107

Collieries

Addis Hill	82
Arthur & Edward (Waterloo)	30, 31, 47, 60-63, 79, 82, 126
Bilson	13, 30
Birchen Grove	43
Bixslade	9
Bixslade Deep Level	10
Bowson	47
Bream Grove	77
Cannop	27, 56-59, 68, 94, 96, 104, 118, 125
Cinderford Bridge	15
Churchway	144
Clement's Tump	44
Cross Knave	95
Crump Meadow	10, 13, 17, 30-31, 32, 118, 120

Dan's Drift	77	Barrett, William	13	Protheroe, Edward	9. 18, 30, 32
Darkhill	44, *91*	Beacham, William	117	Ralls, Richard	121
deep pits, the	47	Beauchamp, Frank	117	Ralls, Thomas	121
East Cannock (Staffs)	82	Bennett, Thomas	144	Read, George	92
Eastern United	35, 65-66, 76, 82, *100*, 121, 128, 129, *138*, 160	Blandford, Charles	112	Richard, James	45
East Slade	79	Blandford, George	112	Richardson, John	30, 32
Ellwood	146	Blandford, Henry	112	Ries, Samuel	159
Flour Mill	*52*, 146	Blandford, Ryland Harris	112	Ridler, James	145
Foxes Bridge	17, *30*, 32-33, 116, 117, 124, 163	Borlase, J. G.	157	Ring, Richard Charles	94
Glyncarn	95	Boucher, Joseph	170	Shackleford, William	170
Harrow Hill	82	Boucher, William	170	Shepherd, James	85, 86
Hawkwell	47, 144, 163	Boulton, Ernest	155	Silvey, Frank	98
Haywood	47, 144, 145	Brain family	28	Silvey, Gilbert	98
Hopewell	43	Bright, Alfred Charles	144, 163	Silvey, Thomas	96
Hopewell Engine	145	Brown, Amos	27	Spillers	169
housecoal	17	Bryant, Walter	153	Stone, James	144
Lightmoor	14, *16*, 17, 25,33, 34-38, 65, 76, 82, 92, 110, 112, 117, 121, 125, 140, 160	Buck, David	45	Stone, Samuel	119
		Burdess, William	79	Sully, family	14
Lydbrook	*16*, 39, 126, 146, 162	Chivers, Jacob	47, 144, 163	Sully, James Wood	18, 85
Mapleford Engine	145	Cole, William Henry	118	Sully, John	85
Meadow Cliff	144, 146	Collins, Mansfield	108	Sully, J. Norman	86
Moira (Leics.)	113	Cooper, John	155	Sully, Thomas	18, 85
Nags Head	41, 89	Crawshay, Charlotte	71	Teague, James	7
Nelson	144	Crawshay, Edwin	25, 47, 72, 144, 159	Teague, Moses	32, 159
New Bowson	79	Crawshay, Henry	25, 32, 34, 71, 144, 160	Thomas, Alfred	108
New Fancy	13, 17, 18, 20, 23-24, *84*	Crawshay, William	32, 34, 160	Thomas, J. T.	*13*
Norchard	41, 48-51, 130	Crawshay, William Jnr	163	Thomas, Richard	162
Northern United	67, 130, *138*, 160	Curwen, Herbert	155	Thomas, Sydney J.	*13*
Parkend	18-24, 85	Daniels, Nathaniel	159	Tingle, William	45
Park Hill	17	Davis, G, of Broadwell Lane End	17	Trotter, J.	18, 85
Pillowell	15, 42, 145	Davis, John	45	Turner, James Edward	152
Pluds	39	Deakin, Thomas	18	Turner, William Henry	152
Princess Royal	48, 52-55, 77, 115, 126, 127, 128, 140	Deakin, Thomas Carlisle	84	Twining, Lewellin	118
Rudge	145	Dott, Thomas	45	Wagstaff, William	15
smaller collieries	41	Dyke, Thomas	52	Washbourn, F. G.	163
St. Vincent	*91*	Ford, Mr	170	Watkins, Fred	155, 158
Speech House Hill	13, 14, 17, 25-26, 53, 145	Fox, Samuel	163	Watkins, Richard	158
Speedwell	27	Fryer, William Henry	157, 163	Weedon, Richard	145
Speedwell Newbridge	144, 145	Gollop, Francis	145	Whitehouse, Benjamin	159
Thatch	89	Gollop, James	145	Whitwill, Mark	118
Trafalgar	*13*, 15, 17, 28-29, 88, 89, 92, 107, 121	Goold, Aaron	13, 31	Williams, Richard	146
Union	146	Goold, Alfred	14	Vincent, John	15
Venus & Jupiter	17, 146	Goold, Charles A.	31, 32	Vivian, Sir Hussey	170
Wallsend	13, 44, 145	Goold, Tom	31		
Wellington	146	Gosling, Frank C.	108	**PLACES**	
Wimberry	14, 17, 27, 145	Greenham, Charles	159	Appledore	139
Woorgreens	45, 113	Guest, Sir Josiah John	163	Berkeley	111, 146
Iron Mines		Gwilliam, Thomas	155	Bilson	7
Crows Nest	145	Haddingham, Mrs	72	Birmingham	121
Easter	157, 163	Haddingham, Stephen	71, 170	Bixslade	146, 149
Fair Play	163	Hale, Aaron	27	Blakeney	13, 146
High Meadow	145	Heyworth, Captain	157	Bradford-on-Avon	95
New Dun Pit	158	Hockaday, Frank Step	84	Bream	17, 157
Park	77	Hockaday, W. L.	43	Bridgwater	13, 14, 18, 85-86, 117, 147
Shakemantle	157, 160	Holden family	79	Bridport	121
Staunton	145	Holford, George	19	Bristol	118, 119
Westbury Brook	163	Holmes, Simeon	13, 15, 41, 42, 89	Brixham	66
Wigpool	13, 163	Holmes, Simeon Oaks	42	Bullo	9, *11*, 41
Ironworks		Howell, Noah	44	Bullo Pill	7, *13*
Cinderford	13, 14, 34, 157, 160, 163	Illingworth family	79	Cardiff	104, 105, 169
Parkend	14, 157	Jackson, Mr Robert	18, 19, 25	Chalford	113
Soudley	31, 157 , 161, 163	James, John	159	Cheltenham	113, 114
Stocksbridge	163	James, Richard	25	Chepstow	7, 123
Other Industries		Jones, George	155	Chipping Norton	*75*
bitumen manufacturers	165	Jones, William	157	Churchway	14
colour works	157	Jones, William J.	108	Cinderford	10, 17, 18, 47 , 110, 157
Industrial coal user	126	Jordan, William	25	Clevedon	114
Lydney Gasworks	146	Kelham, Richard	86, 101	Clevedon Gasworks	*62*
Staple Edge brickworks	13, 145	Kilmister, J. W.	36, 37	Clifton, Bristol	118
Whitecroft Patent Fuel Works	15, 42, 145	Langford, William	153	Clutton	101
Quarries		Langham, Goodrich	144, 155	Coleford	7, 109, 130, 149
Bixslade	*12*, 14, 150, 152	Latham, Arthur	44, 83-84, 145	Culmstock	86, *87*
Clee Hill	154	Letcher, Edwin Marcus	144	Dudbridge	128, 146
Dark Hill	150, 152	Linneker, James	146	Dunkerton	101
De Lank	153	Lovering, John	104	Drybrook	*28*
Drybrook	149	Mabbett, John	111, 146	Dursley	112, 127
general	141	Maclean, M.	56	Eastville, Bristol	119
Hallatrow	153	Maggs, Colin	146	Fishponds, Bristol	98, 119
Point	150	Mansfield, George	109	Gloucester	7, 105, 115, 139
Porthgain	153	Meek, Godfrey	144, 146	Hempstead, Gloucester	129
Portland	153	Montague, William	32, 159	Howbeach	13
Shakemantle	149	Moody, Albert E.	111	Kerne Bridge	83, 122
Wimberry	14 , 150	Moorby, W. G.	146	Liverpool	121
Stone Works		Morgan, Ada	72	Llanelly	159
Bixslade	152	Morgan, Arthur	76, 145, 163	London	121
Fetterhill	152	Morgan, Edwin Percy	76	Loudwater	121
Parkend	150, 151	Morgan, Fred.	71, 72	Ludlow	154
Point	150, *154*	Morgan, G. F.	163	Lydbrook	7, 13, 83
Speech House (Cannop)	151, *153*	Morgan, Henry	72	Lydney	7, *11*, 13, 17, 108
Tinplate Works		Morgan, Rose Lillian	76	May Hill, Monmouth	131
Hawkwell (Cinderford)	157, 163	Morrell, James	146	Merthyr Tydfil	34
Lydbrook	13, 157, 162, 163	Morrell, Robert	146	Mierystock	149
Lydney	13, 14, 39, 157, 159, 162, 163	Morris, Charles	159	Milford Haven	22
Parkend	159	Mushet, David	9, 27	Milkwall	157, 163
		Mushet, Robert	7, 27	Minchinhampton	126
PEOPLE		Mushet, William	27	Mitcheldean Road	83
Aldridge, Robert, E.	111	Neville, W.	153	Monmouth	7, 83, 122, 123, 130
Baker, Charles	144	Nicholson, Thomas	18, 85	Montpelier, Bristol	98
Baker, Frederick	144	Payne, Edwin R.	150	Moseley Green	15, 146
Baldwin, Edward	27	Peglar, Thomas	44	Nailbridge	144
Barrett, James Michaelmas	157	Powell, John	146	Nailsworth	126, 127
Barrett, Osman	32, 157, 163	Pritchard. John	108	New Milford	13

183

Newnham	*106*, 118	Drybrook Road Station	28	coal tips	*11, 14*
Newport	7, 95, *124*, 125	Fetterhill Sidings	91	Crump Meadow	*10*
Oxford	146	Forest of Dean Branch	13, 14, 15, *30*, 32, 34, 79, *155*	Forest of Dean Railway Co.	7, *10,11*
Parkend	7, 146	Forest of Dean Central Railway	13, 15, 23, 44, 145	Milkwall Tramroad	157
Pillowell	13, 17	Fosse Cross Station	113	Monmouth Railway Co.	7,
Princetown	*81*	Great Western	14	names painted on	9
Reading	121	Haie Hill tunnel	7	Oakwood Tramroad	7, *163*
Redcliffe Hill, Bristol	99	Hereford, Ross & Gloucester	83	Severn & Wye Railway & Canal Co.	7, *8, 9, 10,* 13, 14, *18*
River Severn	7	Highworth Branch	119	tolls on	7
River Wye	7	Lawrence Hill Station	119	wagons	*8, 9, 10, 12*
Ross	83, 122, 123, 130	Lightmoor Railway	34	Wigpool Tramroad	13
St. Fagans	*75*	Lydbrook Branch	39, 149	Wimberry Tramroad	*8, 14*
St. Phillips, Bristol	96, 99	Lydbrook Junction	43		
Salisbury	92	Lydney Town Station	108, 145	**WAGONS**	
Sharnel Street, Isle of Grain	165	Lydney Station	13	Broad Gauge	13-15
Sharpness	7, 111, 168, 169	Lydney Junction	71	hired wagons	90
Sling	157, 163	Marsh Sidings, Parkend	17, *163*	requisitioning of	38
Stratford, E. London	165	Midland & South Western Junction	113, 119	Tramroad	8-12
Stratton, Wilts	119	Midland Railway	33, 111, 127	transporter wagons	14
Stroud	113, 115	Mierystock Sidings	60-63	**Wagon Builders & Suppliers**	
Swansea	124	Mineral Loop, the	13, 15, 17, 23, 28, 32, 34, 145	Adams & Co.	15
Swindon	13, 139	Mitcheldean Road & Forest of Dean Junction Rly	144	Albion Carriage Co. Ltd	171
Swindon Electricity Works	*81*	mixed gauge	13	Baxendale & Heald	146
Taunton	116, 117	Monmouth Troy Station	22, *63,* 122, 123	Bennett, E. H.	104
Totterdown, Bristol	94	New Mills Siding	41	Blockley, B. P.	162
Unstone, Yorks	146	Newnham Station	13, *106*	Bridgwater Engineering Co.	86
Wapping Wharf, Bristol	99	Oakwood Branch	52	British Wagon Co.	35, 37, 49, 147
Waterloo	39	Point Quarry Sidings	150	Bristol Wagon Co.	13, *170*
Wellington	117	Railway Clearing House	29, 35, 37, 143	Bristol & South Wales Waggon Co.	*13*
Weston-super-Mare	89, 95	Ross & Monmouth Railway	131	Bolton Wagon Works	124
Whimsey	13, 14, 144, *163*	St. James Station	113	Boucher, Joseph	13, 41, *170*
Whitecliff	149	Severn & Wye Railway & Canal Co.	13, 14, 17, 139, 143, 149, 162	Bullo Pill & Forest of Dean Wagon Co.	170
Whitecroft	*4,* 13, 169			Bute Supply Co.	35
Wimberry	13, 14, 149	Severn Bridge, the	7, 111, 127, *141*	Butterley Wagon Co.	119
Woodchester	128	Severn Tunnel, the	86	Cambrian Wagon Co.	165
Yorkley	17	Sling Branch	157, 158	Charles Roberts	26, 117, 165
		Sling Siding	44	Cheltenham & Swansea Wagon Co.	13, 14, *18, passim, 170*
RAILWAYS		South Wales Railway	7, 9, 11, 13	Derbyshire C&W Co.	86
Awre Station	13	Speech House Road Station	17	Edmunds & Radley	37
Berkeley Road	111, 112	Speedwell Siding	28	Edwards & Brown	35, 72, *75*
Bicknor Siding	17	standard gauge	13	Forest of Dean Wagon Co.	170
Bicslade Wharf	150	Stoke Gifford	139	Gloucester Wagon Co.	7, 13, 15, *18, passim,* 147, *170*
Bilson Junction	*13,* 14	Stroud Branch	127	Harrison & Camm	37, 169
Bilson Yard	15, 31, 32	Swindon Town Station	119	Ince Waggon & Ironwork Co.	*65, 66*
broad gauge	7, 9, 13-15,	transporter wagons	14	Lincoln Wagon Co.	7, 37, 65-66, 118,146
broad gauge conversion	13	Tufts Junction	145	Midland Carriage & Wagon Co.	86, *154*
Bugle Station	*59*	Upper Lydbrook Station	17, 43, *59,* 125, 126	Newnham & Bullo Wagon Works Co.	170
Bullo Station	13	Waterloo Sidings	39	North Cental Wagon Co.	84, 145
Chippenham	120	Whimsey (Cinderford Goods)	163, 165-167	Pickering, R. Y.	168
Churchway Branch	79, 144	Wimberry Sidings	14	Scottish Wagon Co.	170
Clifton Down Station	118	Wyesham Junction	155	Shakleford & Ford	18, 34, 145, 170
Coaley Junction	112	Wye Valley	155	Standard Wagon Co.	35, 53, 171
Coleford Branch (S&W)	91, 146, 157			Standard Wagon & Carriage Co.	171
Coleford Branch (GWR)	155	**TRAMROADS**		Wagon Repairs Ltd	38, 47, *61, 71*
Coleford Station	154	Bicslade Branch	9, *12,*	Western Wagon Co.	7, *13, passim*
Cooper's Siding	*155*	Bullo Pill Railway Co.	7, 18	Yorkshire Wagon Co.	48

A classic Forest of Dean coal train scene. A rake of 35 loaded wagons from Eastern United Colliery passes slowly through Soudley on the Great Western's Forest of Dean Branch having just paused to pin down sufficient wagon brakes for the descent to Bullo at 1 in 48 - 1 in 50. Some of the wagons can be identified –Parkend, Renwick Wilton, Baldwin.